GLASS TOWNS

KEN FONES-WOLF

Glass Towns

INDUSTRY, LABOR, AND
POLITICAL ECONOMY
IN APPALACHIA,
1890–1930s

UNIVERSITY OF ILLINOIS PRESS

URBANA AND CHICAGO

Library of Congress Cataloging-in-Publication Data
Fones-Wolf, Ken.
Glass towns : industry, labor and political economy
in Appalachia, 1890–1930s / Ken Fones-Wolf.
p.   cm. — (Working class in American history)
Includes bibliographical references and index.
ISBN-13: 978-0-252-03131-1 (cloth : alk. paper)
ISBN-10: 0-252-03131-8 (cloth : alk. paper)
ISBN-13: 978-0-252-07371-7 (pbk. : alk. paper)
ISBN-10: 0-252-07371-1 (pbk. : alk. paper)
1. Glass trade—Appalachian Region—History.
2. Appalachian Region—Economic conditions.
I. Title.
HD9623.U46A645   2007
338.4'76661097409041—dc22   2006017933

For Liz, Colin, and Kasey

PETE FELIX

At one time in the mountain state
And many years ago
Pete Felix could blow window glass
As very few could blow.

Pete Felix in those early days
Had manners and was neat
Was known for his fine living ways
And called glass blower Pete.

His friends and fellow mechanics
Were workers highly paid
And training their apprentices
They kept the tricks of the trade.

The art had come from time of kings
Beyond the middle ages
And windows even one foot square
Commanded princely wages.

And in the land of many hills
There was lime and sand and gas
The countryside had in plenty
All things to make the glass.

But Pete could see machines and age
Creeping with stealthy pace
Yet vowed that lacking eyes or brains
Machines couldn't win the race.

Till changes came at rapid rate
Altho he said "It can't be done"
Machinery had him out of date
A dozen sheets to his one.

And now his sons and his grand sons
Make progress many ways
Drawing and cutting window glass
Since Pete's glass blowing days.

Now science plays a part with skill
And safety up to date
Where finest sheets of glass are still
Made in the mountain state.

— Oscar Wood,
  unpublished poem, ca. 1950s,
  Oscar Wood Papers, West Virginia
  and Regional History Collection,
  West Virginia University

Contents

Illustrations

Maps

Acknowledgments

While this work has taken a long time to complete, it received a jump start from two excellent historians, Richard O'Connor and Fred Barkey. Their scholarship provided excellent models, and their willingness to welcome a newcomer to the fold was nothing short of magnificent. Also important was my early familiarity with the West Virginia and Regional History Collection at West Virginia University. I spent fifteen months there as a manuscripts curator, and it was there that I first came across the records of the Window Glass Cutters League of America, which started me on this journey. Over the past fifteen years, I have spent a good deal of time there and have been helped immeasurably by John Cuthbert, Harold Forbes, Michael Ridderbusch, Christy Venham, Lori Hostuttler, and the rest of the staff, who have been terrific colleagues. Likewise, the staffs of the West Virginia State Archives, the Ohio Historical Society, and West Virginia University Libraries have been very helpful.

I was fortunate enough to spend nearly a decade as a labor educator at the Institute for Labor Studies and Research (ILSR) at West Virginia University. My bosses there, John Remington and Stephen Cook, as well as my colleagues, were supportive of my desire to continue historical research (although often with some ironic humor) even amid the more pressing demands for information on contemporary issues. More important, my contact with trade unionists throughout the state gave me a deep appreciation for the tremendous energy, commitment, and compassion that exists in the labor movement, despite the enormous hurdles that it faces. I may not always agree with their policies, but I greatly respect their desire to improve the lives of working people. During my tenure at ILSR, I was also fortunate enough to get to know Joseph Powell, the former president of the state AFL-CIO and a former window glass cutter. To the many workers who came to my classes after a long day of work: I now confess that I learned more from you than you did from me. I hope that we also had some fun together.

In 2000, I was privileged to join the History Department in the Eberly College of Arts and Sciences at WVU (with tenure, no less). The College, under the direction of deans Duane Nellis, Rudy Almasy, and Mary Ellen Mazey, has been generous with financial support to complete research, travel to conferences, and support summer writing. In 2004, I received one of the first Woodburn Professorships, which gave me a boost at a critical time. My colleagues in History have welcomed me, despite a somewhat nontraditional career path, and made the department a wonderful place to work. I especially thank the chairs, Robert Maxon and Robert Blobaum, who have set high standards but have also offered much support. In the department, Liz Fones-Wolf and Ron Lewis have given considerable time to this project. In particular, Ron has taught me much about West Virginia and Appalachia, suggested sources, shared enthusiasm for a project that adds complexity to our understanding of Appalachian industrialization, worked with me on an edited volume, and responded to more of my ideas than anyone. Through it all, he has been a much-valued friend and a model scholar from whom any historian could learn a great deal. Thanks is not nearly enough. West Virginia University has also enabled me to become friends with some excellent young scholars. Four deserve mention for contributions they have made to this project: John Hennen (now at Morehead State University), Paul Rakes (at West Virginia Institute of Technology), Diane Barnes (at Youngstown State), and Lou Martin, currently at work on the history of the working class of the Ohio River Valley. I also owe a debt to the work of Mike Workman and Jeffrey Cook. More recently, some other fine young professionals at WVU have helped me with maps that show more than words can tell. In particular, Jason Ruehl in the History Department, Tim Hawthorne of the West Virginia State GIS Technical Center, and Jesse Rouse and Christine Titus of the National Geospatial Development Center created maps on a tight schedule. Gail Bardhan and Jill Thomas-Clark of the Corning Museum of Glass and Debra Basham of the West Virginia State Archives helped me track down some photos at the last minute. All have put me in their debt.

Because glass was such an important part of many people's lives, I have been invited to address many groups in the state, and every time I have learned something new from the experience. I thank the South

Charleston Historical Society, the Belgian-American Heritage Society of Clarksburg, and Dean Six's glass collectors group for listening to me more than once. At these events, I met Vickie Zabeau-Bowden, Clara McCann, Renee Bastin, and many other children and grandchildren of glassworkers who shared memories, information, and even some family documents that gave me additional insights. When he heard of my interest in glass, Paul Myers, a business agent with the American Flint Glass Workers and a former Fostoria worker, gave me a box of material in the hopes I would write a history of Fostoria. I hope I have fulfilled at least part of his expectations. Finally, I thank the West Virginia Humanities Council and its superb director, Ken Sullivan, who provided a research fellowship, and was supportive when I set aside this project to work on a collection of essays with Ron Lewis, entitled *Transnational West Virginia: Ethnic Communities and Economic Change, 1840–1940.*

I was delighted that the University of Illinois Press thought this project was worth encouraging, especially because the press has lists in both Appalachian and labor history. Consequently, I had the benefit of getting support from two editors, Judy McCulloh and Laurie Matheson, both of whom are terrific. The Press was also willing to send the manuscript to a reader from each area. I thank my anonymous Appalachian reader for some very useful suggestions about technology and making certain that I did not miss anything important in the regional context for this story. Thanks, too, to David Montgomery, who amazes me with his insights, his commitment, and his generosity; he is a role model for all historians.

Over the years, I have presented parts of this research at conferences and in published form in journals. I thank the scholars who have made thoughtful comments and suggested new ways of looking at things. In particular, Craig Phelan (who also shepherded through a piece in *Labor History*), Mary Blewett, Betsy Jameson, Trevor Bain, John Inscoe, Fred Barkey, David Javersak, Marlou Schrover, Leo Lucasson, and numerous anonymous readers have commented on papers or article submissions. I only wish I could have answered all their questions. I published two articles in *Labor History*, "From Craft to Industrial Unionism in the Window-Glass Industry" (winter 1995–96): 28–49, and "Transatlantic Craft Migrations and Transnational Spaces" (Aug. 2004): 299–321. I also published "Immigrants, Labor and Capital in a Transnational Context," *Journal of American Ethnic History* (winter 2002): 59–80; "A Craftsman's Paradise in Appalachia," *Journal of Appalachian Studies* (fall 1995): 67–86; and "Work, Culture and Politics in Industrializing West Virginia," *West Virginia History* (1999–2000): 1–23. I thank the publishers and readers of all of those journals for their consideration and for the rights to use some material from those earlier efforts.

Finally, there are those sweetest debts, the personal ones that you can never repay. My mother, Ruth MacDougall, my brother, Ron Fones, and my sister, Geri Severs, have always encouraged me and taken pride in my efforts. Three role models from years ago made me want to be a historian. I did not acknowledge them in my first book, so I do so now. Keith Olson, Jim Gilbert, and the late Stuart Kaufman were mentors at a key time for me. I would probably not be where I am without their kindness and example.

When I wrote *Trade Union Gospel,* I dedicated it to my children, with the hope that their generation would do better. Colin and Kasey have certainly not disappointed. Colin works as a researcher for the labor movement and is a budding historian in his own right. He is fortunate to be putting his values to work in the real world. Kasey wanted nothing to do with history (and who could blame her) but she is one of the most humane young persons I know. She will become an excellent clinical psychologist in the near future. They make me proud and humble. For Liz, there are no words that can convey how much she means to me; everything I think about writing sounds trivial and insignificant compared to all that I owe her. Our colleagues, our neighbors, and our friends would all agree with me that the old descriptive phrase "his better half" (my apologies if this is politically incorrect) is rarely as accurate as it is in this case. For this book, I acknowledge her support, her insights, and her willingness to kindly coax and cajole. If only she would take responsibility for its faults. But, alas, only I am to blame for those.

Introduction

In 1909, the *Commoner and Glassworker*, a weekly journal for workers in the glass industry, praised the resources of the Mountain State: "West Virginia possesses all that is necessary to make a state great and prosperous. . . . She is a great storehouse of natural wealth, and is richest in resources of any state in the union, and although they are almost intact, as yet, development is bringing them to the markets of the world."[1] Although the extraction of the state's reserves of coal, oil, natural gas, lumber, and other resources was actually well underway by 1909, the newspaper suggested that the state was far from reaching its economic potential. In fact, the process, the politics, and the timing of industrialization in central Appalachia left the region with an underdeveloped economy despite its natural advantages. Even today, the state ranks near the bottom in most economic categories. Through the example of the glass industry, this book explores the development of northern West Virginia and tries to understand why things did not turn out differently.

The goals and energies of two separate sets of capitalists in the last decades of the nineteenth century set in motion forces that helped transform northern West Virginia's political economy. One group, glass manufacturers, faced conditions that encouraged them to restructure their industry to lower production costs. This involved experimentation with marketing trusts, corporate organizations, mergers, new technologies, and increased scales and new social relations of production. But at this time, the most important element in achieving the glass manufacturers' overarching strategy of reducing costs was relocating their factories near ample and inexpensive supplies of natural gas.[2] West Virginia became one of the chief beneficiaries of this new spatial division of labor. The state's share of the industry's wage earners climbed from 3 percent of the nation's total in 1890 to 12 percent a quarter century later, to 15.3 percent by the onset of the Great Depression.

During the same decades, a second group of entrepreneurs, those who eventually pioneered the coal, oil, and natural gas industries in the Mountain State, hoped to make West Virginia part of the great "manufacturing belt." This highly developed region included "all of New England and most of the other northeastern states," according to political scientist Richard Franklin Bensel.[3] The West Virginia entrepreneurs, men like Henry Gassaway Davis, Stephen B. Elkins, A. B. Fleming, and Nathan Goff Jr., among others, already controlled lands rich with coal, oil, and natural gas, fuels essential to the second industrial revolution taking place in America. By the end of the century, they had succeeded, through Herculean efforts, in crisscrossing their lands with railroads and pipelines, and were seeking markets for their abundant fuel resources.

While many of these businessmen were content to become the wealthy agents of such powerful corporations as Standard Oil, some of the more visionary local capitalists saw an opportunity to use the state's natural resources to build a diversified economy that would include value-added manufacturing. In many respects, these two perspectives would wage a struggle over the political economy of this portion of central Appalachia. A glass industry in the middle of restructuring figured heavily in that contest. This book, then, is about these two processes—industry restructuring and the push for economic development in northern West Virginia—and the ways they intertwined to transform the social relations of the region.

For the concept of industrial restructuring, I learned much from economic geographers who have described in theoretical terms changes that were documented in my research on the glass industry and the slow economic development of West Virginia. To Doreen Massey, economic geography is "the spatial organization of the relations of production (defined in the widest sense of that term)." She adds: "new spatial divisions of labour (forms of economic uneven development) are thorough re-workings of the social relations which construct economic space."[4] For scholars of industrial restructuring, the theory asserts "that industries in crisis will make various strategic moves to rationalize production and revive sagging profits in the spheres of finance, organization, production and employment" and that these moves typically involve "workplace relocation."[5]

Indeed, by 1890, the various branches of the glass industry—tableware, containers, and windows—were at a critical juncture that was the result of changes in production costs. During the previous decade, wages had climbed from less than 45 percent of production costs to nearly 55 percent. The value of imported glass increased from $5.1 million to $8.2 million, but more than doubled in windows and tripled in containers.[6] If the theory of industrial restructuring is accurate, we would expect to see a range of strategies in investment, corporate reorganization, new technologies, and new spatial divisions of labor aimed at solving this crisis. In fact, that is exactly what occurred. Indiana's share of glass industry employment jumped from under 7 percent to 25 percent. Older centers of the industry—Pennsylvania, New York, and New Jersey—all saw their shares decline. Even that movement understates the new spatial division of labor. Pennsylvania remained the largest glass-producing state, but much of its capacity moved out of places like Pittsburgh and into small towns like Kane or Jeannette. Companies also entered marketing trusts and merger agreements to enhance their power, or introduced continuous tanks and semiautomatic machines into larger factories to better control labor costs. All these strategies were part of an era that one historian calls the "revolution in glassmaking."[7]

If this process, as explained in theoretical terms, appears predetermined or dominated by just one group in a search for cheap labor, such was not the case. The restructuring of the 1890s also involved a new group of capitalists who did not understand the delicate balance achieved through the cooperation of labor and management in regulating output, according to a longtime industry veteran who testified before a congressional committee in 1900. This new group entered glass manufacture because of opportunities provided by the development of natural gas fields and the use of gas for the innovative continuous tank furnaces, with the result that "the output of glass very soon was more than the demands of the country could consume."[8] (See map 1.)

Nor were capitalists the only people behind workplace relocation. In window glass and—to a lesser extent—glass tableware, groups of workers unhappy with the changing social relations of production pooled their resources and built cooperative factories in such places as Matthews, Indiana, Pt Marion, Pennsylvania, and Salem, West Virginia.

Finally, the restructuring did not occur with a single, dramatic shift. After a decade of prosperity, glass manufacturing confronted another crisis in 1909, when the value of glass produced lagged woefully behind this industry's share of the total industrial workforce. A new round of restructuring was needed; Indiana would rapidly lose ground as a center of glass

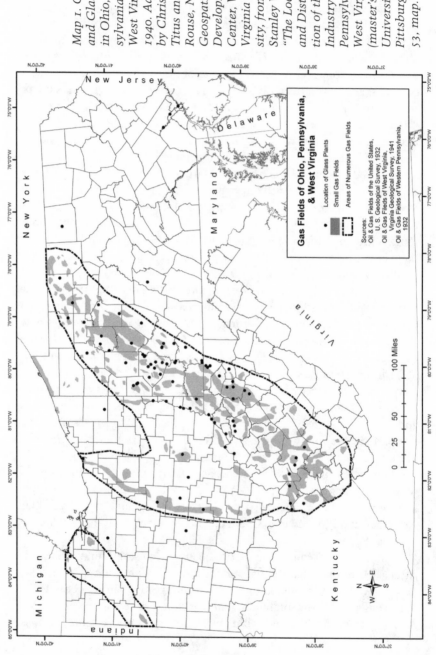

Map 1. Gas Fields and Glass Plants in Ohio, Pennsylvania, and West Virginia, ca. 1940. Adapted by Christine Ann Titus and L. Jesse Rouse, National Geospatial Development Center, West Virginia University, from Robert Stanley Weiner, "The Location and Distribution of the Glass Industry of Ohio, Pennsylvania and West Virginia" (master's thesis, University of Pittsburgh, 1949), 53, map.

Gas Fields of Ohio, Pennsylvania,
& West Virginia

•   Location of Glass Plants
    Small Gas Fields
    Areas of Numerous Gas Fields

Sources:
Oil & Gas Fields of the United States,
    U. S. Geological Survey, 1932
Oil & Gas Fields of West Virginia,
    Virginia Geological Survey, 1941
Oil & Gas Fields of Western Pennsylvania,
    1932

100 Miles

0   25   50

production, replaced by Ohio and West Virginia before World War I. Thus, this book complements the exciting research of Jefferson Cowie, who has greatly expanded the historical framework of what modern scholars have labeled (somewhat incorrectly, as it turns out) deindustrialization. Instead, industry restructuring must be seen in the context of a "constant ebb and flow of investment, industrial production, employment and cyclical behaviour."[9] Some of the benefits of a study of industry restructuring covering an earlier period are the insights it provides into the texture and complexity of the process.

Another benefit is linking these new spatial divisions of labor to their impact on workers and communities. Massey notes that restructuring represents "whole new sets of relations between activities in different places, new spatial forms of social organization, new dimensions of inequality and new relations of dominance and dependence."[10] At the same time, studies of such changes have a tendency to underestimate the problems caused in the older sites of production and overestimate the advantages gained by new sites in the changing landscape of uneven economic development. For workers in the industry, as well as the communities they construct, the social relations of production will inevitably be different in both areas.

Consequently, the first part of this study explores the restructuring of various branches of the glass industry. This section builds upon the work of two excellent glass industry historians who wrote more than fifty years ago, Pearce Davis and Warren C. Scoville. They both offered insightful overviews of the technological revolution that transformed the glass industry between the 1880s and 1920. Davis was particularly concerned with the role tariffs played in the rise and decline of the "bilateral monopoly" of unions and employers in glassmaking and the impact of the subsequent mechanization on labor–management relations. Scoville concentrated on the activities of a particular group of entrepreneurs who were instrumental in breaking the "bottleneck" to industry expansion represented by handicraft techniques and strong unions.[11] While both are outstanding industrial histories, neither is particularly attentive to the local complexity of industrial restructuring or the implications of these social processes for the uneven development of regional economies. These are important components of my study.

This first part contains two chapters. Chapter 1 examines the rise of the dual monopoly imposed by the cooperation of labor and capital in the various branches of the glass industry, as well as the crisis this system faced in the 1890s. As Davis and Scoville note, the dual monopoly emerged as a result of both politics (in the shape of protective tariffs) and the labor process, which relied on skilled workers and handicraft techniques longer than was the case for many industries. After 1890, older firms found themselves trapped in locations that enhanced the power of workers and diminished the benefits employers received from urban sites (agglomeration economies) like Pittsburgh.[12] New companies and entrepreneurs, using new technologies, gravitated to sites offering cheaper fuels and land. The competition these new firms brought made the former costs of production prohibitive and necessitated an industry restructuring.

Chapter 2 turns to the impact of restructuring on workers and their communities at both ends of that process. Restructuring not only set the industry in motion but also recomposed the workforce. Factories that made a more substantial commitment to expensive machinery often reduced their use of women and children. Reform movements that pressured government officials at new sites of production undoubtedly offered an additional incentive to eliminate child labor. At the same time, the desire for larger numbers of unskilled laborers and semiskilled operatives both caused a reshuffling of industry veterans and led to the recruitment of new sources of labor from outside the region and frequently outside the continent. Glassmaking in the United States had always relied on immigrants as craftsmen; worker moves preceded "capital moves."[13] Restructuring merely added to the foreign character of workers at both ends of the occupational ladder. Finally, restructuring elicited reactions from those skilled workers who had benefited from the dual monopoly. Some accepted new opportunities, some contributed to the relocation of production by opening cooperative factories or family-owned firms, and some tried to resist change by turning to politics. Few would have perceived moving as completely unprecedented; after all, many had far-flung, even transatlantic, family connections. However, virtually all could acknowledge the changing social relations of production.

Having explored the background of an industry that would play a major role in the economic development of northern West Virginia, I then shift the angle of vision. In the remainder of the book, I look at the region and some specific communities that were the purported beneficiaries of restructuring. As employers, workers, and technologies were transforming glass manufacturing, capitalists in the Mountain State hoped to drastically alter the economy of their home. When West Virginia separated from Virginia in 1863, a core of the state's Republican political leadership looked to the industrial North for their model. They fashioned a government that emphasized economic modernization, hoping to join the dynamic economies of Ohio and Pennsylvania rather than follow the

agrarian path of their southern neighbors. Unfortunately, many of the resource-rich counties that the Republicans included within West Virginia's
boundaries were undeveloped economically and controlled politically by
a "buckskin elite" who ruled through a system of patron-client relationships and dominance of the county courthouses. One school of thought
attributes Appalachia's slow industrial development to the persistence
of this corrupt system of clientelism, which held considerable sway in
West Virginia in the 1870s and 1880s.[14]

Although this political balance certainly delayed West Virginia's economic growth, other factors contributed. Banking policies, until 1863 in
Virginia and subsequently in the nation, left the Mountain State without
capital resources for private investment; antiquated tax policies prevented
the state from building the necessary infrastructure; and a forbidding terrain made it difficult to get products to markets.[15] Nevertheless, by the
1880s, some key leaders in both the Republican and Democratic parties
understood the opportunities awaiting development. The ensuing two
decades were a time of industrial transformation, as the penetration of
railroads opened up the extraction of timber, coal, oil, and natural gas to
incredible energies and capitalist investments. The problem with this
development, according to a second interpretation of Appalachia's underdeveloped economy, was its control by outsiders. In the 1960s and 1970s,
scholars Ronald Eller, Helen Lewis, and John Alexander Williams stressed
the stultifying impact of absentee ownership of the region's resources
and the development of a colonial political economy. Particularly devastating for West Virginia were the entrepreneurs (Williams called them
compradors) who sold or merged their assets to outside corporations for
personal gain and political influence, and then used that influence to
pursue policies that prevented the state from reaping any benefits from
its natural wealth.[16]

A subsequent group of scholars refined these arguments, acknowledging that the "morality play" of good and evil that became the reign-
ing paradigm for Appalachian studies could not encompass all of the
diversity within the region, nor could it account for the many social
forces determining the fate of Appalachian economic development. The
colonial framework painted mountain people as helpless victims and
ignored those places where local entrepreneurs pioneered and sustained
commercial and industrial development. Moreover, the colonial model
ignored complex social relations within the region, often falling prey
to a geographical determinism. Economic development in the region
was far more varied than these early scholars suggested, and it certainly
predated the piqued interests of outside capital. Moreover, Appalachia

received a steady stream of immigrants and migrants—Irish, Germans, African Americans, Hungarians, Italians—that shatters the image of a homogeneous mountain people.[17] Even the most important advocate of the model in West Virginia, John Alexander Williams, subsequently confessed to its "inadequacies."[18]

The image of the domination of Appalachia's politics and economy by outside capital was more difficult to erase, however, even as scholars turned to a more nuanced interpretation of industrialization. In the 1980s, a new group wrote of Appalachia as a periphery region of uneven economic development that was dependent on the investment capital of the core regions that had already achieved a self-sustaining development. Drawing on the insights of economic theorist Immanuel Wallerstein, Appalachianists like David Walls, Paul Salstrom, Richard Simon, and Ronald L. Lewis emphasized the difficulties of overcoming the region's economic backwardness, but without casting all the blame on malevolent capitalists or greedy *compradors*.[19] Still, these competing theories of development lead us to a similar end. Investment from the financial centers accumulating capital in the great manufacturing belt of the northeastern and north-central states targeted resource extraction, not independent development. Railroads and pipelines siphoned off or hauled away the hardwood trees, coal, oil, and natural gas that the state had in abundance. These resources fueled the value-adding manufacturing plants elsewhere. Creating a balanced, self-sustaining development in West Virginia did not concern bankers in New York, Philadelphia, or even Pittsburgh.

Once in place, core regions seem to accrue even more benefits, cementing their dominance. However, economic geographers remind us that "leading industrial territories do not inevitably stay in the lead, despite the many advantages leadership confers, nor are lagging territories condemned to eternal backwardness, despite their many handicaps."[20] Northern West Virginia, the area that received a considerable share of the benefits from a restructuring glass industry, represented the promise for an alternative to the state's otherwise limited performance in balanced, independent development. Glass manufacturing, many boosters believed, might help create the much-needed home market for the state's fuels, leaving the coal, oil, and gas industrialists less dependent on outside markets.

The second part of this book, then, is an attempt to appreciate the efforts made but also to understand the limitations of indigenous groups in fashioning a different political economy. Some of those individuals John Alexander Williams identified as *compradors* actually made more than casual nods in the direction of investing the wealth gained from coal, oil, and natural gas into a diversified economy that also included value-added manufacturing. Particularly in the northern part of the state, boosters believed that West Virginia was primed to become a part of that great manufacturing belt. Already by 1890, Ohio County in the northern panhandle was one of the forty-eight most developed counties in the United States, measured by a range of factors developed by political scientist Richard Bensel. His map comparing the levels of economic development on a county-by-county level show that the panhandle and the counties comprising the upper Monongahela River valley—the area covered by this study—were above the national average in several categories, a stark contrast to the region to their south.[21] The arrival of glass factories after 1890 seemed to offer the possibility that this region might move into the industrial core.

Chapter 3 explores the changing political economy of West Virginia in the decades spanning its rapid industrialization, as well as the emergence of the "development faith" of its political and economic leaders. While the dual monopoly in the glass industry approached its crisis, entrepreneurs in the Mountain State were waging a battle with railroads and courting the attention of investment capital, hoping to transform the region. These entrepreneurs also had to transform a political culture within the state that seemed little inclined to foster development. Proponents of development, as John Alexander Williams made clear, resided in both parties. To him, that was one of the problems—the agents of outside capital controlled state politics and effectively excluded all criticism or alternatives.[22] However, the fact that both Democrats and Republicans wanted to develop the state's timber, oil, gas, and, especially, coal resources need not obscure some important differences. The Democratic Party sought to achieve this development with a minimal investment from government and to compete for markets principally through a low-wage, low-cost strategy. Republicans, following the political economy of most of the Northeast, opted for a strategy that relied on high tariffs and the gold standard, and was more accommodating to the wage demands of industrial workers.[23] Because the Republicans won this struggle and controlled the state during the decades when the glass industry was in crisis, West Virginia, particularly the northern counties, became a more inviting location for new glass factories and for glass industry craftsmen. But there were also limits to the progressivism of Republicans, as was evident when the state failed to significantly reform its tax code in 1904.

After establishing the background of West Virginia's political economy, I then move to case studies of three towns that became glass manufacturing centers. Each of these represents a concentration of a different sector of the industry—tableware, windows, or bottles—and each emerged as a "glass town" through a different combination of factors. Like the RCA production locations Jefferson Cowie studied, they highlight the fact that there were both winners and losers in the changing spatial organization of the relations of production, and they offer an opportunity to examine the reworking of the "social relations which construct economic space."[24] Each of these towns also represented the hope of local citizens and entrepreneurs to remake the political economy of their area and, if all went as planned, the state in which they lived.

Chapter 4 investigates the arrival of the glass tableware industry in Moundsville, a small town on the Ohio River just south of the much older glass manufacturing center of Wheeling. In fact, Moundsville was the second stop in a relocation process that actually began with manufacturers taking resources out of Wheeling for more promising opportunities in Indiana. Tableware was the branch of the industry least impacted by the technological revolution at the turn of the century. This does not mean that it was unaffected by industrial restructuring. Tableware manufacturers moved for cheaper fuels, created mergers and combinations to take control of markets, and developed strategies to weaken the American Flint Glass Workers' Union (AFGWU). Workers responded to the changing social relations of production with a commitment to craft unionism and a political mobilization that challenged the development faith. Ultimately, the compromise achieved by workers and the Fostoria Company in Moundsville fostered a stable "regulatory unionism" that gave the company a commanding presence in town.[25] Unfortunately, that accommodation did little to stimulate further investment in Moundsville, as other industries avoided what had once been a promising location.

The next case study involves the window-glass industry and its concentration in Clarksburg, a town of modest size and the county seat of Harrison County in the upper Monongahela River valley. A very different constellation of forces brought the glass industry to Harrison County. In window glass, restructuring led to the emergence of a marketing trust and to greatly increased scales of production, but window manufacture was only gradually able to make technological improvements that challenged craftsmen's control over the production process. Meanwhile, the largely immigrant skilled workers had their own ideas about restructuring. Many of the Belgian and French craftsmen pressured their union for help in establishing cooperative factories in areas where they could get cheap gas and land, and they upset the delicate balance that controlled window-glass output. In Clarksburg, these immigrants and their children also built new communities on the outskirts of town where they could exert influence over local politics, much to the dismay of the Republican boosters who had initially attracted them to the benefits of Clarksburg and north-central West Virginia. For a generation, window-glass craftsmen built a "craftsman's paradise" that paid high wages, gave them considerable control over the relations of production, and enabled them to wield political might and cultural independence. Clarksburg became the center of hand-blown window-glass manufacture. Workers' power, however, rested on a realistic acceptance of declining wage rates that enabled their factories to stay productive. When even larger corporations entered the industry with new technological advancements during World War I, the teetering paradise collapsed. In an ironic twist, however, Clarksburg attracted one of the new industry giants, making this town's contribution to the story of restructuring even more complex.

Just a dozen or so miles down river from Clarksburg, a series of glass companies struggled to establish a manufacturing base in Marion County. Chapter 6 examines the arrival and transformation of the glass industry in Fairmont, a county seat that served as the base for the most powerful combination of indigenous coal operators, the group that eventually built the Consolidation Coal Company.[26] This chapter perhaps best captures the competing visions of economic development in the state. The resource extractors in Marion County were Democrats who believed strongly in limited government and a low-wage, nonunion strategy to capture markets for their coal, oil, and natural gas. Although they initially were also interested in investing some of their profits in local glass companies and other manufacturing ventures, they pulled back when they discovered that some of these industries also brought militant and politically aware union workers. Throughout this period, Fairmont coal barons were fighting a pitched battle against the unionization of their miners. As a result, the glass companies that hoped to take advantage of inexpensive fuels in the area strained to attract enough investment capital. That dynamic began to change when more highly mechanized plants arrived, bringing with them more employer-friendly production relations. This trend peaked when the Owens West Virginia Bottle Company built the world's most technologically advanced (and nonunion) bottle factory in Fairmont in 1910. Unfortunately for Fairmont, within a decade, the coal industry would be in trouble, significantly limiting the available pool of investment capital in the region.

The concluding chapter briefly takes the story of the industry, the workers, and their communities through the 1930s. Much of West Virginia's glass industry looked very different in 1940 from 1910, but the process of restructuring did not strip the state or my three case study towns of all of their glass factories. Glass continued to be one of the largest manufacturing industries in West Virginia, but its share of capital investment, as well as the annual earnings of glassworkers, gradually declined below the state averages. However, the triumph of industrial unions and a liberal Democratic Party in the state meant that wherever glass manufacturing survived, the social relations of production were dramatically altered. In each of these towns and in each of the branches of the industry, that transformation took a different form.

In the first half of the twentieth century, glass manufacturing certainly complicated the political economy of West Virginia and Appalachia. It was, unfortunately, never enough to completely remake the region into an area that had a balanced and self-sustaining development. First, the glass industry was not steel or autos, industries that grew in importance and value and attracted growing shares of investment. Glass could contribute to, but not transform, the region's economy. Second, the state's mountainous terrain, which had delayed its economic development, also posed problems for modern factories. Flooding river valleys with strong winds sweeping off steep slopes were hardly conducive to the sprawling plants of twentieth-century manufacturing, even in the glass industry.[27] Furthermore, during the critical decades of West Virginia's economic transformation, 1890 to 1920, the arrival of glass factories and their high production costs relative to the value of output seemed to limit the ability to attract other manufacturing. For example, Ernest Weir moved his primary location of tin plate production out of Clarksburg when glassworkers built their craftsman's paradise, and Fairmont's coal operators increasingly funneled their capital into coal after their experience with glass manufacturing. Finally, economic geographers remind us that less developed regions are not doomed to remain so, but they also caution that moving from the periphery to the core requires a substantial effort. Repeatedly, West Virginia's political and economic leaders have refused to do the things—reform taxes, invest in infrastructure, develop industrial policies—necessary to make that move possible.

GLASS TOWNS

PART I

The Restructuring
of the Glass Industry

I   *The Emergence and Crisis*
of the Dual Monopoly

At the turn of the century, when union and corporate leaders in the glass industry went to Washington, D.C., to testify before the
United States Industrial Commission, they appeared to represent a model
of mature labor–capital relations. The National Glass Company, which
controlled about 75 percent of pressed and blown glass tableware industry, consolidated nineteen separate companies in four states into a "combine." It allowed the American Flint Glass Workers Union (AFGWU)
to organize its factories that had previously operated nonunion, and it
negotiated a trade agreement governing wages and working conditions
for nearly ten thousand workers. Similarly, the union members who
made glass bottles and jars, as well as those who made window glass,
were covered by national trade agreements that resulted from collective
bargaining. Denis Hays, president of the Glass Bottle Blowers Association
(GBBA), perhaps best captured the sentiments of the process:

> We may argue for a week, but always with the best of feeling, and they
> tell us that they come now, knowing that they must meet arguments, not
> bluster, and that their business is far safer with an organization among
> the blowers for this reason: Every bottle has a different price according
> to the different grades of skill and the time required to blow it. A manu-
> facturer must know what his competitor pays for this kind of work.[1]

In short, the national trade agreements that ruled much of these three
branches of the glass industry had helped eliminate cutthroat competition for the benefit of both employers and workers.

3

Beneath the confident surface, however, glass men revealed some insecurity about the immediate future. John Kunzler, president of the AFGWU, acknowledged that one-fourth of his trade operated nonunion, representing a threat to the union, and the two National Glass Company executives hinted that many heads of the individual companies that had formed the "combine" were not necessarily committed to operating as union shops. James Campbell, a former president of the Window Glass Workers Local Assembly 300, noted the "unfortunate" divisions that had led to dissension in the flat-glass industry. Even Denis Hays fretted. He testified that the Glass Bottle Blowers were powerless to protect fully trained apprentices from having to work several additional years at reduced pay, while increased specialization and improved furnaces meant that bottle blowers made "double the number of bottles and more than he did fifteen years ago." More threatening to Hays was the prospect that employers would use new semiautomatic machinery to increase production and eliminate skilled workers.[2]

The testimony taken in 1899 and 1900 offers insight into the glass industry at a moment of calm during an era of turbulent transformation. Technological developments, the use of new fuels, shifts in tariff policies, fluctuating markets, and the emergence of trusts and combinations all contributed to the restructuring of the various branches of the glass industry in the 1890s. Yet the testimony shows a surprising fealty to the "bilateral monopoly" of labor and capital that had ushered in an era of dramatic growth and prosperity for both employers and workers, and for good reason; the glass industry in the 1880s had virtually doubled its capital, its workforce, and its product while paying among the best industrial wages in the country.[3] It was during the tumultuous decade of the 1890s that the glass industry gained a major presence in West Virginia. In a fifteen-year period beginning in 1890, West Virginia glass plants and the capital invested in them would expand by a factor of five, and its numbers of glassworkers would triple.[4] The changes taking place at that time had a significant impact on the nature of the industry in the Mountain State, as well as on the political economy of the towns that became home to hundreds of glassworkers who flocked into West Virginia.

This chapter will survey the nineteenth-century social relations of production in the three branches of the glass industry that migrated into the state—tableware, containers, and windows. Despite some similarities, each developed in unique ways that shaped the organization of firms, the composition of the workforce, the labor relations, and the political activism that characterized the particular branches of the industry and thus the regions where they emerged. By the end of the century, however, the "dual monopoly" structure of industry, which relied on labor–management cooperation in the regulation of output, was in crisis.

Industrialization of Glassmaking

Although glassworkers in the 1890s would often refer to themselves as craftsmen, their trade began to change significantly as early as the 1820s. Until then, glass production was a small-scale, local affair, relying on the skills of European-trained craftsmen. The glassblower made the entire product, typically assisted only by an apprentice or helper. He had learned to make a wide variety of articles—tableware, bottles, windows—since flexibility was one of the essential elements of early glassmaking. Indeed, early glasshouses did not specialize, but rather responded to demand. Master craftsmen gradually increased the supply of skilled labor by training apprentices, who might remain for a time as journeymen before establishing themselves as masters.[5]

The 1820s marked an early watershed in the industrialization of glassmaking, according to Dennis Zembala, perhaps the most thorough student of the industry's technology. A number of factors contributed to the expansion of domestic glass manufacturing in the antebellum decades. First, glasshouses began to specialize in a particular branch of the industry. Factories producing just window glass or bottles emerged after 1800, hiring glassblowers who had mastered only a particular part of the trade, one that they could improve through constant repetition. Furthermore, these factories continued to grow in size, increasing the numbers of glassworkers who had learned only a part of the craft.[6] Second, these glass factories began subdividing the labor process. Instead of a single craftsman with a helper making the entire product, glassmaking increasingly relied on a "shop" system in which a larger number of assistants could perform many of the routine tasks where skill was less essential.[7] Through specialization in the item produced, as well as in the tasks performed, American glass producers greatly expanded production in the first half of the nineteenth century.

A third factor contributing to the industry's growth was the tariff. Although periods of heavy protection (1824 to 1832 and 1842 to 1846) alternated with more moderate import duties, tariff protection kept American glass and glassware prices and the costs of production higher than in European countries. Between 1860 and 1890, the government rewarded the extensive lobbying from the glass industry with "a new era of heavy tariff protection," which helped American producers steadily increase their share of the rapidly growing domestic market.[8] Clearly, import duties gave American glass manufacturers some assistance with a growing industry, but there is debate over the tariff's impact on the fourth factor affecting glass manufacturing—technology. Several scholars assert that the high tariffs retarded technological improvements and impeded efforts to lower production costs. Dennis Zembala, on the other hand, notes the steady development of machines in glassmaking, especially molds and presses that reduced the skill required for glass bottles and tableware. By midcentury, in every branch of the industry, glassworkers had a number of devices that decreased the manual dexterity and the talent needed to make glass items. As early as 1879, a glass industry journal could assert (incorrectly, as it turned out): "before another decade passes, glass factories can be operated without the employment of a single skilled laborer, as scarcely a week passes without the issuing of a patent for some new device for simplifying and cheapening the work of production."[9]

A final factor in the industrialization of glassmaking in the nineteenth century emerged from innovations in furnace design and the use of new fuels. Until 1800, glasshouses relied on wood for their furnaces, which tied them to rural settings with plentiful forests. The switch to coal in the first half of the century resulted in a dramatic geographical shift of the industry away from the Northeast toward the Midwest, especially western Pennsylvania. Since fuel was about one-third of the cost of production, glass factories moved to where coal was easily available and built larger furnaces that enabled factories to melt five times more "metal" (the term used to describe the molten glass ready to be worked) than earlier glasshouses. Thus, when Joseph Weeks prepared his famous *Report on the Manufacture of Glass* in 1880, Allegheny County, Pennsylvania (Pittsburgh), alone accounted for more than one-fourth of the nation's glassmaking capacity.[10] The migration of the industry to new and better sources of fuel had not ended, however. The improvement of the Siemens furnace ushered in a shift to natural gas and eventually led to the development of continuous tanks that allowed an even larger scale of production. By the 1890s, the glass industry was on the move again. When Henry Clay Fry, president of National Glass Company, testified at the Industrial Commission hearings, he mentioned the vast expansion of factories in Indiana, Ohio, and West Virginia, resulting from efforts to take advantage of cheap natural gas, the industrial infrastructure, and the blandishments of boosters in those states.[11]

Industrialization thus transformed glassmaking in the nineteenth century. Specialization in the items produced, as well as the tasks performed, had altered the production process. If a glassworker from 1780 could have walked into a factory in 1880, he would have recognized most elements of the process, but he would have been astounded at the ways that teams of men and boys relieved the blowers of much of the work. Likewise, he would have been amazed at the output that resulted from the cooperation of shops as well as the variety of molds, tools, and mechanical devices that glassworkers had at their disposal to "work the metal." Finally, he would have been surprised at the urban settings of the factories, the size of the furnaces, and the numbers of workers. But these changes did not occur uniformly across the various branches of the glass industry. For example, while tableware factories had grown to an average of 173 workers, window-glass factories remained less than half that size. While presses and molds drastically reduced the skills required in tableware, they had less impact on bottle making and even less on windows.[12] Thus, each branch had its own particular historical process of development affecting workforce composition, wages and working conditions, unionization, and political outlook. However, all three faced a crisis in the 1890s. To understand the process, it is necessary to look at industry restructuring in each branch of glassmaking, focusing on the last two decades of the nineteenth century.

The Flint Glass Industry

Industrialization achieved its earliest and most significant impact on the flint glass industry, particularly in glass tableware. Although the making of tumblers, goblets, bowls, and so on required the greatest amount of skill in its preindustrial phase, the successful use of molds, and especially presses, took much of the skill and artistry out of this type of work. Molds enabled blowers to easily shape glass at the end of the blowpipe into a uniform size and style, greatly speeding up the process. Presses took that a step further. *Hunt's Merchants Magazine and Commercial Review* described the process in 1846:

> The first thing done, is for one of the men to dip an iron rod in the melted glass, and move it about until he has a sufficient quantity of the fluid mass on the end of his rod; he then holds it over the hollow of the mould, and, with a pair of shears, cuts off what he judged to be just enough to constitute the tumbler. Instantly the other man brings down the follower with lever power, and the melted glass is so compressed as to fill the cavity of the mould. He then turns his mould bottom up, with a little blow, and the tumbler drops red hot upon the stone table. One of the boys, with an iron rod having a little melted glass on its end, presses it on the bottom of the tumbler and it slightly adheres. He then holds it in the mouth of a glowing furnace, turning it rapidly, till it is almost in

a melted shape, when the third man takes it, and whirling the rod and tumbler on a sort of arm of a chair, he holds a smooth iron tool against the edge of the tumbler, till all the roughness is removed from its edges, when a boy takes the rod from him, and by a slight stroke on the end of it, drops the tumbler, and places it in a hot oven to cool gradually.[13]

This method could turn out a tumbler every forty seconds, making it a considerable advance on the path to mass production. Indeed, Deming Jarves, who was one of the first to successfully press tumblers in the 1820s, recalled the hostility of glassblowers who feared being displaced: "my life was threatened, and I was compelled to hide from them for six weeks before I dared venture in the street or in the glass house, and for more than six months there was danger of personal violence should I venture in the street after nightfall."[14]

Glass craftsmen did not consider press operators to be skilled workers before the 1860s. Moreover, most consumers considered the ware the pressers made to be of inferior quality, so that glasshouses using this technology filled the cheaper ends of the market. In the decades after the Civil War, however, pressers improved their status to a level roughly equal to that of blowers. In part, this improvement resulted from experiments in the composition of the glass itself, substituting lime for the red lead (litharge) used in flint glass. This substitution reduced the cost of the raw materials while improving the quality and durability of the product. In addition, because lime glass became rigid more quickly than flint glass, it improved productivity. Between 1860 and 1880, demand for pressed glass products grew substantially. At the same time, manufacturers, like Addison Thompson, recognized the skill that pressers developed. When asked by the Industrial Commission if pressing were purely mechanical, Thompson replied that there was "a great deal of skill involved" in judging the amount of material to be pressed as well as the speed, the touch, and the pressure to be applied to the lever.[15] When Weeks undertook his study of the glass industry in 1879, pressers could expect to average about $3.50 a day, making as much as $5.00, a rate comparable to blowers, most of whom were working with glass molds.[16]

The creation of the AFGWU in 1878 united those workers who exerted some control over the production process in the glass tableware industry. Workers had made several previous efforts; in 1858 they formed a Glass Blowers Benevolent Society that disappeared after several unsuccessful strikes during the Civil War, and Pittsburgh area flint glass workers formed a union in 1866. During the early upsurge of the Knights of Labor in the 1870s, Pittsburgh "flints," as they were known, took advantage of the flurry of activity in the center of the nation's glass industry and established themselves as Local Assembly 281, which quickly spread among the glass plants of the Ohio River Valley. By the time the flints decided to form a national union, organization had spread to New York, Philadelphia, and as far west as St. Louis.[17] The timing of organization was fortuitous; the industry was on the verge of recovering from the depression of the 1870s. Indeed, the industry as a whole had stagnated throughout the decade, but expansion in the 1880s would be dramatic. Consequently, in 1879, the AFGWU successfully struck for a 15 percent increase in wages.[18]

Over the ensuing two decades, the flints, in tandem with employers, in effect regulated the industry. The union negotiated terms and conditions of employment for roughly one-third of the workforce—pressers, blowers, finishers, decorators, engravers, mold makers, and cutters. In an industry that made such a variety of products, the union organized members into departments (there were fifteen such departments) for the purpose of bargaining with employers who made particular items. Each department was responsible for negotiating rates for a "move," the number of items that a shop should produce in four and a half hours (a half-day's work). Although a move was an expected minimum production quota (since union members were pieceworkers), the union also enforced a maximum level so that the fastest workers would not drive down "move" rates or put slower craftsmen out of work.[19] The AFGWU locals also established rules governing the conduct of business, the acceptance of new members, enforcement of the contract, and each member's relationship to his employer and his fellow workers. Particularly important was inducting new members into the culture of the craft. Since apprenticeship lasted only a year, the union was vigilant in enforcing its code; it routinely disciplined members for discussing union business with management and for breaking production quotas, as well as for drinking on the job or making "slanderous" comments about the union.[20]

Unionization brought stability to the industry in the 1880s, but not without a struggle. Ohio Valley flints struck employers in 1883 to combat a proposed wage reduction, and pressers engaged in a nationwide work stoppage in January 1888 that lasted for more than three months.[21] Still, the glass tableware industry expanded dramatically during the decade, aided by a protective tariff for some products and by the improvements in pressed-glass branches that made American pressed ware the best in the world (see table 1.1). Industry capacity grew at such a rate that imported tableware ceased to be an important factor in the industry, amounting to less than 15 percent of the domestic market.[22]

As it expanded in the late nineteenth century, the glass tableware industry workforce became increasingly adult and male. At the onset of

Table 1.1: Glass Tableware Industry, 1880–90

Year	Number of establishments	Number of workers	Wages paid (millions)	Value of product (millions)
1880	91	12,640	$4.452	$ 9.568
1890	125	22,178	$9.469	$18.601

Sources: Data from Joseph D. Weeks, "Report on the Manufacture of Glass" in U.S. Census Bureau, *Tenth Census (1880): Report on Manufactury* (Washington, D.C.: Government Printing Office, 1883), 14; U.S. Census Bureau, *Eleventh Census (1890): Report on Manufacturing Industries,* pt. 3 (Washington, D.C.: Government Printing Office, 1895), 332–33).

the union era, adult men made up only 65.3 percent of the workforce. More than 3 of every 10 tableware workers were boys or girls under sixteen, and 1 of every 25 was an adult woman. A decade later, men made up nearly three-fourths of the workforce, and women over age sixteen made up 7 percent. Children, while still present, declined from 30 percent to 20 percent of the workers. Although some women occupied skilled jobs in etching and decorating, most women and children were concentrated in the unskilled and semiskilled jobs. In 1890, they were 43 percent of the unskilled workers and 29 percent of the operatives, but only 8 percent of the pieceworkers (the best paid workers in the factory).[23]

The union ensured that at least some workers shared in the benefits associated with the industry's expansion. The adult, male pieceworkers (most of the unionized employees) made slightly over $662 a year in 1890, well above the average yearly industrial earnings of just under $490. Male operatives and semiskilled workers averaged $489 a year, and unskilled men just $330. The averages for women in the various categories ranged from $143 to $244, and for children from $124 to $179. Labor costs during the decade increased as a share of the total costs of production from 46.5 percent to 54.7 percent. Clearly, the protective tariff was necessary to reduce foreign competition and keep the factories profitable.[24]

The *rapprochement* achieved by the AFGWU and the glass manufacturers showed cracks in the 1890s. The development of gas-fueled furnaces and the availability of cheap natural gas in Ohio, rural western Pennsylvania, and especially Indiana dispersed the industry but also increased the domestic competition. Indiana's numbers of glassworkers jumped from 3,000 to 13,000 in the 1890s, composing fully one-quarter of the industry. One industry executive claimed that many of the new companies entering the business "were strangers, so far as understanding how to do the business part of it. . . . The output of glass very soon was more than the demands of the country could consume," leading to price slashing and the failure of many plants. In addition, the lower rates of the Democratic Party's Wilson tariff (1894) increased imports by 48 percent, further destabilizing the industry.[25]

The competition resulting from growing competition increased employer concern over rising labor costs. Their solutions involved attempts to restructure the industry in ways that led to conflict with workers. In 1893, a group of sixteen tableware companies that had formed a "combine" called the United States Glass Company decided to break with the AFGWU and operate nonunion. The flints engaged in a costly five-year battle against the combine, but eventually succeeded in forcing ten of the companies to give up on the nonunion strategy. Those remaining firms, however, took advantage of the high unemployment resulting from the economic depression of the 1890s to replace union workers, managing to keep control of about 25 percent of the tableware industry.[26] More significantly, the end of the decade brought the introduction of semiautomatic machines that reduced the numbers of skilled workers needed to maintain production and undermined the union in the lamp chimney, jar, and tumbler branches of the industry.[27] Once begun, the mechanization of other branches followed, affecting most of the blown and pressed ware industry by the 1920s.

In the more tumultuous decade of the 1890s, male workers were still earning wages above the average for manufacturing, but they did not fare as well as they had in the previous decade. Unfortunately, the census does not provide the same breakdowns by category of labor, but male wages as a whole increased only from $511 to $524. The composition of the workforce was also changing. The number of women in the industry doubled, increasing their percentage to about 7 percent, but the numbers of children began a steady decline—they were only about 1 out of every 8 workers in the industry. Wages improved more rapidly for women, rising from $171 to $238 during the decade.[28]

To union men, this was a dangerous trend; they worried that some employers had begun substituting women for men in the mechanizing glass tableware factories. Not surprisingly, male workers decided in 1899 to lodge complaints against the growing number of women in glass factories. Flints in Indiana asserted that, while the moral atmosphere of a glass factory was "infinitely better than a few years ago," it was nevertheless "such as to make the employment of young women and girls therein a menace to society." In particular, it was the notion of men working in intense heat, "with just as little clothing on as possible," that appeared to present the problem. But that had not seemed to bother the glassworkers of 1880—suggesting that protecting jobs during a period of turmoil was a stronger motive.[29] If so, these protests appear to have been successful, as the AFGWU reached new agreements with employers at the turn of the century. By 1905, men made up more than 80 percent of the pressed and blown ware workforce, while women and children began not only a relative but also an absolute decline in numbers.[30] Undoubtedly, one reason for the decline of women and children was the enactment of protective legislation in the states that made up the industrial belt. Laws regulating the employment of women and children began to reduce their numbers in the glasshouses.[31]

Women and children were not the flints' only concern. Employers and the AFGWU cooperated in other practices that restricted access to jobs in the industry. In addition to limiting female employment, unionized plants excluded immigrants and African Americans. The AFGWU charged immigrants $50 to join—in contrast to the $3 initiation fee for workers completing the union's apprenticeship—but immigrants still managed to gain a foothold in nonunion plants. Moreover, a few companies experimented with the use of black strikebreakers. Not only was the union outraged, but even the *National Glass Budget*, the voice of the employers, worried about the implications. The *Budget* editorialized:

> The introduction of black labor into one of the highest waged industries of the northern states is an industrial event which even the negroes of Pennsylvania have shown little appreciation of. Once introduced he is there to stay. He is attentive to his work. He has shown himself appreciative of good wages and enhanced social position accruing therefrom. He was not wanted in the trade either by striking workmen or by manufacturers resisting the demands of the workmen. The latter had to have him and they took him. And the flint glass workers' union is not likely to pull him out, initiate him, and send him adrift with a working card in his inside pocket. The case of Sambo is interesting, and will bear watching.[32]

Aside from a few isolated cases, there was no great upheaval in the composition of the glass tableware workforce. When the U.S. Immigration Commission studied the industry in 1911, men had increased their percentage of the workforce to 81.5 percent, while African Americans constituted only 0.3 percent. Although immigrants made up about three out of every ten tableware workers, almost half of the immigrants were of German, French, English, or Irish heritage—groups that had a long history in the industry. Unfortunately, the report does not break down categories of work by ethnicity, but undoubtedly, south and east Europeans in the factories were relegated to the unskilled and semiskilled positions and were not a threat to union jobs.[33]

Despite all the potential threats to peace that emerged in the restructuring of the 1890s—intense competition resulting from industry relocation and expansion, mechanization, corporate combination, and potential replacements for union labor—the glass tableware industry began the twentieth century on a cooperative note. Nineteen companies created a second combination, the National Glass Company, which controlled about 75 percent of the market. In contrast to the United States Glass Company, the new combine welcomed the unionization of its various plants. Even Henry Clay Fry, president of the National Glass Company, who had operated a nonunion plant in Rochester, Pennsylvania, for twenty-six years, allowed his workers to join the union. The protection of the Republican Party's Dingley Tariff (1897) also reduced imported glassware and facilitated labor–management harmony. During the first years of the twentieth century, the AFGWU expanded from about 7,200 members to 9,800. The two sides negotiated a series of yearly agreements covering wages, working conditions, the ratio of apprentices, and the adoption of new machinery, ushering in a period of calm that seemed to benefit both employers and workers. Yearly wages for male workers jumped from $524 to $623 per year between 1900 and 1905, while tableware manufacturers became competitive enough to venture into the export markets. In essence, the AFGWU and the National Glass Company helped bring stability to the industry, serving the interests of both parties.[34]

This stability rested on the idea that the union could help the employers regulate competition. Of course, helping create this stability were a number of other factors, including relatively high tariff rates, the recovery from the depression of the 1890s, and the resurgence of labor union growth generally. Also important was the intellectual environment of the turn of the century. Progressive employer groups like the National Civic Federation (NCF) were experimenting with a new formula for industrial peace—the national trade agreement. The NCF promoted the notion that collectively bargained agreements between employer associations and unions could stabilize and equalize labor costs throughout an industry, thereby removing cutthroat competition that hurt prices and wages and potentially led to conflicts that disrupted markets.[35]

The agreement between the AFGWU and the National Glass Company was just that sort of national trade agreement. But company president Henry Clay Fry only reluctantly acceded to the new spirit of the times, and only because he had joined an industrial combination that included a majority of union firms. Still, he warned: "I had a very pleasant life in the manufacturing business with nonunion labor." Moreover, he believed that "a factory properly managed and organized with nonunion labor gives men a better chance to be free and independent—allows them to grow, and they are better men."[36] Consequently, the "dual monopoly" of the union and the National Glass Company that regulated glass tableware at the turn of the century teetered precariously on a fragile scale balanced with a number of factors. As the industry began a new period of expansion and relocation into places like West Virginia, and as it developed new technologies, that balance was in jeopardy.

The Glass Bottle Industry

Production of glass bottles and containers was closely allied to that of glass tableware through most of the nineteenth century. Indeed, the AFGWU competed for union jurisdiction over bottle blowers until after 1900.[37] Bottle blowers used molds and the shop system much like the flints; by midcentury, the typical shop consisted of a blower, a gatherer, and a finisher, helped by four boys. Blowers were more skilled than pressers, requiring a deftness of hand and control of their lungs as they blew into the mold. But the division of tasks and the constant repetition of mold production made the process a "monotonous routine" as early as the 1840s, according to Dennis Zembala.[38] After 1870, the process involved a gatherer, who would gather and partially inflate the required amount of glass on a blowpipe and hand it to the blower, who then placed it in the open mold. A mold boy sat on a low stool at the foot of the blower's bench and closed and opened the mold as required. Another boy cleaned the pipe, while a "snapping-up" boy put the unfinished bottle in the "glory hole" for the finisher (called a "gaffer"), who shaped the lip on the neck of the bottle. Finally, yet another boy carried the bottle to the lehr for annealing.[39]

The common glass (or green glass) bottle industry grew up in New Jersey and eastern Pennsylvania, and that area remained a center of bottle manufacturing through most of the nineteenth century. In 1890, those two states still accounted for 52 percent of the industry. In fact, the first glass bottle blowers union appeared at the Wistarburg, New Jersey, glass works in 1846 and survived for a decade. After the Civil War, bottle blowers began to organize in the "western" factories (the Pittsburgh area), and in the 1870s they affiliated with the Knights of Labor. Eastern bottle blowers formed a separate organization in the 1870s, finally joining with their western counterparts in the Knights in the 1880s. The eastern and western branches finally left the Knights to form the United Green Glass

Workers Association in 1890, changing the name of the union in 1895 to the Glass Bottle Blowers Association (GBBA).[40]

By 1880, green bottle works differed from flint glass factories in particular ways, helping to separate those represented by the GBBA from those claimed by the AFGWU. Green glass plants were only slightly smaller on average (159 workers, compared to 173 for flint glass factories) although they were more heavily capitalized (by about 16 percent). Bottle works, however, were decidedly male environments in 1880; they were far less likely to employ women or girls. Adult men made up 74 percent of the bottle workforce, but only 65 percent of tableware workers. Women represented only 2 percent of bottle workers. Children (particularly boys) were important to production, making up about 1 out of every 4 workers. The most significant difference was in the melting of the batch. Green glass factories used open pots, while the batch for flint bottles was melted in covered crucibles to protect the glass from discoloration. When the industry began to use the much cleaner burning gas furnaces, the differences in the two branches of bottle making disappeared, leading to much more intense competition between the AFGWU and the GBBA.[41]

Union strategies also separated the AFGWU and the GBBA. The bottle blowers relied less on restricting output and more on restricting access to the trade. For example, the AFGWU apprenticeship lasted only about a year, while bottle blowers served four years. In addition, setting a stricter ratio of apprentices to journeymen was one of the issues that led to the formation of the GBBA. In 1886, eastern bottle blowers in the Knights refused to take on any new apprentices until all blowers were fully employed, but western blowers compromised on the issue. Then, in 1887, eastern blowers left the Knights, and manufacturers began a lockout to enforce apprenticeship rules favorable to employers. Eventually, the eastern and western factions united behind efforts to control the supply of skilled labor, and the fledging Green Glass Bottle Blowers (later to become the GBBA) forced employers to grant a ratio of one apprentice to every fifteen journeymen.[42] But glass bottle blowers imposed no restriction on output. Improvements in molds and teamwork enabled bottle blowers to double and triple output, and increased demand for bottles meant that the workers did not produce themselves out of work.[43]

The GBBA's strategy of restricting access to the trade rather than output led to considerable prosperity for union members in the 1880s. While unskilled and semiskilled men earned only $277 and $438 per year, respectively, pieceworkers (union members) earned on average almost $765 per year, making bottle blowers one of the best paid types of industrial worker. Under this system, labor costs as a percentage of the product skyrocketed, from just under 40 percent to over 52 percent during the decade. Because the prices of bottles were dropping during the decade, the profit margins in the bottle industry were less than in tableware.[44]

The bottle blowers paid a heavy price for their strategy, however. Denis Hays, the president of GBBA, told the Industrial Commission that the bottle blower "to-day makes double the number of bottles and more than he did fifteen years ago. . . . Years ago it was all day work; now we work night and day, double turns." While Hays acknowledged that improved methods, tools, and furnaces made it possible for a blower to earn $25 a week, it came at "an enormous cost of energy and vitality." Despite high wages, Hays felt the "workingman does not get as much out of the social improvements of these times as other and less useful people."[45] Experienced bottle blowers worried that the pace of labor in the hot factories also shortened the work-life of the craftsman. One explained to the Bureau of Labor Statistics: "The chances for the older men are becoming less each year. . . . So with this increased expenditure of energy he is shortening life by burning the candle at both ends."[46]

Aside from the physical toll, GBBA strategy encouraged manufacturers to look for machinery to substitute for the blowers. For years the American industry had lagged behind European competitors, safe in their tariff-protected markets. But the increasing labor costs during the 1880s encouraged experimentation. In 1896, the Atlas Glass Works in Washington, Pennsylvania, began operating a semiautomatic machine that had "a revolving hand-operated table and five molds, and used compressed air for glass-blowing purposes" (see illus. 1).

Although it required two skilled workers to operate it, the machine quadrupled output. The appearance of semiautomatic machines coincided with the shift to gas furnaces in the bottle industry, creating even greater havoc. Thus, new bottle plants in search of cheap natural gas and no longer in need of large numbers of craftsmen settled in Ohio, Indiana, and Illinois, part of a major restructuring. Many of these new plants refused to negotiate with the union, opting instead for the machines. When the GBBA met to open negotiations with the manufacturers in the summer of 1897, 30 percent of the bottle plants were operating nonunion.[47]

Once underway, the mechanization of bottles and jars proceeded rapidly. The *National Glass Budget* could crow in the summer of 1898: "Of the making of machinery to displace the 'gentilhomme de verre' there is now no end. Fact is that inventors, infringers and imitators are tumbling over each other in their hot haste to get there first."[48] The GBBA seemed powerless to prevent the migration and mechanization of the industry.

Illus. 1. In 1908, Lewis Hine took this photograph of a semiautomatic bottle machine that "blows 4 milk bottles at a time" in the Travis Glass Company, Clarksburg, West Virginia. Hine promoted the machine because the plant manager claimed that it would help him replace child labor. Skilled bottle blowers probably viewed the machine differently. Reprinted from a photograph in the National Child Labor Committee Collection. Courtesy of the Library of Congress.

In 1899, the union struck against wage cuts in New Jersey, but without success. One glassworker poet lamented:

> "For strikin' doesn't pay down 'ere, our trade is goin' west,
> It never will come back again, tho' we do our level best;
> They're gettin' up some new machines, to blow us out for good,
> An' to win out 'gainst th' iron man is just not in the wood."[49]

By 1901, semiautomatic machines made most of the wide-mouth jars in the country.

After a brief flirtation with resistance, the GBBA decided to pursue a strategy of accepting the machines and claiming the machine-operating jobs. Denis Hays negotiated what at the time seemed a breakthrough agreement with the giant Ball Brothers Company's plants in Marion and Fairmount, Indiana. The agreement called for a reduction in piece rates of 47.5 percent, which Hays claimed was a victory. It may have saved the union, but it just as surely leveled the wages in the industry. Because the Census Bureau did not separate bottles and jars from tableware in its 1905 report on manufactures, it is difficult to gauge the full impact of the mechanization of the 1890s. But by using New Jersey as an indicator, since the bulk of the state's pressed and blown glass production was bottles, it is possible to get some indication. Average yearly wages for men over age sixteen in New Jersey's glass factories actually dropped by 4 percent over the decade, from $532 to $511. Machine operators did not fare much better. In Illinois, where new plants tripled the value of bottle production in the 1890s, annual earnings were only $491.[50] Restructuring altered the social relations of production everywhere.

Still, Hays sounded optimistic when he testified before the Industrial Commission in March 1899. The GBBA had reached an agreement with several of the largest bottle-producing companies, such as Ball Brothers, and he was confident of organizing many of the nonunion shops. Hays had taken the GBBA into the American Federation of Labor and would soon win for his union jurisdiction over some two thousand flint bottle makers who had been members of the AFGWU. His optimism had some merit as well. Improvements in the economy and the efforts of manufacturers to achieve some stability enabled wages to creep up after the turn of the century. One factor encouraging employers to seek stability was the amount of capital invested in machinery. Between 1900 and 1905, the average capitalization per firm jumped by 24 percent, from about $151,000 to $187,000. But in New Jersey and Illinois, states where bottle manufacturing dominated, the average capitalization was over $300,000. Restructuring in the glass container industry was in the direction of mechanized, capital-intensive, mass production.[51]

Bottle blowers, despite the introduction of molds early in the nineteenth century, had commanded among the highest industrial wages. Until the 1890s, skilled craftsmen in bottle plants maintained their earnings better than the glass tableware workers. Then a revolution in technology rapidly transformed the industry. As early as 1910, this revolution would result in the construction of a fully automated factory in the expanding natural gas fields of north-central West Virginia.

The Window Glass Industry

In contrast to those in the tableware and bottle industries, workers and even employers in window-glass manufacture asserted the industry's imperviousness to change. One Pennsylvania manufacturer told an 1880 Census Bureau enumerator: "No labor-saving machinery and improvements have been introduced, and there very probably never will be any, into the manufacture of ordinary cylinder glass. The strong-limbed, muscular, and powerful-lunged animal known as man is the best machine ever invented, and no improvement has been made since his introduction into the manufacture of window glass more than 300 years ago."[52] Although many in the industry took a false comfort in such attitudes, industrialization had changed the manufacture of window glass significantly even by 1880.

Most American plants used the German cylinder method of window-glass making. This method involved a blower or his apprentice gathering and inflating a gob of glass on the end of a blowpipe. The blower repeated this several times until he had a sufficient amount for the job. He then swung the inflated gob over his head to form the "shoulders" of the cylinder, and followed by swinging it in a pendulum motion in a "swinghole" to elongate the cylinder and achieve the desired thickness (see illus. 2). At that point, the cylinder was cracked off the pipe and also at the closed end, with a strand of hot glass touched by a piece of cold iron. The cylinder was then reheated and cracked lengthwise, and taken to another furnace, where it was flattened on a smooth stone by reheating while the glassmaker worked on it with a wooden paddle. The flattened glass pane was then taken to an annealing oven, and eventually the cutting table. Until the 1830s, the master glassmaker directed the entire process, but by the Civil War the division of the process had resulted in four distinct crafts—gatherers, blowers, flatteners, and cutters—each responsible for a particular part of the process.[53]

Over the next two decades, the industry fluctuated greatly. The division of labor increased productivity and lowered the price of glass, enabling a dramatic expansion of the industry during the postwar years. In 1860, there were only thirteen window-glass factories, employing 1,416 workers; a decade later, there were thirty-five factories and 2,859 workers. The growth, combined with the tariff protections of the Civil War era, allowed American producers to increase their share of the domestic market from 65 percent to 72 percent while continuing to pay high wages. Labor organizations emerged in the Pittsburgh area, where nearly one-third of the window industry was located. Then, industry growth slowed in the

Illus. 2. Window-glass workers holding the pipe and glass cylinder over the swinghole. Undated photograph in the Window Glass Cutters League of America records. Courtesy of the West Virginia and Regional History Collection, West Virginia University Libraries.

1870s as a result of the severe economic depression. Still, by 1880, there were fifty-eight window-glass establishments employing 3,890 workers. Employers undoubtedly used the hard times and destructive competition to squeeze concessions from the craftsmen. The 36 percent increase in the size of the workforce produced a 75 percent increase in the value of the product, despite falling prices during the decade.[54]

As the industry recovered from the depression, window-glass crafts-men mobilized to gain control of their trades. Coinciding with the emer-gence of the Knights of Labor as a considerable force in the Pittsburgh area labor movement (which was also the center of the window-glass industry), the gatherers, blowers, flatteners, and cutters formed local assemblies of the Knights. In 1877, all the glassworker assemblies in Pittsburgh formed the first National Trades Assembly, a short-lived district that soon broke apart due to disagreements between workers in the various branches of glassmaking. In 1880, however, the separate window-glass assemblies merged to form Local Assembly (LA) 300, which actually functioned as a national trade union for the four window-glass trades. Although that structure conflicted with the general philosophy of the Knights, which emphasized geographical districts including local assemblies from a variety of industries, LA 300 received the support of the Knights' hierarchy to become a national trade assembly with a good deal of autonomy.[55]

Local Assembly 300 ushered in the "dual monopoly" era of window-glass production. The union quickly became a national organization, negotiating the terms and conditions for 1,500 skilled workers at annual meetings with the manufacturers. Included were strict rules covering apprenticeship (generally lasting three years) that limited apprentices to sons or brothers of LA 300 members. The union also restricted the amount of glass produced in a week and stipulated rules on virtually every aspect of the production process, including crew size, work pace, and prices for the various sizes and thicknesses of window glass.[56] The advantages of sharing control with the union were not immediately apparent to all employers. As the industry showed some promise of growth, new factories needed skilled tradesmen, and they turned to immigrants. Declining conditions in Belgium, in particular, made Belgian window-glass workers a potential source of craftsmen. Local Assembly 300 responded by leading a successful strike against employers in 1882, and then followed up its victory by hiring former congressman Benjamin F. Butler to draft the nation's first contract labor bill to prevent employers from importing labor under contract.[57] Although LA 300 would later recruit between 600 and 700 Belgian glassworkers to help expand the American industry in 1885, the union would exert vigilance against an oversupply of skilled labor.

Eventually, employers saw some benefit as well. In a highly competitive industry that imported around one-quarter of the window glass needed for domestic consumption, reducing wage and production variations brought stability. In addition to production quotas and standardized wages, LA 300 also instituted July and August shutdowns for factories, both to relieve members from toiling near hot furnaces in the summer months and to reduce stocks to keep prices higher. Particularly because startup costs for new factories were generally quite minimal, LA 300 became an ally in reducing competition. In 1880, window-glass plants employed only seventy-nine workers per establishment, less than half the size of bottle and tableware factories. Thus, companies maintained their market share because the union effectively regulated the ability of companies to enter the industry through its control of skilled labor.[58]

The first decade of the bilateral monopoly lived up to the expectations of the members of LA 300. Average yearly earnings in window glass jumped from $550 to $669 as the industry nearly doubled its workforce and the value of its product. Tariff rates remained high, enabling American companies to actually increase their share of the domestic market. The greatest beneficiaries were the skilled workers. While yearly earnings averaged $372 for unskilled workers and $611 for operatives and semiskilled workers, the pieceworkers (LA 300 members) averaged a whopping $943, making them a true "labor aristocracy." Wages in window glass rose from 42.4 percent of the value of the product to 56.1 percent, the highest of any of the branches (see table 1.2). The gatherers, blowers, flatteners, and cutters who made up LA 300 accounted for nearly four of every ten workers in window-glass plants.[59] And, in contrast with the tableware and bottle industries, window-glass production was almost exclusively an adult male domain. In 1880, only three females worked in window glass; a decade later the census reported none. Children under age sixteen also declined during the 1880s, from 3.4 percent to 2.7 percent of the workforce.

The next decade was not so kind to the window-glass workers. In the late 1880s, window manufacturers finally began to adopt the continuous tank furnace, which had been in use in Europe for a decade. Until then, the batch for window making had been melted in clay pots inside the brick furnaces. Craftsmen were at the mercy of the charging, melting, and cooling process, which typically took ten to fifteen hours to complete. Furnaces held from six to fifteen pots, depending on the size of the factory, and each pot held around five hundred pounds of batch, enough for a day's work by one blower. The pot-furnace process was inefficient, wasting fuel in the melting and cooling stages, during which

Table 1.2: Production Costs in the Glass Industry (Percentage of Product)

		1880	1890
Tableware:	Wages	46.53	54.65
	Materials	34.41	26.48
Bottles:	Wages	39.85	52.27
	Materials	43.18	30.44
Windows:	Wages	42.39	56.09
	Materials	36.64	30.10

Source: U.S. Census Bureau, *Eleventh Census (1890): Report on Manufacturing Industries*, pt. 3 (Washington, D.C.: Government Printing Office, 1895), 314.

time no glass was being produced, and wasting glass in the "unworkable metal residue left in the bottom" according to window-glass historian Richard O'Connor. Furthermore, the process also deteriorated the pots, which required constant replacement.[60] English and Belgian window-glass manufacturers began experimenting with the more efficient regenerative furnaces developed by Friedrich Siemens in the 1860s. In the early 1870s, Siemens added a continuous melting tank to the process, replacing the pots. The tank melted, fined, and prepared the batch for working in one continuous operation. By the end of the decade, Siemens and the European producers had overcome the "slightly seedy" texture of tank glass, as well as problems arising from the placement of the gathering holes and temperature regulation.[61] The tank did not alter the process of making glass, but it did enable employers to build larger factories and operate around the clock in shifts, thereby producing much more glass.

The American industry proved much slower to adapt. Finally, Pittsburgh glass manufacturer James Chambers took a trip to Belgium to study tank technology in 1887. Two years later, he opened a huge new facility, complete with the regenerative furnace and continuous tank, in Jeannette, Pennsylvania. Chambers placed an advertisement for 72 blowers, 72 gatherers, 28 cutters, and 16 flatteners, but the plant had an even greater capacity, about four times the average window-glass factory of 1890. Aggregate numbers, which suggest that plant size actually decreased during the 1890s, hide a more complex reality. In fact, many small cooperative factories were established in the decade, but the large tank factories would garner the lion's share of the industry, increasing from just 8 percent of the total capacity in 1889 to 68 percent in 1898. Furthermore, since the tank operated much more efficiently with natural gas, it dispersed the industry into Indiana, Ohio, West Virginia, and rural western Pennsylvania, away from its former union stronghold of Pittsburgh.[62]

The restructuring of the industry had serious repercussions for LA 300. An increasing flow of immigrants took advantage of new opportunities in the gas belt, while older members remained in declining areas. The union experienced upheaval, with ethnic hostilities and regional divisions leading to bitter battles for control of LA 300, ultimately resulting in the rise of a new leader, Simon Burns, backed by the growing number of Belgians in the trades. To add to the complications, cutters and flatteners felt that Burns ran LA 300 principally for the benefit of the blowers and gatherers, who had backed his election, and the smaller trades left the union to form their own single-trade groups.[63]

Compounding these divisions were two other factors. First, the depression of the 1890s and the resulting stagnation in the domestic market left the industry overextended. Output had been at 66 percent of the existing capacity in 1890, but stood at only 36 percent in 1900. As a result, a significant portion of the 4,500 skilled workers in the industry were periodically out of work, often making glass for only six months or less in a year. Annual earnings in the industry plummeted to below the average for all industrial workers between 1893 and 1897. A second factor was the appearance of the industry's first marketing trust, the American Window Glass Company. The appearance of this trust in 1898 triggered an intensification of competition that led to plant shutdowns and lower wages, particularly since the trust included many of the large tank-furnace plants. Its attempt to control a significant share of the domestic market threatened many of the small companies that had dealt fairly with LA 300.[64]

By 1900, despite little actual change in the process used by skilled workers, the window-glass industry was deeply divided. The American Window Glass Company plants included 1,729 pots (a term still used to designate the number of spots for blowers, even though factories were using tanks), while 1,170 plants remained independent. Even the independents were divided between proprietary companies, some of which had formed their own combine, and cooperatives. The workers were equally fragmented; gatherers and blowers remained in LA 300, while the cutters and flatteners each had their own organization. In addition, snappers, long considered an essential part of the production team but denied entry into the union ranks, began exploring the possibility of forming their own union.[65] Wage rates remained high, but total earnings were unstable due to periodic unemployment.[66] In the chaos that reigned at the turn of the century, some factories were idle for half the year. Meanwhile, the modest cost of starting new factories in the gas belt encouraged many to enter the business, destroying the stability of the "bilateral monopoly."

What looked like chaos to some represented opportunity for others, however. Indiana had benefited from the shift to gas-fueled tank furnaces in the 1890s, but cheap natural gas there was not as abundant as had previously been believed. After 1900, West Virginia became the new haven for small proprietors and glassworker cooperatives trying to escape the control of the American Window Glass Company trust. Unfortunately, the window-glass craftsmen could gain only a temporary reprieve from the development of new technology in their branch of the industry.

Glass Men and a Restructured Industry

The turmoil that characterized the 1890s spawned a number of experiments by employers to stabilize the industry. Until the middle of the century, the men who ran the glass industry were themselves descendants of the preindustrial glassworking families. One such family, the Stangers, traced their roots in American glassmaking back to the eighteenth century in Wistarburg, New Jersey. In 1820, Solomon Stanger and his four brothers opened their own glasshouse in Glassborough, New Jersey, twenty miles from Philadelphia. By 1850, members of this family managed at least four separate glass factories, including one west of the Alleghenies. One of the most prominent enterprises in the Pittsburgh area likewise owed its existence to a family of German craftsmen, descendants of Charles Ihmsen, who came to the United States in 1795. His sons William and Christian became partners in an enterprise near Pittsburgh that innovated in the use of molds in bottle production. By 1860, Charles Ihmsen's grandsons, Charles and William Jr., employed over five hundred glassworkers in five separate plants, "each with specialized equipment designed to expedite the mass-production of a single product," according to Dennis Zembala. Moreover, the children and grandchildren of many more former artisans served as foremen and glasshouse managers as well as journeymen.[67]

These close connections to a glassworking fraternity had helped usher in the bilateral monopoly era in the industry. Manufacturers relied on the abilities of skilled workers because they had risen through the trades. In particular, the concentration of glasshouses and craftsmen on the south side of Pittsburgh was home to generations of craftsmen who had worked for the same family-owned factory. This made the area a seedbed for the unions that emerged in all three branches of the industry, each of which had roots in the Knights of Labor. Although the early unity of all glassworkers did not last, as the growing specialization of labor meant that each trade jealously guarded its prerogatives, there remained a powerful "craftsman's ethos" that included manufacturers. Employers accepted the unionization of their workforce (at least the 30–40 percent considered to be craftsmen) with relative equanimity. This is not to suggest that they did not blanch at and even threaten their skilled workers, but labor peace came with minimal animosity. Owners like James Chambers and Samuel McKee developed close personal ties with their workers, some of whom were national union leaders. Of course, the benefits of tariff protections helped; the unions adjusted their wage scales in tandem with the price of glass, working with employers to ensure profitability.[68]

This cohort of factory owners and managers shared a common heritage with their skilled workers. Employers and union members often showed a mutual respect that bordered on friendship. When owners and managers retired or moved on, their former employees often presented them with watches or other gifts, and employers often reciprocated when union leaders retired. Similarly, they frequently shared political interests; most glassworkers, like their employers, were Republicans because the party supported high tariffs. Both the industry journal and the workers' magazine typically endorsed glass men for office regardless of position in the factory. For example, when Local Assembly 300 leader James Campbell sought to gain appointment as the chief Pennsylvania state factory inspector, his former employer, James Chambers, interceded on his behalf. In another glass community—the northern panhandle of West Virginia—glass workers and manufacturers joined together to pick Republican candidates who supported high tariffs for the industry.[69]

Manufacturers who emerged from the culture of the craft continued to play an important role into the twentieth century. Michael Owens, who would become one of the giants in the glass industry, had been a union member and had been blacklisted for his activities during a strike. His partner, Edward Libbey, was the son of a glassworker who had long ties to the glassmaking fraternity.[70] Such men as Owens and Libbey, like McKee and Chambers, increasingly came to believe in technology and improvements. Glassmaking was a highly competitive industry, and the startup capital necessary for new factories had been modest until the 1890s. Since labor represented a significant portion of production costs, the manufacturers with considerable experience understood that a potential competitive advantage depended on labor-saving inventions. They worked closely with a new glass industry fraternity emerging after the Civil War, one composed of machinists and mold-makers. The iron foundries and machine shops of Pittsburgh and the Ohio River valley made the region a center not only for the unionism of skilled workers but also for the technological inventions that made skilled workers less important. Working with glasshouse owners, foremen, and craftsmen who had ideas for molds, presses, and other devices for glass manufacturing, machinists and molders revolutionized the industry. Practical metal workers claimed patents for air blowers, more intricate molds, and more powerful and faster presses. The accumulation of the work done in these shops, by men outside the ranks of the glassworker unions, led to the development of semiautomatic and eventually automatic glassmaking machines.[71]

At the same time, a new generation of manufacturers joined the industry. These new men did not rise out of the glassworker fraternity and did not share their predecessors' loyalty to the interests of craftsmen. Addison Thompson and Henry Clay Fry, who created the National Glass Company that dominated glass tableware, began as clerks, not craftsmen. Nathan B. Scott, a glass manufacturer and U.S. senator from West Virginia, started as a salesman; and the general manager of the American Window Glass Company, William L. Monro, entered the industry as a lawyer.[72] Some of these men had little use for unions. Fry, for example, demonstrated his lack of understanding of the union pride that skilled workers had when he asserted:

> If the labor organizations could have their best men as their managers, I believe it would be a good thing, but generally the people who come to the front in labor organizations are demagogues; they are the men usually who can do the most talking—glib of tongue—but are wanting in true manliness or interest in their fellow workmen or the manufacturers. They are men generally too lazy to work themselves and want what they call a snap or easy position.[73]

When the labor costs of producing glass increased significantly between 1880 and 1890, and when unions proved less successful in providing stability in the turbulent 1890s, employers began to search for their own means of controlling conditions in the industry. These new manufacturers put their confidence in business strategies, hoping that pools, trusts, and combinations would supply a much-needed stability. In tableware, two major combinations of individual companies controlled most of the industry; in window glass, the American Window Glass Company accounted for about 60 percent of the production capacity; even in bottles, the manufacturers had two associations that set prices. These trusts recoiled against a reliance on the cooperation of unions, and some employers hoped that restructuring would provide a solution.[74]

Thus, when the U.S. Industrial Commission investigated the glass industry in 1899 and 1900, it found an industry at the precipice of dramatic change. Some entrepreneurs believed that cooperation among the various factories could restore stability; some still clung to the bilateral monopoly that they created with unions of skilled workers; others hoped that machines would give them a competitive advantage. Despite the turbulence that shook the industry in the 1890s, each group had reached a temporary truce with their skilled workers, acknowledging the important stabilizing role that unions had performed. But beneath that calm surface, potential conflict swirled.

During the nineteenth century, glass manufacturing had thoroughly in-dustrialized, and the artistry and artisan status of preindustrial craftsmen came to an end. By 1880, the industry ranked twenty-eighth of 331 Ameri-can industries in terms of numbers of workers employed, and fifty-third in value of output, despite its lack of mechanization. Still, an array of molds, presses, and other devices routinized much of glass manufacturing, enabling the industry to lower costs and expand the domestic market. If not quite resembling an assembly line, the production of bottles, cheap tableware, and even windows was certainly moving toward mass produc-tion. The pace of change then accelerated during the 1890s.[75]

Despite some similarities, each branch experienced its transforma-tion in unique ways. Restructuring resulted in different industrial strate-gies that shaped the composition of the workforce, competition within the industry, wages and costs of production, plant location, industrial relations, and the propensity for mechanization. As glass manufacture faced the twentieth century, all these factors would, in turn, help shape the towns where glass factories operated. For workers in the industry, the development of the various branches meant that three separate unions represented the skilled workers in the industry. With the exception of bottle blowers, few workers crossed into another branch or across the jurisdictional boundaries of their particular organization. Each union de-veloped its own strategy for representing members, while the industrial relations and workforce composition of each branch gave rise to differ-ent political outlooks. To understand how the workers responded to the industrialization of their trades, we must now turn to the occupational subcultures they developed as they existed at the outset of the twentieth century.

2 Workers and the Revolution in Glassmaking

Between 1888 and 1904, the glass industry transformed the small community of Jeannette in southwestern Pennsylvania. In 1887, Pittsburgh glass manufacturer James Chambers journeyed to Belgium to study the latest developments in the furnace technology used in window-glass plants. Continuous tank furnaces, fueled by gas, melted the "batch" for factories in England and Belgium and enabled a dramatic increase in the scale of production. When Chambers returned, he began constructing a huge new plant outside of Pittsburgh, in Jeannette. To work in the plant, Chambers recruited Belgians who were fleeing a glutted labor market and bitter industrial conflict in their native country. Nearly the entire complement of Chambers's skilled workers were Belgians, and Chambers filled the unskilled jobs with local, native-born Americans, mostly young males anxious for industrial work. A decade later, a bottle plant opened in Jeannette, part of the restructuring of the glass container industry. This new factory recruited American-born workers from eastern states to fill the declining number of skilled jobs in bottle making and relied mostly on Italian immigrants (about 175 of the 300 workers) to do the unskilled work. Then, in 1903, the skilled window-glass workers struck when Chambers announced his intention to introduce the Lubbers cylinder glass blowing machines into his Jeannette plant. When the strike failed, most of the Belgians left Jeannette for places where machines had not yet been introduced. American-born workers moved into the machine-tending production jobs, while Italians, Poles, and Slovaks performed the unskilled work.[1]

In the space of fifteen years, industry restructuring had brought successive waves of migrants and immigrants to Jeannette and had given rise to and then reconfigured the makeup of this glass town. With numerous variations, depending on the branch of the industry, the existing local population, and the immigrant groups that were recruited for both skilled and unskilled jobs, the Jeannette story was replayed in communities from Pennsylvania to Oklahoma. The transformation of the glass industry opened up opportunities for new groups of workers, even as the prospects for skilled craftsmen became increasingly grim. Although the industry had never been static, the torrent of technological change in the 1890s greatly accelerated the pace of factory relocation, workforce recomposition, and political reorientation that characterized glass manufacturing communities in the early twentieth century.

This chapter will explore the impact the restructuring of the glass industry had on workers and their communities. I will examine the ways that new technologies altered the gender, ethnicity, age, and skill levels of the workforce in that critical transition period. Such changes, in turn, affected the geographic mobility and the living standards, as well as the social and political ideas, of workers in the industry—particularly those in the highly skilled glass trades. But, as the story of Jeannette makes clear, the social, cultural, and political resources with which glassworkers faced new systems of production were forged in a transatlantic context.[2] To understand how the glass industry transformed towns like Jeannette and, eventually, more than thirty towns in West Virginia, we must pay attention to the culture and the networks created by these people who were constantly in motion.

The Changing Workforce in Glass

What business historian Warren Scoville called the "revolution in glassmaking" had a profound impact on the glass industry. The revolution had two components: the introduction of new machinery and the spread of the corporate form of organization, with its increased reliance on salaried officials. For example, while the numbers of establishments and workers grew by 20.7 and 17.7 percent, respectively, during the 1890s, the amount of capital invested increased by almost 50 percent, and the number of salaried officials more than doubled. Each branch of the industry experienced the revolution in different ways and at different times. In tableware and windows, corporate consolidation and plant relocation were important changes, triggering bitter conflicts in the 1890s, as the United States Glass Company and the American Window Glass Company trust tried to gain control of their industries. In bottle making, the introduction of semiautomatic machinery for wide-mouth bottles in 1896 began a flurry of innovation that led to experiments with fully automatic bottle making by 1903, the same year that American Window Glass Company introduced a cylinder-blowing machine for the production of windows. Mechanization began reducing craftsmen in both industries, holding out the potential for eliminating all skilled labor in the foreseeable future.[3]

Restructuring brought dramatic changes in the composition of the workforce. Investments in machinery, combined with new laws regulating child labor, led to a steady decline in the use of children; between 1890 and 1905, the ratio of children under age sixteen would drop from about 1 in 6 to 1 in 10. At first, employers substituted women, but after 1900, the protests of men and the influx of cheap foreign labor resulted in both a relative and an absolute decline in female employment.[4] Of the just over 19,000 workers the industry added between 1890 and 1905, adult men accounted for 18,000. An increasing portion of those workers were foreign-born. The explosion of immigrant labor from southern and eastern Europe added to what was already a steady flow of glassworkers from Belgium, France, England, and Germany. But there was a clearly defined hierarchy for immigrants in the glass factories. Immigrants from Belgium, France, England, and Germany typically entered the industry in the most highly skilled positions; employers recruited them specifically to expand their complement of craftsmen. Italian, Polish, and Slavic workers, on the other hand, were largely unskilled "birds of passage," filling the lowest paying factory jobs, slowly replacing women and children in the more highly mechanized factories.[5]

The revolution in glassmaking, then, as it reduced the number of skilled jobs in the various branches of the industry, made the workforce increasingly adult and male. By altering the balance of skilled and unskilled jobs, it also changed the mix of foreign and native-born workers. Mechanized glass factories offered opportunities to American-born young men whose fathers were also born in the United States. Some were the sons of skilled glassworkers who adopted their fathers' trade, but most resembled those American-born workers in Jeannette. They were the local workers who moved off the farms of southwestern Pennsylvania and into industrial employment at the bottom rungs of the job ladder. When restructuring occurred and the skilled immigrants departed, American-born men moved into semiskilled production jobs, gaining an advantage over newer immigrants, who took the general labor jobs vacated by native-born men.[6] One category of men declined in relative numbers—the sons of immigrant parents. (See table 2.1.) As the possibility of working at the craft of their fathers diminished during the revolution in glassmaking, many began looking for other avenues of employment. Certainly, skilled glassworkers had the means to help their sons pursue occupations with brighter prospects.

Each branch of the glass industry had its own unique pattern for mixing the American-born with immigrants and their children. For example, in the manufacture of glass tableware, the workforce kept much of the character it had in 1890. Tableware factories had most of the women and children who remained in the industry, including a small portion of women who did the skilled work of etching and decorating. They also continued to recruit immigrants and their children as the bulk of their skilled workers. Germans were the single largest foreign-born group, accounting for one-tenth of the workforce. Moreover, the children of Irish and German immigrants made up another 20 percent of the entire workforce. Both these groups of children had used the relatively open and brief (one-year) apprenticeships to gain access to skilled work. These two ethnic groups rose to leadership positions in the AFGWU, establishing an ethnic niche in the industry. Gradually, however, tableware factories began to add unskilled southern and eastern Europeans for the general labor jobs. By the time the U.S. Immigration Commission studied the industry in 1909, these immigrants made up one-seventh of the workforce.[7]

The revolution in the manufacture of glass bottles created a quite different workforce profile. Over 70 percent of the workforce in bottle plants were American born, and they controlled the remaining skilled jobs. As semiautomatic machines replaced older hand methods, the industry stopped recruiting skilled immigrants. Instead, bottle manufacturers recruited a largely unskilled labor pool from Europe. Italians alone accounted for exactly half of the immigrant bottle workers. As the example

Table 2.1: Changing Composition of Glass Industry Workforce, 1890–1910 by Birth Characteristics

	Native born/ Native parents	Native born/ Foreign parents	Foreign born	Black
1890 Census	39.3%	32.8%	27.2%	0.8%
1900 Census	47.0	29.4	22.8	0.9
1910 Sample	44.3	22.6	31.1	1.9

Source: Compiled from tables 11–13, U.S. Immigration Commission, *Reports: Immigrants in Industries*, pt. 12, *Glass Manufacturing* (Washington, D.C.: Government Printing Office, 1911), 19–24.

of Jeannette illustrated, bottle factories were hiring new immigrants for unskilled laborer jobs and moving native-born workers into semiskilled, machine-tending positions. At the same time, the children of former craftsmen were leaving the industry, recognizing that the prospects for skilled work were rapidly diminishing.[8]

The situation in window glass was perhaps the most complicated of all the branches. Although the continuous tank had increased the scale of production, the hand-blown process of making window glass remained unchallenged until 1903. In that year, the American Window Glass Company trust introduced a mechanical blowing machine that made much larger glass cylinders. The machine operated by drawing glass vertically, while forcing compressed air into a conical "bait" as it was gradually raised from the tank. The cylinder-blowing machine eventually could make cylinders 40 inches in diameter and 25 feet in length.[9] Use of the cylinder-blowing machine, which eliminated gatherers and blowers, began to move the industry toward mass production techniques, but highly skilled and well-paid craftsmen resisted. When possible, they fled mechanizing plants, such as the one James Chambers built in Jeannette, and pooled their resources to establish cooperatives or small family-owned factories practicing traditional methods.

When Immigration Commission investigators sampled window-glass plants in 1909, they found a bifurcated industry. The composition of the workforce reflected that complexity. There were roughly equal numbers of foreign-born and American-born workers with American-born parents (43 percent for each), but only 1 in 8 was a second-generation immigrant (see table 2.2). Equally important, the foreign-born window-glass workers were fairly equally divided between skilled craftsmen (Belgians, Germans, French, and English) and unskilled, "new immigrant" workers. This composite, however, hid the more revealing picture. Where machines made the cylinders, the foreign-born were principally unskilled Italian and Slavic workers; where plants maintained the older "hand-blown" production methods, the immigrants were mostly highly skilled Belgians, English, and Germans. The old-stock Americans held unskilled positions at the hand-blown plants, and rose to semiskilled production jobs in the mechanized plants, as the example of Jeannette and numerous other sites illustrated.[10]

Regardless of where glassworkers fit in the occupational structure emerging at the onset of the twentieth century, the majority of them were on the move. Much of this had to do with the mobility of the industry during restructuring. Eastern states lost an aggregate of nearly seven hundred jobs between 1890 and 1905, and their share of the nation's glassworkers

Table 2.2: Workforce Composition of Glass Industry Branches in 1910 by Birth Characteristics

	Native born/ Native parents	Native born/ Foreign parents	Foreign born	Black
Window glass	43.2%	12.6%	43.1%	1.1%
Glass bottles	51.2	16.8	28.2	3.8
Tableware	38.1	32.8	28.8	0.3

Source: Compiled from tables 11–13, U.S. Immigration Commission, Reports: Immigrants in Industries, pt. 12, Glass Manufacturing (Washington, D.C.: Government Printing Office, 1911), 19–24.

dropped from 24 percent to under 16 percent. Meanwhile, Indiana and Illinois, which benefited from the shift to natural gas, increased their ratio of the industry's workforce from 1 in 8 to 1 in 4. Even within states, there was movement. Pennsylvania's glassworkers increased in number from 18,510 to 20,794, but there had been considerable movement out of older centers like Pittsburgh, where the costs of production were higher and land and fuel were more expensive, to newer glass towns in rural areas such as New Eagle, Kane, and Charleroi. Moreover, as the story of Jeannette made clear, even when the numbers of glassworkers remained constant, a change in technology could trigger a considerable amount of workforce replacement.[11]

The mobility of glassworkers was likely to be higher at the upper than at the lower end of the job hierarchy. Glass manufacturers often looked to the local population for the unskilled portions of their workforce. For example, in Kane, Pennsylvania, glass factories recruited their general labor from among the Swedish young men whose fathers had immigrated a decade earlier for farm land; in Arnold, Pennsylvania, the glass plant relied on local farm boys until they left for better opportunities in the new tin mills. Of course, when an ample supply of local unskilled labor was unavailable, manufacturers did not hesitate to import new immigrants.[12] For skilled labor, however, the expansion of the industry necessitated the recruitment of migrant and immigrant craftsmen, and the industry tapped well-developed traditions of "tramping" artisans and networks of craft information to match the supply of skilled labor with the demand.[13] Different ethnic groups tended to dominate the skilled labor pool in each of the branches, giving each branch its own transatlantic flavor. In window glass, the Belgians were the dominant group during the critical period of industrial transformation; in tableware, German and Irish craftsmen were the major groups; in bottles, it was the English and the Germans.

Older patterns were changing, however. As the glass industry faced a new century, its corporate and technological restructuring reconfigured the workforce. It was older and more masculine, and it was becoming both less skilled and more ethnically heterogeneous. Although branches experienced this transformation unevenly, change affected all in the industry. One aspect of the experience shared by all was that wages in the industry declined. Through the nineteenth century, glassworker earnings were typically well above the average for all industrial workers. After 1907, they were consistently below the manufacturing average.[14] To understand how workers coped with these changes, it is necessary to explore the experiences of different types of glassworkers.

Unskilled Immigrants

In 1904, when the staff of the U.S. Commissioner of Labor prepared a special report on the regulation and restriction of output in the glass industry, there was no mention of activity by unskilled workers. Unionized craftsmen in the window, bottle, and tableware branches of the industry had developed various strategies, codified into working rules, to protect their jobs and the pace at which they worked.[15] But unskilled workers had no such formalized protections. If they worked as part of a team under the direction of craftsmen, they followed the pace set by the team; if they worked as part of the general labor force—lifting, carrying, loading, and unloading—they worked at the pace established by the foreman in the area. As the various branches of the industry substituted machines for older manual production methods, jobs for unskilled immigrants increased. And, while largely silent in terms of organized resistance to the drive system of factory managers, they fashioned their own means of survival.

The revolution in glassmaking in the 1890s dramatically altered the character of immigrants in the workforce. If the percentage of immigrants was growing, most of that growth involved Italians, Poles, Slovaks, Rumanians, and Magyars. They were relatively recent arrivals who came with little industrial experience. Only 5 percent of the immigrants in bottle making reported any previous factory experience; 72 percent had been in farm or general labor. In tableware and window manufacture, where machines had been introduced but a significant number of plants continued to operate with the older methods, more of the immigrants had experience in glass factories, but they were still outnumbered by laborers.[16] The process of mechanization reduced the flow of skilled glassworkers from England, Germany, France, and Belgium, and opened the taps for unskilled peasants from southern and eastern Europe.

The benefits to employers of substituting machinery and unskilled immigrants for skilled labor were substantial. Bottle manufacture showed the greatest impact; the weekly wages of Italians averaged $8.70, while blacks earned $9.98 and Poles $10.73. By way of contrast, skilled Germans who had years of experience earned over $19 a week. In window glass, Italians earned about $11 a week, while skilled workers averaged over $17 per week. Over the course of the year, the earnings of unskilled male household heads made for a meager existence. Italians made roughly $450, Slovaks $513, and Poles $575, during an era when estimates of the minimum necessary to sustain a family of four stood at around $600.[17]

Consequently, unskilled immigrant glassworkers needed other strategies to survive. One strategy involved leaving families behind and sending money home. Many of the immigrants were young and single, but even married men followed this strategy. Of the married Italians in the bottle industry, for example, only 4 in 10 brought their wives to the United States; of the married Poles, less than 1 in 4 did so. These "birds of passage" came for a job. They crowded into hotels or the homes of immigrant families from their native country, and they tried to save as much as possible to improve their position when they returned.[18]

When unskilled immigrants brought their families with them, survival depended on providing room and board for those who traveled alone. Italian, Polish, and Slovak households in glass communities derived between one-twelfth and one-sixth of their income from boarders. Sixty-five percent of Italian households took in boarders; 56 percent of Polish families did likewise. These households averaged between three and five boarders. Adding in the earnings of children (wives of southern and eastern Europeans in glass towns rarely worked outside the home), unskilled immigrant families at least approached, if they did not exceed, the income necessary to survive. Of course, such strategies placed households under heavy pressure. The households of unskilled immigrant glassworkers had almost twice as many persons per room as did those of American-born glassworkers.[19]

Despite their concentration as unskilled immigrants at the bottom of the job hierarchy, Italians, Slovaks, and Poles developed effective means for community building. Churches and immigrant benefit societies played an important role. In one glass community studied by the Immigration Commission, new immigrants accounted for nearly half of the local population of 8,500. They formed eighteen benefit societies with over nine hundred members. For monthly dues ranging from 25¢ to $1.50, these societies provided weekly sick benefits of $5 and death benefits ranging from $400 to $1,000 to ensure some level of security for unskilled glassworkers. In the same community, Slovak, Polish, Russian, and Italian immigrants had established five different Catholic, Orthodox, and Lutheran churches to minister to their communities. Hard work and frugal living showed some results—Slovak glassworkers sent over $30,000 abroad in 1908, and nearly 1 of every 4 were in the process of buying their own homes. Even the poorest group in the community, the Italians, managed to send home $11,500.[20]

Southern and eastern Europeans lacked the means to establish unions and assert some formal voice in setting the terms and conditions of their employment. Nevertheless, in subtle ways, they exerted influence. Networks of countrymen enabled many to move to plants where the pay or working conditions were somewhat better. Similarly, unskilled immigrants were not tied to the glass industry; when higher paying jobs opened in tin mills or coal mines, southern and eastern Europeans voted with their feet for improvements.[21] But their reactions to the new regimen of the mechanized factories rarely surfaced. Many expected to return to Europe and hoped only for steady work so that they might send money home to their families. Others established households that depended on the efforts of all family members to scratch out some security.

Native Sons

If the transformation of the glass industry injected a new group of unskilled immigrants into glass plants, it also increased the numbers of native-born workers who were the sons of Americans. Some of these sons were following those earlier generations of skilled glassworkers, learning the trades of their fathers. Others were able to grab skilled jobs that were auxiliary to glass production, for example, as carpenters, bricklayers, machinists, and so on. But more were young men who sought industrial employment when glass factories moved into their area. The mechanization of factories actually increased their opportunities, in part because most employers preferred to hire native-born workers, rather than new immigrants, in the semiskilled machine-tending jobs. The history of Arnold, Pennsylvania, illustrates the advantages that native-born Americans had over southern and eastern Europeans.

The small town of Arnold, just a few miles northeast of Pittsburgh, became home to a new window-glass plant in 1892. Belgian, English, and German immigrants and their children made up the skilled portions of the workforce, but over half of the six hundred workers were Americans, located principally in unskilled positions. The mix of employees remained virtually the same until 1900, when tin mills opened in New Kensington, just a mile away. Many of the unskilled Americans left for the higher pay of the tin mills, and the Arnold glass factory introduced Italians for the first time. Other Americans gradually gained promotion into the skilled glass trades as Belgians moved to new factories in the Midwest. Then, in 1904, the Arnold owners introduced the cylinder blowing machine, which triggered a strike by the skilled trades. The strike failed, causing the majority of the remaining craftsmen to leave. By 1909, the Belgian, English, and German craftsmen in the flattening and cutting departments made up about 5 percent of the total; Americans, who had moved into machine-tending positions, made up about 40 percent, and the remaining 55 percent were a mix of Italians, Poles, Slovaks, and Macedonians.[22] Thus, American-born workers twice gained advantages over immigrants in improving their conditions; once when they left for the tin mills and again when they moved into semiskilled mechanized jobs and left the least desirable work to new immigrants. This pattern recurred in numerous glass towns in Pennsylvania, Ohio, Indiana, and Illinois.

As a result, the transformation of glass manufacturing placed the native sons in the middle of the job hierarchy. In bottle making, for example, the average weekly earnings reflected this middle status. The most highly paid workers were the skilled German immigrants, a rapidly declining portion of the workforce. They averaged over $22 per week, working at a breakneck pace on semiautomatic machines. American-born workers with American-born parents, who earned $16.87, were several steps removed from the best paid workers. Lowest on the job hierarchy were the new immigrants, Poles and Italians, who made between $8.61 and $10.73 per week. The situation in window glass was similar; second-generation Belgians and Germans averaged nearly 2 dollars a week more than old-stock American workers, who still made 4 dollars more than new immigrants.[23]

These native sons were thus improving their position as mechanization occurred. Although their weekly earnings lagged behind those of the skilled immigrants and their children, their prospects were brighter. As the new mechanized plants gained a growing share of the market, they operated on a more continual basis, without the long summer shutdowns that skilled workers demanded as a respite from the heat in the unionized factories. Consequently, yearly earnings for the native sons operating machinery, by 1909, more nearly approximated those of craftsmen.[24] Their share of the jobs in the industry was growing, while the children of skilled immigrants were declining as a portion of the workforce.

The optimism of the native sons showed through in a variety of ways. They had higher rates of home ownership than other groups, and they tended to claim the best rentals. Because they were more likely to be rooted in the local community, they were often the last fired during layoffs and the first hired when times improved. Of household heads, 68.3 percent reported working twelve months in 1909; the industry average for all workers was 53.8 percent. Local connections also meant that they had more family resources at their disposal. For instance, some households headed by native sons had income from other sources, such as farms or small businesses. Taking all sources into account, the annual income of the families of native sons averaged $901, the highest of any group. Only 1 in 10 had incomes below $500, compared with more than 1 in 4 for all glassworker families.[25]

Despite their improving status, native sons often found it difficult to break into the craft fraternity. The best example of their exclusion involved snappers in the window-glass plants. As glass industry historian Richard O'Connor notes, snappers became an increasingly essential part of the gathering and blowing "shops" in window glass. But until the 1890s, craft rules limited snappers to assisting only craftsmen who needed extra assistance in their strenuous tasks—those who were making very large glass windows or were "temporarily disabled." The increased size and scale of the glass factories that utilized the continuous tank changed that relationship. Instead of blowers and gatherers working in close proximity to the pot in which the glass was melted, much of the work now took place twenty-five yards from the tank. To maintain production, gatherers and blowers needed another team member, the snapper. Snappers thus rapidly became essential to the earnings of blowers and gatherers.[26]

As their duties increased, the profile of snappers changed. Once limited to small numbers of the young sons of blowers and gatherers who expected to enter into an apprenticeship, by 1900, snappers tended to be young men who had little prospect of moving into one of the crafts. Belgian, German, and English craftsmen no longer looked to their sons to find snappers; instead, they preferred men who might be satisfied with a career of snapping. Quickly, conflict emerged. While blowers and gatherers wanted men with experience and some skills, they had to pay the snappers out of their own earnings and thus tried to pay them as little as possible. One snapper wrote to the *Commoner and Glass Worker* about his prospects after working for seven years:

> What encouragement does a snapper have? I never lost a day's work from sickness or any fault of mine; always did my work well; have been cursed by drunken blowers and gatherers; have been offered by more than one

blower and gatherer more pay to leave the man I was working on, but have stayed out the season with the one I hired with at the beginning of the blast; but I had no brother or relative working in the trade and so I am doomed to work for the paltry sum of $6–$7 a week. That is, if I wish to stay in the window glass business.[27]

Native-born snappers clashed with foreign-born craftsmen. When apprenticeships opened, blowers and gatherers "took on" their sons, brothers, or nephews, while "American boys" who had been snapping for ten years, "who had wives and families," were denied opportunities. Moreover, whenever snappers tried to organize their own union and improve their wages and working conditions, the craftsmen's union routinely cooperated with employers to crush the effort. "No one can exploit a common working man, that is a common laborer, like a skilled workman," according to Frank Gessner, the patriotic editor of the *National Glass Budget.*[28] For more than two decades, the snappers tried to gain admission to the unions of skilled workers in the window-glass industry, but the union consistently turned them away. Even as the union faced obsolescence in 1919 and again in 1923, blowers and gatherers refused to consider solidarity with a group of native sons who were instrumental to their work.[29]

As technology and corporate restructuring transformed the glass industry at the turn of the century, American-born young men had advantages over southern and eastern European immigrants, even though neither group had experience in the industry. At the same time, native sons found it difficult to break into the best paying glass trades or to obtain support from craftsmen to broaden union membership. They made their greatest advances in bottle making, where union control was declining most rapidly. However, even those improvements were fleeting. When Robert S. and Helen Merrell Lynd did their famous study of Muncie, Indiana, in the 1920s, few sons of bottle makers wanted to follow in the footsteps of their fathers.[30] The revolution in glassmaking, then, initially gave American-born boys an entering wedge into industrial employment, but further restructuring meant that few would stay permanently in the glass industry.

Women and Children

Some of the most enduring images in the photography of the reformer Lewis Hine involve pictures of young boys on a short stool hunched over molding machines at a glassblower's feet (see illus. 3). Hine captured one of the major criticisms of the glass industry at the turn of the century—its use of child labor. The introduction of the continuous tank made the problem worse; as factories operated through the night, it meant that children were needed around the clock.[31] Addis Thompson, secretary of the National Glass Company, defended the practice at the U.S. Industrial Commission hearings, claiming that "it is almost impossible to do without the small boy in carrying the work over from the presser to the finisher . . . carrying it to the reheating furnace, and to be tempered." Even Denis Hayes, president of the Glass Bottle Blowers, seemed unapologetic about the practice: "Boys come into the factory at 12, 13, 14. Before the child-labor law they went in at 9. I went to work at 12."[32]

The use of child labor was controversial, however, partly because a major campaign led by the National Child Labor Committee (NCLC) targeted the particular evils of glass factory employment for children.

Illus. 3. A glass-blower with a mold boy at the Seneca Glass Works, Morgantown, West Virginia, October 1908. The mold boys sat in that position for an entire "move," which ran about four and a half hours. Photograph by Lewis Hine. From the National Child Labor Committee Collection. Courtesy of the Library of Congress.

In particular, the NCLC was concerned about the health of young boys who worked near the furnace in temperatures typically exceeding 100 degrees, often in cramped positions or on their feet for long periods without breaks. The combination of drastic shifts in temperature when boys left the hot factories in winter and the heavy fumes and dust present at the furnaces were responsible, according to reformers, for high rates of pneumonia, rheumatism, tuberculosis, and respiratory diseases among these boys. They also suffered from cuts, burns, skin irritations, and even eye trouble caused by the furnace glare.[33]

Skilled workers resisted efforts to eliminate children from the factories. Since the majority of craftsmen earned their pay by the piece, they needed as much help as they could get to maintain production and high wages. Thus, they used their sons and nephews as helpers, which at the same time supplemented family earnings and maintained parental supervision. Craftsmen also could begin training their sons for the craft. The *National Glass Budget* recognized the reluctance of skilled workers to give up child labor: "Even the big Belgian who blowed [sic] the big ring in the window glass factory was not ashamed to lay off and let his pot remain spare because his little boy was not on hand to fan his brow, hand him his sweatrag, cracking iron, and obey his commands."[34] Fathers could at times be tyrants in the factory, but they could also use their power to protect kin from abuse. In 1904, when young girls walked out of the Fostoria Company's plant in Moundsville, West Virginia, the Flint Glass Workers came to their aid and had wage cuts restored. Of course, when boys halted work against the interests of skilled workers, such as the 1899 strike of the "shove-in" boys in Pennsylvania, skilled workers could be quite harsh in reimposing discipline, even threatening to recruit strikebreakers.[35]

Manufacturers resisted the NCLC even more vigorously, hoping to keep labor costs as low as possible. As late as 1909, the bottle industry could pay boys as little as $5.85 per week; tableware was worse, paying boys between ages fourteen and eighteen only $5.78 and girls a meager $4.21. Industry leaders argued that the industry could not survive without the speed and agility of children, and that ending child labor would deny boys the opportunity to learn a trade and to contribute to much-needed family income. Employers also rejected the idea that nighttime labor in glass factories prevented boys from receiving an education. The *National Glass Budget* claimed that many successful men began working in the industry at age ten, and advised child labor reform advocates to "turn their attention to such children as are in need of their assistance instead of wasting their energy in an attempt to prevent boys from acquiring a trade and thus fitting themselves for gaining a livelihood."[36]

Despite the opposition of glass manufacturers, between 1890 and 1905, child labor in glass factories shrank from 15.5 percent to 10.1 percent. State laws contributed to the decline, but, more important, glassworkers experiencing the new factory regimen introduced by the technological revolution in glassmaking began to feel less interested in subjecting their children to such a future. One craftsman asserted: "I would rather send my boys straight to hell than send them by way of the glass house."[37] Technology, in fact, while viewed with suspicion by craftsmen, actually reduced the need for boys who could "get about quicker." Conveyors did much of the routine carrying in mechanized bottle factories and in window-glass plants after 1900. The inventor and industrialist Michael Owens even received an unsolicited letter of praise from the NCLC for his innovations that helped eliminate child labor from bottle plants. Only in tableware factories were children still a significant presence by 1910. There, boys and girls age sixteen and under still made up almost 22 percent of the workforce.[38]

Before 1890, women did not make up a major portion of the workforce in American glass factories. At the onset of the revolution in glassmaking, they were only 1 of every 25 glassworkers, limited primarily to decorating, washing, and packing departments in tableware plants. In the United States, a dual monopoly of glassworker unions that negotiated high wages and manufacturers who were protected from wage competition by high tariffs enabled men to keep a tight hold on jobs. This was not the case in European glass factories. At St. Helens in England, women made up 13 percent of the workforce, and in Belgium, large numbers of women worked, even in window-glass plants.[39]

The economic depression of the 1890s and the restructuring of the industry threatened to bring more women into American factories. Agitation for child labor regulations cut the numbers of boys in the industry just as employers looked to new sources of cheap labor to reduce operating costs. Factory managers viewed women as a potential substitute, doubling their numbers during the decade and increasing their percentage from 4.2 to 6.7 percent. This trend brought a vocal response from union men in Ohio, Indiana, and Pennsylvania, who called it a "dangerous and pernicious" trend. They claimed that the heat of the glasshouse frequently forced men to work "half disrobed," which they argued would have a negative moral influence on young women. Union members in Anderson, Indiana, even involved the state factory inspector in their efforts to rid the factory of females. When he found that the young women were all of legal age, he promised to visit the company headquarters and "ask that the girls be discharged, and if the request is not granted he will try to secure an injunction against their employment."[40] Some of this agitation must have worked; women declined in absolute and relative numbers over the ensuing five years, although they continued to be an important part of the workforce in tableware.

Most of these female workers were young girls: two-thirds were aged nineteen and under; seven-eighths were under age 25. Few skilled glass-worker households had wives who worked outside the home. Only 9 of 613 families studied by the U.S. Immigration Commission reported working wives. But clearly, many glassworkers made room for their daughters to work in the years before their marriages. The vast majority of female glassworkers in 1909 were of German, Belgian, English, and French backgrounds—the very groups that dominated the skilled trades. For the majority of female glassworkers, then, the job was temporary, a stage between school and marriage. They made, on average, less than $6 a week, and only 1 in 6 could make as much as $7.50 a week.[41]

The revolution in glassmaking gradually eliminated women and children from those segments of the industry where mass-production technology made its greatest advances—bottles and windows. In ta-bleware, however, the work process still relied more heavily on older methods of production, and decorating, carrying, washing, and packing the ware was not easily mechanized, due to the variety of small items produced. There, women and children maintained a presence, although it is extremely difficult to gauge their reactions to the changes in the glass industry. Only sporadically did their resistance to management practices leave a record.

The Transatlantic Craftsman's Empire

In the early morning hours of July 4, 1898, the French liner La Bourgogne, bound for Europe, sank off the coast of Nova Scotia after colliding with another boat in a dense fog. Among its passengers were three glasswork-ers from Jeannette, Pennsylvania, at least two from Arnold, and one from Alexandria, Indiana. Most noteworthy was the disappearance of "Big Joe" Azelvander, a native of Switzerland. Azelvander was an "extraordinarily large man," able to blow an unusually enormous amount of glass. The National Glass Budget claimed that he could earn as much as $700 a month at a time when many skilled workers earned that much in a year. When Azelvander went down with the steamer, he had more than $20,000 in cash and securities on his person, triggering a search that would eventually recover both his body and his money.[42]

The story of *La Bourgogne's* demise is revealing for more than the personal tragedy of its passengers. It sheds light on the transatlantic movement of skilled glassworkers and their privileged status among wage earners through the end of the nineteenth century. This privileged status shaped an ethos that encompassed attitudes toward culture, politics, and relations with employers. Glass industry craftsmen moved among communities of their trade throughout Europe and the Americas, as well into new centers of production in Russia, Turkey, and Afghanistan. But few places offered better opportunities than the United States. There, glassworkers entered the twentieth century with expectations of a standard of living well above that of the average worker. They also protected access to their trade, so that their sons, brothers, and nephews could pursue the craft, often to the exclusion of native-born workers. However, the restructuring of the glass industry starting in the 1890s posed a significant threat to the culture, politics, and economic welfare of these highly mobile craftsmen. Their various attempts to grapple with these changes had a profound impact on glass towns that emerged throughout the manufacturing belt running from New Jersey to Indiana.

One reason that the United States had been until the 1890s a desirable destination for glassworkers was the slow pace of change there. The industry weekly, the *National Glass Budget,* accused American employers of being "mossback" manufacturers. They were far behind in introducing the technological improvements used in Belgium, England, and Germany. Glass industrialists in the United States had done little to take control of the production process or even the training of key production workers, relying instead on recruiting craftsmen from Europe and on high tariff rates to protect their markets. As a consequence, work remained under the control of skilled immigrants and their children, and wages remained high relative to those in Europe, attracting even more craftsmen. When European glassworkers tried to resurrect an international federation of unions, they found it "impossible to understand the cold indifference of the trades unions of American glass workers, who have no ideas beyond the walls of their narrow lodge rooms, and are limited in their sympathy to the isolated craft interests of their own branch."[43]

At the start of the 1890s, American glass craftsmen maintained fairly amicable relationships with their employers. Workers routinely recognized the important transitions in the careers of manufacturers and managers, and employers celebrated with their skilled craftsmen when valued employees retired or moved into new opportunities. Likewise, craftsmen seemed to take pride in the accomplishments of employers in other walks of life. West Virginia glassworkers supported the political successes of Nathan B. Scott as he became a powerful United States senator, and Ohio craftsmen cheered the efforts of chimney manufacturer J. J. Gill to become a popular congressman. Glass manufacturers in Congress often repaid worker support by promoting tariff restrictions and other issues important to labor. For example, one bottle manufacturer in Marion, Indiana, used his appointment as director of the Indiana state prison to remove prison labor from competition with union jobs. Even James Chambers, the manufacturer in Jeannette, Pennsylvania, who helped bring technological change to window-glass plants, frequently earned plaudits from glassworkers. They appreciated his trade negotiations "with Belgian manufacturers to keep foreign glass out of this [the American] market."[44] These relationships had been a part of the culture of glassworker communities and were slow to disappear. Despite the role of Michael J. Owens in developing technology and managerial practices that eliminated skilled work and collective bargaining, glassworkers in Wheeling, West Virginia, continued to think of him as one of their own and to applaud his tremendous success well into the twentieth century. Even the Socialist president of the AFGWU, Thomas Rowe, considered Owens, the former unionist, a close friend.[45]

Skilled glassworkers held their employers in high esteem for a reason—it paid. While men like "Big Joe" Azelvander were clearly the exception, immigrant and second-generation glass craftsmen expected to earn a good living. In tableware, skilled German craftsmen could earn over $20 per week, well above the industry average for male workers of $14.20 in 1909. In bottle making, nearly 4 of every 10 German immigrants and children of German immigrants earned over $25 per week, in a branch where the average wage was $15.73.[46] Despite the introduction of machinery, the various branches of the industry only gradually cut wages and operated nonunion shops. Instead, the close connections that had developed between craftsmen and manufacturers encouraged many employers to accommodate glassworker unions and give union members the opportunity to operate new machines. Even where mechanization had progressed the most, in bottles, the GBBA made concessions that enabled its members to hold onto high-paying jobs by nearly tripling their productivity. Union president Denis Hays might complain that "with this increased expenditure of energy he is shortening life by burning the candle at both ends," but bottle makers maintained earnings well above the average for industrial workers.[47]

Into the 1890s, skilled immigrant glassworkers were the "labor aristocracy" of the United States. Their living conditions, in contrast to those of the southern and eastern Europeans, reflected their privileged status. They typically earned much more and lived in more spacious housing. Because they were moving within craft communities to specific jobs, French, German, Belgian, and English glassworkers tended to move with their families. They were much less likely to take in boarders, and those families who did took in fewer boarders than Polish, Italian, or Slovak families. But since craftsmen typically hired their own helpers, German, Belgian, and French families were far more likely to have sons and daughters at work. The comparison of German and Slovak families is telling. Slovak families earned one-sixth of their total family income from boarders but only 3 percent from the contributions of children. German families reversed those figures; only 3 percent of their income came from boarders while 20 percent came from the earnings of children.[48] Finally, the lure of craft positions in the glass industry dictated that skilled workers moved with stronger intentions of permanently relocating. Most had learned English at the time they emigrated from Belgium, France, or Germany, and they moved more quickly to become fully naturalized citizens. After five years in the United States, only 13 of 48 Italians in the window-glass industry had even begun the process of naturalization, but 42 of 47 Belgians had done so. In the bottle industry, only 4 of 72 Italians and Poles with five years experience were fully naturalized; 28 of 30 German and Irish workers had completed the process.[49]

Advantages in earnings, incomes, and family conditions translated into a dense craft culture for skilled glassworkers, held together by kin and ethnic networks. In older glass locales, such as the south side of Pittsburgh, the skilled workers were largely the sons of German and English craftsmen who had pioneered the new industrial communities in the 1860s. In the newer glass towns that emerged with the shift to natural gas, the skilled workers were more likely to be immigrants who helped the various branches expand.[50] In both settings, networks connected migrants and return migrants through family, friendship, and attachment to shared places of origin in ways that helped craftsmen move easily within the United States as well as across the Atlantic Ocean. English glassworkers from St. Helens or Belgian craftsmen from Jumet reconstructed communities in Newark, Ohio, or Matthews, Indiana. There, the existence of friendly faces lowered the moving costs for subsequent migrants because they could serve as guides to newcomers on issues of employment and housing.[51]

Equally important, skilled glassworkers moved within an organizational framework of fellow craftsmen that determined the terms and conditions of employment as well as acceptable standards of behavior on and off the job. Local Assembly 300 of window-glass workers established sixty-six "Rules for Working" governing virtually every aspect of production. Included were rules mandating crew size, the pace of work, the times when certain tasks could be performed, and the months of the "blast" when the furnaces were in operation. Committees of the AFGWU met with employers on an annual basis to determine the number of items to be made in each half-day shift (called a "move"), the wages for each move, what to do with faulty items, and the responsibilities for routine maintenance. The GBBA did not regulate output, but did closely monitor access to the craft through long apprenticeships and strict ratios of apprentices to journeymen. The GBBA rules also mandated crew size, the length of the workday, and how long workers were expected to wait at their workplaces while employees fixed "bad glass" or machine breakages.[52]

Union rules and apprenticeships taught young workers the code of the craft and reinforced their attachment to it. Each union had stiff penalties for workers who violated the rules or acted in an "unmanly" manner toward an employer or a fellow member. The AFGWU, for example, disciplined members for discussing union business with management and for breaking production quotas. But the union also fined members for drinking while at work or making "slanderous" statements about the union. Window-glass workers likewise punished such transgressions as stealing rollers, improperly "booking" glass, or shoddy workmanship.[53] Of course, many young workers learned the rules at home as well as at work. Apprentices in window glass needed a family connection (a father, an uncle or a brother) to enter one of the skilled trades. While the bottle and tableware branches were somewhat more open, apprenticing for a craftsman meant more than merely learning the skills. Apprentices also learned the principles of "fairness" that "tightened the bonds of solidarity" among craftsmen and stipulated proper relations between employers and employees.[54]

Upon entering the craft fraternity, glassworkers shared in a culture that transcended the workplace. Picnics, dances, and festivals punctuated the end of the "blast," or the shutdown for repairs, over the Christmas and New Year's holidays. Belgians, in particular, were famous for their "ducases" just prior to the summer hiatus. These carnivals attracted craftsmen from all the neighboring towns and included cooking contests, pigeon races, games, and other entertainments. The *National Glass Budget* noted the transatlantic importance of these events, remarking that the proceeds of the Hartford, Indiana, carnival would "enable the big bluffers to visit their fatherland and return in time for the next fire without spending a cent of their own money."[55] Connections to their European cultural roots united glass craftsmen in other ways as well. Glassworkers were known for their musical talents and often made up local community bands that accompanied local parades and other special events. In Salem, West Virginia, for example, the community band was primarily Belgian window-glass craftsmen; in Muncie, Indiana, German flint glass workers performed a dance program that included the "Flints Waltz," the "Gaffer Quadrille," the "Catsup Blowers' Two Step," and the "Wide Mantle Schottische."[56]

Recreational clubs demonstrated the greater access to leisure enjoyed by glass industry craftsmen, especially during summer shutdowns. In July 1900, the fishing clubs of three glass plants along the Ohio River shared a summer camp in New Martinsville, West Virginia. In addition to boating and fishing, the clubs held joint entertainments that showcased the singing and comedic talents of German, Irish, and English glassworkers. Glass towns in southwestern Pennsylvania and northern West Virginia often alternated competitions in Belgian handball and American baseball, featuring local athletes. Other clubs organized camping trips, rod and gun clubs, and vacation excursions to Atlantic City and Niagara Falls. Commercial travel agencies gave evidence of the affluence of glass industry craftsmen by routinely advertising special excursion rates in the pages of the *Commoner and Glassworker.*[57]

Clubs and societies enveloped glassworkers in an atmosphere of mutual support that also provided important links to transnational communities. In Charleroi, Pennsylvania, for instance, skilled glassworkers congregated in the German Turnverein, "one of the most pretentious buildings in town." There, German, French, and Belgian craftsmen enjoyed a swimming pool, billiards, and weekly dances. The hall also offered special rooms for beer drinking and card playing, favorite pastimes of several of the groups. Although the club admitted some Americans, social gatherings followed the customs of the "old country," while promoting sociability among the different groups making up the skilled workers. In Matthews, Indiana, "the best place of amusement" was the French Club, which had a large reception room and a dance hall that accommodated six hundred people. Reflecting its French and Belgian leadership, the club featured musical entertainment, pigeon races, and dramatic performances, in addition to nightly card playing and beer drinking.[58] Skilled glassworkers also used clubs and fraternal societies to complement union insurance against death and illness or to help families buy groceries at favorable prices. In Pt. Marion, Pennsylvania, and Moundsville, West Virginia, skilled craftsmen dominated branches of the Odd

Fellows, while Belgians began *La Prevoyance*, a benevolent association. French glassworkers in Charleroi operated a benefit organization for co-operative shopping on the Rochdale model, as did the English and Belgian workers in Clarksburg and Salem, West Virginia.[59]

Skilled glassworkers thus blended ethnic and craft subcultures to create a transnational occupational identity. This identity transcended the particular ethnic group, as plants mixed skilled immigrant glassworkers from England, Germany, France, and Belgium, workers who might also have worked for a time in another country. But it was also an exclusive identity, intent on protecting craft prerogatives and potentially passing them on to sons. (It was also an intensely masculine culture.) Through craft rules, kin networks, and an active sociability, glassworkers reinforced their bonds in their new communities. Meanwhile, they kept abreast of developments in Europe through both craft and ethnic publications as well as through the movements of people. For instance, in 1899, Belgian window-glass workers were excited that Albert Delwarte, a leader of the Belgian socialists, came to Jeannette to start a political and economic journal, *Le Bourdon*. They felt that it would have appeal to those "who, under his leadership in his native Belgium, achieved the suffrage for the working class, and in their adopted country, have preserved their manhood and intellectual independence."[60]

Industry Restructuring and the Workers' Political Economy

The restructuring of the glass industry, which shifted into high gear at the end of the 1890s, threatened the transatlantic empire of skilled glassworkers. The GBBA witnessed the rise of a nonunion sector that controlled 30 percent of the industry by 1898. To maintain collective bargaining agreements with such influential firms as Ball Brothers, Macbeth-Evans, and Hazel, the GBBA accepted price list reductions as high as 50 percent on some items.[61] The AFGWU confronted a trust, the United States Glass Company, which sought through combination to gain control over the market for tumblers, mugs, and jars. The trust sought to impose new rules, uniform wage cuts, and "iron clad rules" that, according to AFGWU circular number 14, "demanded that our members shall give up their manhood and leave the union." The trust locked out 1,500 union members in a five-year struggle that cost the flints approximately $1.2 million in strike benefits. Moreover, the AFGWU locked horns with the GBBA in a jurisdictional dispute caused by declining memberships.[62] In window glass, the production process did not diminish the need for the skills of blowers, gatherers, flatteners, and cutters until 1903, but the industry reorganization effected by the introduction of the continuous tank wreaked havoc. The newer gas-belt plants became dominant just as the depression of the 1890s triggered an employment crisis in the industry. Manufacturers took advantage of the situation to slash wages, precipitating regional, ethnic, and craft conflict within LA 300, the union of skilled workers in window glass. By 1897, LA 300 was in disarray, and separate unions of flatteners and cutters shattered skilled labor solidarity.[63]

Some manufacturers were excited by the prospect of breaking the power of skilled workers. As early as 1899, Frank Glessner, editor of the *National Glass Budget*, crowed that the "entire glass working methods of centuries are being revolutionized, cost is reduced and output is greatly enlarged." Four years later, Glessner related a conversation with Robert D. Layton, a former leader of the Knights of Labor, in which Layton spoke of glassworkers' reluctance to believe that mechanization was changing their lives. Layton asked: "Don't you know that no man ever frankly welcomes or accepts an unpleasant truth?"[64] Mechanization was an unpleasant reality for skilled workers. For example, when the U.S. commissioner of labor investigated output in the glass industry in 1904, he discovered that lamp chimney manufacturers had increased output from 250 to 1,300 chimneys per turn, while cutting labor costs in half. Moreover, the machine process had replaced a highly paid blower with a semiskilled feeder. The manufacture of fruit jars followed a similar scenario. A traditional shop of three blowers could make as much as 3,600 jars per day; a machine shop of one presser and one gatherer easily produced 4,300 in the same time. As early as 1898, the *Commoner and Glassworker* began running articles wondering: "Will the Machine Make Tramps?"[65]

Beginning with the depression of the 1890s, conflict between employers and workers in the glass industry escalated. The older mutuality that had bound them together began to show cracks. Reports of confrontations in Washington and Rochester, Pennsylvania, Muncie, Indiana, and Bridgeton, New Jersey, filled the pages of the *National Glass Budget* and the *Commoner and Glassworker*. Denis Hayes, GBBA president, railed against "the great organization of capital" that squeezed bottle workers. He attributed the bitter five-month strike of the GBBA in southern New Jersey to the fact that the "men were bound to a condition of absolute servitude" by powerful corporations that cut wages and denied employees basic civil rights.[66] Such efforts to reduce wages in the tableware industry provoked violent reaction. In Tarentum, Pennsylvania, the Flaccus Glass Company put barbed wire on its fence and recruited guards to protect strikebreakers. Following an injunction against the AFGWU, tempers flared as nonunion workers became increasingly bold, leaving one union member dead and another in jail.[67] The annual struggles became so contentious that the *National Glass Budget* lamented: "There is not the least sign that the day will ever dawn when there will be no trouble" in glass manufacture due to the "labor trust"[68] (see illus. 4).

Unions in all three branches began to think about politics in new ways. The old alliance of employers and employees behind Republican Party high-tariff candidates began to lose support. The *National Glass Budget* sneered that "glass workers are beginning to lose faith in the protecting power of the tariff, and that the trades union, large defense fund, and absence of non-union factories, are not such a safe anchorage and sure shield as they were once deemed to be."[69] Politics took on a more adversarial tone. In the wake of a local labor conflict, the AFGWU in Wellsburg, West Virginia, for example, ran union member John Kunkle on the Democratic ticket against state senator Samuel George, a Republican glass manufacturer. Likewise, window-glass workers deserted the Matthews, Indiana, Republican club in 1902 to run an "independent labor

THE KNOCK OUT DOSE.

LABOR TRUST DOCTOR—"This dose will put you to sleep, my friend. It may produce nausea enough so you will throw it up. If not you will never come to; but don't worry, we'll run the business for you."

Illus. 4. "The Knock Out Dose." Antiunion cartoon featuring Thomas Rowe, president of the AFGWU, and Denis Hayes, president of the Glass Bottle Blowers Association. From National Glass Budget, *February 10, 1906. Courtesy of* National Glass Budget *and the* Glass Factory Directory.

ticket." Even Denis Hayes began to wonder if his traditional support for Republican candidates was the correct policy. He singled out David M. Parry, leader of the National Association of Manufacturers, "whose radical utterances have done more to create a bitter feeling than those of any man now before the public."[70]

Increasingly, formerly Republican glassworkers began to consider more radical alternatives. The 1899 AFGWU convention officially endorsed the international socialist movement, and Socialist Thomas Rowe moved into the union's presidency in 1903. Likewise, the window-glass workers' LA 300 put forth a Socialist candidate for its presidency in 1898.[71] More persistently, in towns where glassworkers made up a significant portion of the population, independent labor and Socialist tickets began to appear. In March 1900 in Muncie, Indiana, flint glass workers led a ticket that advocated municipal ownership of public utilities and promised an eight-hour workday with a minimum wage for all city workers. But Marion, Indiana, where city voters elected several Socialists to council positions, captured the prize for the "most socialist town" in the state. The Indiana Socialist Labor Party had four glassworkers on its statewide ticket in 1900, including members of the GBBA and the AFGWU.[72] But Indiana was not the only state where the revolution in glassmaking prompted political activism. In Findlay and Toledo, Ohio, glassworkers gained office, as was the case in southwestern Pennsylvania and the northern panhandle of West Virginia.[73]

In some cases, radicalism had a transatlantic flavor. In particular, Belgian window-glass workers imbibed a political culture in which unionism and socialism mixed easily. Concentrations of Belgians in Charleroi, Jeannette, and Pt. Marion, Pennsylvania, raised funds through union assessments, as well as social events, to support strikes by the Parti Ouvrier Belge (Belgian Workers Party) to win both improved working conditions and full political citizenship. They read the newspapers from Belgium and hosted important Socialist activists from their homeland.[74] Glass manufacturers, of course, worried that Belgians absorbed too much of that culture. The *National Glass Budget* complained that conditions in the window-glass industry were contentious because of "the economic teaching received at the hands of the *Partie Ouvrier.*" While *Budget* editor Frank Glessner admired the "jolly, jovial and sunny-souled" character of the Belgians, he choked on the political and economic ideas that they brought to the glass industry in the United States.[75]

Especially disturbing to glass manufacturers was the appearance of worker-owned cooperatives, which employers associated with a dangerous foreign disruption of industry stability. Success in window glass rested precariously on careful regulation of output and markets. The depression years of the 1890s upset that balance, and manufacturers had turned to a marketing trust, the American Window Glass Company, to restore the balance in their favor. However, improvements in the market brought new competitors into the industry and led to overproduction. When strikes closed Belgian window-glass plants in 1898 and 1900, profits soared for American firms. However, the relatively low costs of entering the industry led to a flood of new independent firms, raising supply and wages, which triggered declining prices and excess capacity.[76]

A major component of the threat to stability in the window-glass industry was the rise of cooperative plants, especially those formed by French and Belgian craftsmen who disliked the changes introduced by the continuous tank. During the 1890s, these skilled workers had gained a leading role in LA 300, and they used this power to direct union policies toward helping worker-owned cooperatives. By 1900, LA 300 had loaned $29,000 to seven separate cooperative plants. Together with the independents, they controlled 42 percent of capacity, seriously limiting the control of the window-glass trust. The *National Glass Budget* bemoaned this intrusion of these "clannish" workers but also recognized that the French and Belgians were the "most energetic" cooperators, because "they are as a rule closer students of economics than the average American workman."[77]

The real danger was that the average American workman might learn the lessons of the French and Belgian window-glass workers. Cooperatives, in fact, became a part of worker strategies in other branches of the industry. In 1896, the AFGWU considered loans to flint bottle factories in Hyde Park, Pennsylvania, and Ottawa, Illinois, and to workers in Bellaire, Ohio, to begin a lantern factory. In 1899, the flints followed up their endorsement of socialism with a union-controlled cooperative in Summitville, Indiana. With the elevation of Thomas Rowe to the presidency of the AFGWU in 1903, the prospects for careful regulation of output in the tableware industry appeared to be in jeopardy, due to Rowe's "socialistic doctrines" and "insane mania" for cooperatives.[78]

As the nineteenth century closed, the harmony of interest with which employers and skilled workers had begun the 1890s was under much stress. Union leaders like Rowe and Denis Hayes protested that owners and workers were no longer neighbors and friends. Meanwhile, the voice of the manufacturers warned unions of the futility of struggle against the machines. "In all these cases," claimed Frank Glessner, "the workers have been taught to rely on the power of organization to retard industrial progress, and so firm has become their conviction not only in the efficiency of their organization, but [also] in the rightfulness of their cause" that, he said, they had chosen to pursue policies that worked against their fellow workers and to the disadvantage of the industry.[79]

With the industry in turmoil, one of the ways employers could try to compete was to move to where fuel costs were cheapest and silica sand was plentiful. In the 1890s, those areas had been southwestern Pennsylvania, Ohio, and Illinois. After 1900, one of the most promising states was West Virginia. Between 1900 and 1905, the number of glass factories in the state more than doubled, and it jumped past New York, Maryland, and Massachusetts to become the sixth largest state in glass production. During the ensuing fifteen years, West Virginia's share of glassmaking would increase, ranking it behind only Pennsylvania in 1920.

As the glass industry prepared to take advantage of the abundant natural resources of West Virginia, employers and workers were enmeshed in industry restructuring. A revolution in glassmaking was remaking workforces and work processes. Technology, employer designs, and union strategies altered the gender, ethnicity and skill levels of workers and affected their opportunities, standards of living, and politics. But the revolution in glassmaking affected each branch of the industry differently. As new glass communities emerged in the Mountain State, the dynamics of change in the particular branches of the glass industry left an imprint on the society, culture, and politics of glass towns.

PART II

Glass Towns and
Political Economy
in West Virginia

3   The Development Faith
and the Glass Industry

The restructuring of the various branches of the glass industry came at an opportune moment for West Virginia. Entrepreneurs were
just beginning to tap the incredible reserves of coal, oil, and natural gas,
energy resources critical to the second industrial revolution. Although
the Baltimore and Ohio Railroad had opened north-central West Virginia
to the possibilities of economic development as early as the 1850s, only
the Ohio River towns, like Wheeling, enjoyed significant growth and
developed a manufacturing base. Much of the mountainous state seemed
impermeable. Furthermore, through the 1880s, state politics rested se-
curely in the hands of men for whom industrialization had a limited
appeal. That changed rapidly after 1890, as a flurry of railroad building
connected rich deposits of coal, oil, and gas to national markets and created for key political leaders a faith in economic development that soon
won over the electorate. Resource extraction, in some areas controlled
by powerful outside interests, surpassed agriculture as the dominant
economic activity of the state.[1]
    For some West Virginia entrepreneurs, the opportunities opened by
rich fuel resources led to a modified version of this development ethos.
Particularly in the northern portion of the state, where a modicum of
urban, industrial development had preceded the boom in resource extraction, local boosters saw the potential for attracting manufacturing
enterprises to the region. They believed that the growth of a manufacturing base would create a domestic market for energy resources while also

helping to expand opportunities for merchants and real estate developers. Boosters in the small railroad towns that doubled as county seats and banking centers—Clarksburg, Fairmont, Moundsville—had visions of greatly increasing the local population and business activity.[2]

Few industries offered West Virginia boosters a more inviting target than glass. The technological changes that introduced the continuous tank placed a premium on supplies of natural gas, which the state could furnish in abundance. Ample deposits of silica sand and inexpensive land for factories offered additional lures. These assets complemented the availability, in close proximity, of skilled glassworkers, due to the earlier concentration of glass manufacturing in southwestern Pennsylvania and Ohio. Finally, the relatively modest capital investment required to enter the industry encouraged small firms, cooperatives, and even novices to take advantage of an expanding market. For all these reasons, glassmaking became one of the most important manufacturing industries in the state in the early twentieth century. This chapter will explore the factors that left West Virginia economically underdeveloped until the 1890s as well as the hopes of some that the industry could promise a different future.

Unequaled Opportunities

In 1891, A. B. Fleming, the governor of West Virginia, proclaimed that the "vast possibilities of the State are as yet scarcely realized." He noted that railroads, people, and investment had "swept heedlessly by" the state, unaware of its millions of acres of virtually "untouched" valuable original forests and "vast mineral resources." According to Fleming, no other state possessed such cheap and abundant raw materials or offered "such conspicuous opportunities for safe and profitable investment of capital."[3]

To the men who had separated West Virginia from Virginia during the Civil War, Fleming's words would have signaled deep disappointment. Many of the fathers of the statehood movement rejected the traditionalistic political culture of the Old Dominion that placed power in "hereditary and cumulative" offices commanded by cliques of local elites lodged in county courthouses. In the words of John Alexander Williams, the new statehood leaders "borrowed an Ohio broom to sweep away Virginian cobwebs." What this meant was that West Virginia's creators preferred a new political system that promoted education, democratic reforms (the secret ballot, annual elections, a reorganized judiciary), and policies favoring a more modern commercial and industrial economy.[4] This perspective, in part, reflected the disproportionate influence of Wheeling in the proceedings of the founding conventions, for which it served as the host city. Wheeling was a burgeoning industrial town, more like its close neighbors in Ohio and Pennsylvania than its distant cousins in Virginia. Two out of three heads of households in Wheeling were born out of state and out of the South, being either migrants from Connecticut, Pennsylvania, and Ohio or immigrants from Germany and Ireland. They wanted schools, railroads, tariffs, and tax policies favorable to industry, not a limited government content with the traditional agricultural economy.[5]

The founders of statehood, however, confronted a population that did not share their outlook. Indeed, the inclusion of counties south of the Kanawha River and east of the Monongahela River within West Virginia's boundaries meant that perhaps one-third of the state's voters sympathized with the Confederacy. A much larger portion opposed the racial and economic policies of the Republican Party once the war ended. Governor Arthur I. Boreman bolstered the party's short-term prospects by disfranchising ex-Confederates, but the debate over extending the suffrage to African Americans sparked by the Fifteenth Amendment split the Republicans. Liberal Republican William H. Flick sought to unify support for black suffrage by restoring the voting rights of ex-Confederates in 1870.[6] The plan backfired. Democrats regained control of the state and immediately called for a convention to rewrite the West Virginia constitution. Gone from power were the founding fathers of statehood, who in many ways had "prefigured the corporate capitalists who in time would dominate West Virginia business and politics," according to John Alexander Williams. Gone, too, was the new political culture they had introduced. For the next two decades, the Democrats ruled, bolstered by a traditionalistic political system inherited from antebellum Virginia that restored the courthouse cliques. From 1872 to 1895, Democrats won 64 percent of the seats in the West Virginia House of Delegates and over 70 percent of the state senate seats. Only once in those years did the Democrats fail to control both houses of the legislature.[7]

During its generation of state rule, the Democrats sent mixed messages to entrepreneurs, due to party factionalism. In some counties, lawyers and ex-Confederates made up a conservative faction that exploited the complex land registry system to line their pockets and facilitate the transfer of land to speculators. There was also an "Agrarian" wing that was highly critical of industrial capitalism. Finally, there was a bloc known as the "Kanawha Ring," which operated out of Charleston law firms.[8] As a result, Democrats pursued conflicting agendas that did little to encourage industrial development or a manufacturing sector. The party divided on protective tariffs that benefited industry and shifted capital from the agrarian South to the industrializing North, and many Democrats opposed a rigid adherence to the gold standard, which the bankers who controlled capital felt was essential to securing their investments. Furthermore, there was little in most nineteenth-century Democrat platforms that appealed to the interests of organized industrial workers—only meager support for restricting immigration or convict labor, and virtually nothing that strengthened the bargaining position of workers over wages and working conditions.[9]

In fact, most of West Virginia remained undeveloped through the reign of the Democrats. In 1880, nearly half of all manufacturing jobs in the state were in the northern panhandle (Wheeling and its neighbors on the Ohio River), which retained a Republican base throughout the era. These counties traced their industrial traditions back to antebellum times, and remained committed to industry and commerce. In fact, the panhandle's control of nearly half of the state's manufacturing highlights the lack of modern, diversified development elsewhere. Four out of every five iron and steel workers resided in Ohio, Marshall, Brooke, and Hancock counties, as did 85 percent of glassworkers, 65 percent of brick and tile makers, and half of foundry and machine shop employees. Outside the panhandle, only coal, sawed lumber, leather, and salt (natural resource industries) kept the state from having virtually no industrialization at all. Still, more than two-thirds of West Virginia's labor force toiled in agriculture.[10]

However, West Virginia's location at the southern fringe of the great manufacturing belt that swept from New England through the Great Lakes north of the Ohio River meant that at least a few farsighted Democrats saw the opportunity to enrich themselves by supporting the development of the state's natural resources. Two Democratic U.S. senators from West Virginia, Johnson Newlon Camden and Henry Gassaway Davis, often acted against the mainstream of their party on issues of economic development.[11] During the 1870s and 1880s, Camden and Davis, both men who absorbed the religion of development, exerted considerable influence on the leadership of the state party. Camden, operating out of the Parkersburg area, by the late 1870s had obtained "complete control of West Virginia [oil] production." Davis rose to influence in the eastern portion of the state, developing a company that supplied coal and timber from the upper Potomac River region. Both men tied their fates to resource development. In Camden's case, he tired of competing against the beneficial shipping rates extracted by John D. Rockefeller's Standard Oil Company. Unable to beat the enemy, Camden merged his operations into

Rockefeller's during the economic depression of the 1870s. He served in
the U.S. Senate from 1881 to 1887, often placing Rockefeller's interests
above those of West Virginia. Davis had accumulated resources by supplying the Baltimore and Ohio (B&O) Railroad with coal and railroad ties,
but he used his two terms in the Senate (1871–83) to attract a powerful
group of investors for a rail network connecting the vast coal and timber
resources of the upper Potomac fields to the main east-west trunk line
of the B&O.[12]

Thus, by the time of Governor Fleming's statement in 1891, West
Virginia was certainly no longer a secret. Especially in the sparsely settled
southern coal fields, the rush to exploit the region amounted to a virtual
feeding frenzy. During the 1880s, such noted national business figures as
J. P. Morgan, John D. Rockefeller, Collis P. Huntington, and E. H. Harri-
man hurriedly built railroads connecting the state's coal fields to important markets. Other entrepreneurs speculated in coal lands, purchasing
deeds dating back as far as the Revolutionary War. Although the state had
long ago reclaimed these lands, since the original deed holders had neither registered their claims nor paid taxes, speculators persuaded friendly
judges to void subsequent sales, evict current landholders, and reinstate
the earlier titles. By 1900, according to historian David A. Corbin, "absentee landowners owned 90 percent of Mingo, Logan, and Wayne counties and 60 percent of Boone and McDowell counties." These absentee
owners included men with enormous influence in business and political
circles.[13]

The role of absentee ownership is part of a long debate about the
causes of the lagging economic development of West Virginia. Because
outsiders owned such large portions of the resource-rich southern coal
fields, the state lacked the means to develop self-sustaining economic
growth. In fact, in a gloomy but insightful report in 1884, the West Virginia Tax Commission cautioned against just such a condition. The
commission noted that, regardless of the construction of railroads, the
opening of mines, and the influx of workers, "if the entire enterprise is
owned by non-residents, if all the profits belong to persons who reside
abroad, if those who are permanently identified with the locality do not
participate in the harvest, the State is going backwards." The agents of
powerful nonresident capital, the commission advised, were "emissaries
of injurious schemes," buying up the state's resources and manipulating
politics to the benefit of private interests.[14] Drawing on such examples,
Helen Lewis, John Alexander Williams, Ronald Eller, and other scholars
explain the truncated economic growth of the state through a model of
"internal colonialism." This model explains the ongoing poverty of West

Virginia as the result of political, economic, and cultural domination by powerful corporations operating outside the region. Their ownership of land and mineral rights doomed the state's ability to promote a more diversified, self-sustaining growth.[15]

Other scholars, however, warn against interpreting too widely the experience of the southern West Virginia coalfields. Michael E. Workman and Richard M. Simon remind us that other parts of the state developed differently. The northern panhandle has already been mentioned, but it was not the sole exception (see map 2). The process of industrialization in the upper Monongahela valley also broke with the pattern of nonresident ownership that channeled investment into a single industry, coal. Instead, much of the development in this region built more gradually from a base of local (albeit small-scale) commercial activity and capital accumulation begun earlier. Coal, oil, and natural gas were important, but Harrison, Marion, and other north-central counties nurtured manufacturing enterprises as well.[16] But this area never became a fully developed region with "the ability, the finances, and the will to generate the conditions for further development internally." Simon and Workman, among others, explain this by drawing on a theory of world capitalist systems that emphasizes the dependent relationship of certain regions. According to this theory, the global spread of capitalism causes regions to develop collaterally but not equally. Later developing regions (peripheries) become dependent on core regions and are unable to overcome the barriers to self-sustaining economic growth. As applied to West Virginia, this model explains the state's economic backwardness as a consequence of its lack of capital and human resources and its inability to generate sufficient internal investment that could keep profits in the state.[17]

Certainly, West Virginia's industrial development had much to overcome. Despite its wealth in natural resources, the increasing concentration of manufacturing in the United States made it difficult for new areas to compete. By 1889, nearly three-fifths of all manufacturing jobs were located in just thirty-four industrial areas, and those same areas maintained their share of manufacturing employment over the next forty years. This was the core. These centers of manufacturing, according to Richard Simon, built on their early advantages. Their population growth provided large markets, a labor pool attractive to new industries, and fertile fields for further investment in new products and advanced technologies that only enhanced their advantages. Peripheral areas (like West Virginia) that had lagged behind in industrial development thus faced enormous obstacles in changing their relationship to the core.[18]

Even though West Virginia, especially its northern counties, abutted

Map 2. *West Virginia Industrial Regions, ca. 1900. Produced by Tim Hawthorne for the West Virginia State GIS Technical Center, 2005.*

the fringes of the core industrial region, Mountain State capitalists faced barriers. The state's agricultural sector declined in the post–Civil War years, unable to compete with the fertile soils and mechanizing farms of the Midwest and the Plains. Moreover, West Virginia suffered the lingering effects of Virginia's antipathy to commercial and industrial development, particularly in its western counties. Many West Virginia counties had no bank at all as late as the 1890s. The state ranked near the bottom in holdings of stock in national banks, and in 1891 West Virginia had just forty-nine state banks with deposits under $9 million. Combined, the total investments in both state and national banks amounted to only $5 million, a paltry sum for a state with 760,000 people.[19] As economic historian Paul Salstrom notes, such limited assets made the region dependent on imported capital, which was "less likely than local capital to finance local markets, and particularly to finance local markets that were supplied by local production."[20]

People in the northern panhandle and the upper Monongahela valley were doing their best to overcome those obstacles. Considering several factors that demonstrate industrial development—manufacturing activity, accumulation of wealth, integration into capital markets, participation in technological change, and the skill level of the workforce—political scientist Richard Bensel calculates that these areas were above the national average in at least two of the categories and, in several counties, three. On his map of relative development, the northern panhandle and upper Monongahela counties make up the southern limits of the most advanced region. Not surprisingly, most of these counties, which made up the state's First Congressional District, returned majorities for Republican candidates beginning in the 1880s, if not earlier.[21]

Prodevelopment Democrats had injected an enthusiasm for industry in one wing of the party, but they never ruled the party unchallenged. Although Camden and Davis built a modern political organization that relied on effective communications, fundraising, patronage, and bureaucracy, they could not completely "tame" the other factions, according to John Alexander Williams. By the late 1880s, Davis, for one, wondered if his party could serve as the vehicle for attracting capital investment and spurring industrialization, especially once the national party moved increasingly toward free-trade and soft money planks in its platform.[22] In a state so unevenly reaping the fruits of economic development, the problem was how to shift the balance of power.

The Republican Party and the Development Faith

During the 1880s, as key individuals in the state embraced the faith in industrial development (what I will call the "development faith," following the lead of the historian John Alexander Williams), many linked that faith to coal. Whether they enticed outside speculators or generated investment from within, coal seemed like the most marketable commodity and thus the key to subsequent development. In 1893, at the Columbian Exposition in Chicago, for example, Governor William A. MacCorkle claimed: "It is an axiom of political economy that the coal, iron and heavier products will attract the lighter products, cotton, wheat and wool and each of their products and manufactures."[23] For coal to drive West Virginia development, however, some coal operators argued that they needed tariffs to protect their markets against foreign (especially Canadian) imports. Others argued for a low-wage, low-cost formula for competitiveness.[24]

The most consistent advocates of protective tariffs were the Republicans. As the development faith spread, so too did support for the party. The Republicans provided links to the founders of West Virginia but, until the 1890s, won election only in the First Congressional District in the state. This district included the northern panhandle and the upper Monongahela River valley, where railroad building, coal mining, manufacturing, and banking were already progressing. In fact, this district had more manufacturing capital and produced more manufacturing value than the other three districts combined.[25] Republicans stressed their attachments to the Union cause in the Civil War, especially through support of soldiers' pensions, but they also emphasized a development-oriented economic program. In particular, the party believed that tariffs would "give employment to the labor and capital of this country" and that government surpluses could be spent on internal improvements and education, what scholars today call the "social capital" that would attract further investment capital.[26] That philosophy migrated into West Virginia along with railroads, investment capital, and industrial development. It increasingly won over voters in the coal mining and industrial counties during the 1880s, particularly as party constituencies began to more closely match party economic agendas. The Republican gubernatorial candidate in 1888, for example, received letters of encouragement from coal miners in Fayette County as well as factory workers in Ohio County.[27]

The eventual triumph of the Republicans awaited only new leaders and a more professional party organization. Supplying the missing ingredients, as well as some much-needed funding, was Stephen B. Elkins, son-in-law of Henry Gassaway Davis. In fact, the Democrat Davis actually encouraged his Republican son-in-law to enter politics because he was so discouraged by the low-tariff policies of his own party. Elkins, born in Missouri in 1841, had risen to prominence in Republican circles in New Mexico in the 1870s. In 1875, he married Davis's daughter Hallie, and became a partner in the family's extensive Maryland and West Virginia enterprises. Although he continued to wield influence in the Republican party from his homes in New York and Washington, D.C., he did not enter politics in West Virginia until his father-in-law pressed him to do so as a result of his growing frustration with the state's Democrats. Elkins's close friendship with President Benjamin Harrison enabled him to assume leadership of the party after 1890. In particular, state Republicans appreciated the money that Elkins could bring to party coffers, from his own substantial wealth as well as his connections. One Republican leader sarcastically rejoiced that they could now entice votes from mountaineers who needed "encoinagement."[28]

Despite steadily growing popular support, the Republican ascendancy did not occur until the depression of 1893 rocked the Democrats. Because the party trumpeted its protectionist, hard money program, Elkins hoped that the economic calamity would crush the free-trade, soft money, Democrat opposition in the state. As the depression worsened, strikes and labor unrest swept across the state, and Republicans put the blame for them on Democratic policies that they claimed discouraged high wages and capital investment. Many political leaders in both parties, particularly those who placed industrial development at the top of the state's agenda, blanched at the proposed Democratic tariff reductions in 1894. They believed that these reductions, in large part authored by West Virginia Democrat William L. Wilson, would disadvantage the state. In particular, the Wilson-Gorman tariff opened a major chasm between Wilson and Davis and split the state's Democrats.[29]

This was all the help the Republicans needed. Elkins worked throughout the winter and spring to save some protections for coal, and then turned his attention to unifying the party to defeat Wilson in the November elections. His confidants predicted the impact of the Wilson-Gorman tariff: "free coal and iron meant Republicanism in West Virginia."[30] They were right. Elkins watched as the Republicans swept to a surprising landslide victory in West Virginia, electing all four congressmen and gaining a 29–vote majority in the state legislature. Davis felt vindicated by his party's defeat and his son-in-law's triumph. More important, he expected some rewards: "I hope and believe that the result . . . will be to considerably increase business in the country and we should get our share," he wrote to his nephew.[31] The real payoff came to Elkins in January 1895, when the state legislature elected him to the U.S. Senate. In the nomination speech, Alex R. Campbell revealed what the party expected. He noted that Elkins was the right man to develop the "unexplored wealth of coal, iron and minerals" in the state. Not only could he obtain "home capital" but also he could go into the "monied centres" and command attention.[32] The development faith had an important advocate in the U.S. Senate.

Elkins still needed to complete his organization of the state's Republican Party to guarantee unswerving support for his policies. After a generation out of power, much of the party's energy went into securing patronage positions for loyalists. To cite just a few examples, Nathan B. Scott, a Wheeling glass manufacturer, banker, and investor in coal and oil, wanted an appointment as commissioner of internal revenue; John W. Mason, a Fairmont lawyer and mine owner, sought a position in the Treasury Department; Parkersburg newspaper editor A. B. White hoped to become a collector of internal revenue. Elkins worked hard to keep their loyalty: Scott obtained a seat in the U.S. Senate in 1899; Mason obtained a judicial appointment in 1900; and White became governor in 1901.[33] Elkins also needed to walk a tightrope among national party candidates to obtain the maximum benefits for West Virginia. In 1896, for instance, he cultivated the presidential aspirations of both Pennsylvania senator Matthew Quay and Ohio congressman William McKinley so that he could win support for a $1.13 million appropriation for dams between Fairmont and Morgantown. Elkins reminded his followers: "I do not think such success would have come to us had we been fighting the Presidential candidates that are here," and warned that "in the interests of the State we had better keep up these good relations."[34] If the party had hoped to put a man in the Senate who could bring development dollars to West Virginia, then Elkins tried his best to deliver.

The realignment of politics resulting from the critical election of 1896 solidified the Republican Party in the state for the next thirty years. When the Democratic Party attached its fate to William Jennings Bryan and his opposition to the gold standard, those areas in the state hoping to entice outside capital became firmly committed to the Republicans. Political scientist Richard Bensel asserts that "the intersection between Bryan's electoral support and congressional voting on gold may have been the closest tie between popular voting behavior and legislative policy-making in history." In West Virginia, the critical elections of 1894 and 1896 signaled a dramatic shift to popular support for the Republican economic program, and their representatives voted for sound currency and high tariffs. For those attaching the state's future to the development faith, the results were electric. Between 1895 and 1931, Republicans held 60.5 percent of the House and 70.3 percent of the state senate seats. Only three times did the party fail to rule both houses of the legislature.[35]

The Republican triumph did, in fact, accelerate dramatic changes to West Virginia. Elkins threw his influence behind the resumption of high tariffs that protected coal, and the state became a prime target for investment. In the 1890s, despite the years of depression from 1893 to 1897, population increased by nearly 46 percent. The patterns of that growth demonstrate even more clearly the changing nature of the state. The growth occurred in two concentrations, the first being the eleven counties along the Ohio River (commerce and industry) and the second in the ten leading coal counties. These concentrations accounted for only one-third of the land in the state, but two-thirds of the population increase. In fact, jobs in coal increased from 5 percent of the male labor force to 9 percent during the decade.[36] Once begun, the industrial transformation picked up pace. After 1900, the Ohio River counties and the principal coal counties together accounted for four-fifths of the population growth until 1920. By 1910, the combined numbers of men in manufacturing and resource extraction topped the numbers in agriculture (see table 3.1).

It is important to further distinguish this transformation within the principal coal counties. The six southern coal counties accounted for few manufacturing jobs, aside from those directly related to coal (coke production) and one railroad center (Bluefield). Coke production is a low-wage industry conducted with relatively little capital investment. In short, the investment attracted by the southern coal counties was of the sort that historians have associated with the theories explaining the economic backwardness of West Virginia. These were the counties where powerful nonresident investors dominated and took the state's mineral wealth to fuel the factories of the Great Lakes region. They and their agents recruited large numbers of blacks and southern or eastern European immigrants, constructed makeshift towns completely controlled by the company, and made the region as nearly as possible dependent on coal.[37]

The panhandle and the northern coal counties did not fit that pattern. The panhandle built on its early industrial development and its advantages in cheaper water transportation on the Ohio River. The four panhandle counties accounted for more than one-fourth of all new manufacturing jobs between 1890 and 1930, keeping its share of manufacturing in the state above 30 percent. At the same time, the upper Monongahela valley of West Virginia, a 10–county coal region built around Harrison, Marion, and Monongalia counties, experienced an economic takeoff. Improvements on the Monongahela River and the opening of the Monongahela River Railroad in 1890 sparked the boom. The population more than doubled between 1890 and 1920, with Harrison leading the way with a growth of 293 percent. The main county seats (Clarksburg, Fairmont, and Morgantown) grew from towns with a combined population of under 9,000 to almost 58,000 during those years. Although coal was a

Table 3.1: West Virginia Male Workforce Distribution, by Industrial Sector

Industrial sector	1890	1900	1910
Agriculture	57.7%	49.6%	40.2%
Trade & Transportation	11.0	12.2	12.1
Services (professional & personal)	5.4	4.9	5.8
Manufacturing	18.7	20.7	25.6
Resource Extraction	7.2	12.6	16.3
Total Male Workforce (000's)	202	295	394

Source: U.S. Census Bureau, *Thirteenth Census (1910): Population* (Washington, D.C.: Government Printing Office, 1914), 529–30.

critical component here, the number of manufacturing establishments more than doubled, and the average manufacturing wage surpassed both the state and the national averages.[38]

Equally important, these two regions did not follow the example of the southern coal counties in relying almost exclusively on outside capital. The northern panhandle included a significant number of local elites who invested in the industrialization of the region's iron and steel, nail, pottery, glass, leather, and tobacco factories.[39] The upper Monongahela valley developed much later, but much of the investment also came from local capital. The Watson family and A. B. Fleming in Fairmont, the Goff and the Lowndes families in Clarksburg, Alston G. Dayton in Philippi, George Sturgiss in Morgantown, and John T. McGraw in Grafton were among the men who honeycombed the region with railroads and built fortunes and power by adopting the development faith. This group, however, split on party affiliation and economic thinking. While all could agree that railroads were essential to prosperity, their visions of economic development diverged. Democrats (the Watsons, Fleming, McGraw) believed that a low-price strategy would enable coal operators to export fuel resources and accumulate investment capital. Many Republicans, in contrast, worried about exporting all of the state's energy resources. They hoped to attract more diverse investment and create a balanced development strategy that included high wages and value-added manufacturing.[40]

Particularly appealing to Republican proponents of the development faith was the emphasis on protective tariffs. As coal production soared, West Virginia operators needed to capture distant markets, especially the Great Lakes region. While Elkins preached the benefits of high tariffs to keep out coal from Nova Scotia, Democrat operators felt they could best achieve this with a low-wage, nonunion strategy. Thus, agreement on the desirability of development masked important policy differences. Of course, tariffs also benefited the fastest growing manufacturing industries in the state, glass and steel. Not surprisingly, then, a strong candidate to join Elkins in the U.S. Senate in 1899 was Nathan B. Scott. Born in Ohio in 1842, Scott was a Union Civil War veteran. In 1865, he located in Wheeling, where he became a glass manufacturer, banker, and coal and oil speculator. As the Republicans came to power in the 1890s, Scott's political fortunes soared. He gained favor not only among the manufacturers in Wheeling's steel, glass, and pottery factories but also with the growing numbers of manufacturing workers there because of his support for protective tariffs and immigration restriction, issues that protected the high wages and profitability of these industries.[41] With Scott on the

Senate Committee on Mines and Mining and Elkins on the Committee on Interstate Commerce, West Virginia industrialists felt that their interests were well represented.[42]

Another division in the development faith involved tax policy. Democratic proponents of industrialization believed that limited taxation was essential to attracting capital investment. The state's constitution required fair and uniform taxation, but placed the burden of taxes on owners of real estate at rates of twenty-five cents for every one hundred dollars of assessed value, plus an additional ten cents for education. The problem was that the assessment of value and the collection of taxes remained in the hands of local authorities. In sparsely settled counties where nonresident corporations held a commanding influence, the assessments severely understated the real value. For example, the valuation of railroad property actually declined between 1894 and 1900 by half a million dollars, despite a 25 percent increase in mileage. Especially in counties where coal was king—McDowell, Randolph, and Marion, for example—the average value per acre of real estate declined in the 1890s, despite the presence of huge mining corporations and the growth of new towns.[43]

This system generated considerable animosity. On the one hand, counties with a more diversified economy and a more politicized citizenry insisted on more accurate valuations. But this meant that property owners in these counties—primarily in the northern panhandle—paid much more in state taxes. On the other hand, many objected to the growing deficits in the state budget. Republican-dominated legislatures in the 1890s expanded the state bureaucracy as government took on a growing number of responsibilities in a more modern industrial society. Organized groups of small businessmen and industrial workers pressed government for regulatory agencies and the provision of new services. Demands ranged from pure food laws and railroad regulations to child labor laws and factory safety inspections, so that by 1899, the projected state budget was approximately $200,000 above expected revenues.[44]

By 1901, the clamor for tax reform could no longer be ignored. The legislature convened with a strong reform contingent, led by the president of the Wheeling Board of Trade, George A. Laughlin. Moreover, the outgoing governor, also a Republican from Wheeling, endorsed an increase in the license tax on all corporations. Opponents of increased taxes averted political disaster by agreeing to a commission to study tax reform, and managed to fill it with conservative industrialists, including Elkins's partner and father-in-law, Henry Gassaway Davis. But the commission's report in 1902, as well as the new governor, A. B. White, gave an unexpected boost to progressive forces in the state. The report recommended that property taxes go to the localities but required uniform annual assessments from the state tax commissioner. For state funds, the commission proposed a combination of license taxes (that hit saloon owners more harshly than mine owners) and a small severance tax on coal, oil, and natural gas, but one that carried a guarantee in the state constitution that rates would remain low.[45]

Even these modest changes generated a considerable backlash from Democrats and the agents of nonresident corporations. Elkins supported the reforms, hoping to hold the Republicans together and eliminate the possibility of more sweeping changes. He wrote to Governor White, "I am satisfied the gas and oil interests will submit to any reasonable taxation, and we don't want to impose any other; the coal men may stand out, if so we could compromise with them, and then we could treat the railroads fairly and I believe they would be satisfied."[46] Elkins was wrong. Democratic operators successfully recruited some disaffected Republicans and forced the reformers to retreat. Eventually, the legislature passed a compromise proposal in a special session in 1905, which represented a small shift in the tax burden toward the corporations but omitted the proposed severance tax on coal, oil, and gas.[47]

Reformers at the turn of the century thus failed to restructure the finances of the state. Some Republicans, especially a group of Progressives in the more diversified industrial areas of the northern panhandle and the northern coal counties, hoped for different results. They believed, like Governor White, that companies engaged in resource extraction "should pay taxes for miners' hospitals, inspectors and education" among a host of other activities that a modern industrial state should provide.[48] Although White eventually capitulated on the severance tax in the interest of Republican harmony, many in the party felt that increased corporate taxes, as well as a tax on the exporting of the state's energy resources, might encourage more investment in manufacturing industries that would add high-paying jobs, increase the urban population, and create a growing home market for goods and services. At the same time, tax revenues would enable state government to invest in education, roads, services, and infrastructure, the social capital that could generate the conditions for further development.

Instead, a combination of low-wage resource exporters (both Democrats and Republicans) and agents of the large nonresident corporations thwarted reform. Key were men like Henry Gassaway Davis, A. B. Fleming, and Alston G. Dayton, each of whom promoted a low-cost export strategy for coal. They did not worry about the uneven development or the policies that funneled investment into coal and other extractive industries, and for good reason. None other than the governor of the state, George Atkinson, told a group of businessmen in 1897: "West Virginia, my friends, is the *eternal center* of coal and gas and oil and timber and of stalwart Republicanism also." Conservative politics and plentiful resources had created a "New Old Dominion."[49]

Gas and Glass in the Mountain State

The transformation of West Virginia occurred simultaneously with the restructuring of the glass industry. Although coal became the dominant force in the state's economy, it was the development of natural gas fields that attracted the glass industry. Critical to the restructuring of the glass industry had been the shift to gas-fueled, continuous tank furnaces in the late 1880s. This change permitted glass manufacturers to build much larger factories and achieve economies of scale. At the same time, these early technological changes coincided with a boom-and-bust atmosphere in the markets for glass (explored in the previous chapter) that led to disastrous increases in production capacity just before the depression of the 1890s bankrupted many firms. In response, firms in each of the glass industry branches—windows, bottles, and tableware—formed marketing trusts, engaged in mergers, or made other arrangements to try and stay afloat. They used these new corporate strategies to undercut handicraft control and reduce labor costs. Thus, the industry experienced the entire gamut of industrial restructuring: technological changes, managerial changes and reorganization, and sociopolitical changes that modified the division of labor and power relationships of the production process.[50]

This restructuring process also entailed a geographic relocation of the industry. At the start of the 1880s, glass factories were concentrated in the towns and cities of southwestern Pennsylvania and Ohio due to the proximity of raw materials, fuels (at that time coal), and markets. The switch to natural gas was bound to bring relocation, especially since the ratio of fuel costs to the value of the product in the glass industry was very high. Another factor in relocation was the desire to change the labor relations in the industry. The previous concentration of the industry in cities like Pittsburgh gave unionized workers a strong base. Manufacturers seeking to lower labor costs believed that building bigger plants in rural areas would tip the scale of power away from workers and toward employers.[51] The initial beneficiaries of this relocation process were Indiana, rural western Pennsylvania, and southeastern Ohio. By the end of the 1890s, however, West Virginia began to attract considerable attention from glass manufacturers.

The use of natural gas as an industrial fuel actually had a long history in West Virginia. As early as 1815, salt makers on the Kanawha River drilling for brine struck a gas pocket that caught fire, halting work. In 1841, William Tompkins, a local "inventive genius," managed to construct a crude system of pipes to bring gas into his saltworks, which he used as fuel to boil the brine. But few West Virginians saw the potential of gas. Not until 1889 were any new productive areas developed. By then, improvements in drilling, tools, casings, and fittings opened up the potential for the industrial use of natural gas. The rich gas fields that entrepreneurs were tapping in rural western Pennsylvania stretched down the western half of the full length of West Virginia. By 1904, state geologist I. C. White estimated that the natural gas coming to the state's surface was worth $100,000 per day. White noted problems, however. The state was piping out 200 million cubic feet daily "to Pittsburgh, Cleveland, Toledo, and intermediate points," and another 200 million cubic feet were being wasted due to inefficiency. White wanted the state legislature to intervene to ensure that West Virginians realized the value of its assets.[52]

The desire on the part of some entrepreneurs to create a domestic market for natural gas spurred boosters to explore the glass industry. Glass manufacture had some history in the Mountain State. Glass plants first emerged in Wellsburg in the northern panhandle as early as the 1810s. The opening of the National Road through Wheeling encouraged many of the early plants to relocate there. By the 1830s, Wheeling had at least three glass factories, which relied on easy transportation down the Ohio River to supply tumblers, lamp chimneys, jars, and even some crown window glass to the growing frontier markets. The city also played a major inventive role in the glass industry. The community of "creative glass mechanics" in Wheeling, according to glass historian Dennis Zembala, introduced a number of mechanical devices that greatly increased the productivity of glass tableware manufacturing. In addition, the inventor William Leighton, who worked for Hobbs, Brockunier Company in Wheeling, developed the soda-lime formula that revolutionized flint glass.[53] However, the industry never expanded beyond the panhandle until after 1890.

The restructuring of the glass industry in the 1890s gave West Virginia a new chance. The state had an abundant supply of the most important fuel, and its land prices were modest. It also had ample supplies of most of the other elements that went into glassmaking—sand, lime, soda ash—and the north-central and Ohio River counties were relatively close to the supply of skilled labor that was then underemployed in Ohio and southwestern Pennsylvania. Finally, the railroad building boom that was underway in West Virginia provided easy transportation access to markets. Boosters in such small towns as Moundsville, Paden City, Fairmont, Morgantown, and Clarksburg looked at glass as a potential development industry; glass manufacturers and even some glass workers eyed the Mountain State as a fertile field for investment. The *National Glass Budget* commented in August 1900: "West Virginia has natural gas, plenty of excellent sand, and an unexcelled supply of coal, and bids fair to take a higher place in the glass industry during the next decade."[54]

Still, the state did not find it easy to attract glass plants. In 1890, there were only seven, employing 1,371 workers in the state, all concentrated along the Ohio River. These plants represented merely a slight expansion of Wheeling's early development of the flint glass industry. By 1900, West Virginia had sixteen glass factories, employing nearly two thousand workers and representing just about 3 percent of the nation's capacity. Interestingly, the first two window-glass plants opened during that decade, one in Clarksburg and one in Mannington. Both of these plants were cooperatives, transplanted from Indiana where the gas fields were not nearly as rich as West Virginia's. Both cooperatives cut deals for cheap gas with local gas producers.[55] During the ensuing five years, glass manufacturing took off, especially in the upper Monongahela valley. By 1905, the state had thirty-nine plants (about 10 percent of the nation's total) employing 3,673 workers (just under 6 percent of the industry). Fifteen of the twenty-three new factories made window glass, but the better paying window factories were relatively small, employing only about 20 percent of the state's glassworkers.[56]

The glass industry's early growth in West Virginia, while impressive, also suggests some of the limits the industry confronted in wielding influence, compared to that exerted by the industries that focused on resource extraction. Many of the glass plants coming to the Mountain State were small, family-owned or cooperative enterprises. Indeed, the average capital investment in West Virginia glass factories was about $110,000, less than half of the national average and only one-third of the average value of Pennsylvania factories. In the higher value building glass (windows and plate glass) segment of the industry, the contrast is yet more striking. West Virginia's window-glass plants averaged only about forty workers and just $99,000 in capital invested per establishment. Indiana's plants were roughly double those figures, while Pennsylvania's factories averaged 154 employees and whopping $488,000 in capital invested.[57]

The glass industry pointed proudly to its political influence in the state. Both the *National Glass Budget* and the *Commoner and Glassworker* emphasized the fact that one of the industry's own, Nathan B.

Scott, was a Republican senator from West Virginia. But by 1900, Scott was more heavily invested in coal and oil, and he retreated from his involvement with the Central Glass Works. He supported protective tariffs for the glass industry, but served as chairman of the U.S. Senate Committee on Mines and Mining. When glassworkers in the northern panhandle supported tax reform that proposed a severance tax on coal, oil, and gas, Scott worked behind the scenes to make certain the severance tax was eliminated.[58] In short, the profits to be made from West Virginia's glass industry paled in comparison to the bounty to be reaped from coal. Likewise, the weight that such small-scale capitalists in the glass industry brought to politics was no match for the elephant that coal represented.

Of course, boosters hoped that attracting some initial investment in the glass industry would lay the foundation for further development. Once the factors—fuel, resources, transportation, and labor supply—were in place, they would draw additional capital. By World War I, promoters of the glass industry could take pride in their accomplishments. During the early twentieth century, the Fostoria Company in Moundsville expanded into the largest glass tableware factory in the country. In 1910, the Owens West Virginia Bottle Company opened the most modern, completely mechanized bottle factory in the world in Fairmont. Between 1914 and 1917, the two giants of the flat-glass industry—Libbey-Owens-Ford and Pittsburgh Plate Glass—began mass-producing window glass with the latest technologies in South Charleston and Clarksburg.[59]

At the end of World War I, the glass industry employed more workers than any other manufacturing industry in the state, passing the twelve thousand mark, if clerical and supervisory employees are included. It accounted for 15 percent of West Virginia's manufacturing jobs and five of the twenty-nine factories in the state with five hundred or more workers. The state's glass industry also improved its position in the national industry. Between 1909 and 1919, it surpassed Indiana and Ohio to become the second largest glass-producing state in the nation, and had narrowed the gap with Pennsylvania from roughly a 4-to-1 to a 2-to-1 ratio, based on the number of glassworkers and value of product.[60] Clearly, additional restructuring in the industry had only enhanced the attractiveness of West Virginia. But the growth of the industry increasingly reflected the investment patterns in much of resource extraction—control by outside interests. The mechanized bottle and flat-glass plants were owned by corporate interests headquartered in Toledo, Ohio, and Pittsburgh. The Owens and PPG interests routinely threatened to take their business elsewhere when they objected to local labor conditions, political movements, or fuel costs.[61]

More important, the manufacturing interests in the state never accumulated the political power that the coal industry had. In 1919, all manufacturing combined employed 23.8 percent of the workforce; coal alone accounted for 18 percent. At the same time, most of the investors in the glass industry were content with the accommodations made by the state's Republicans: protective tariffs combined with cheap fuel and low taxes. They also benefited from Stephen B. Elkins's influence on the Interstate Commerce Commission, preventing discriminatory rates against West Virginia companies.[62] Consequently, despite the quite impressive development of a manufacturing industry in the north-central and Ohio River region, the glass industry entrepreneurs were relatively minor players in state politics.

This became increasingly so when workers in the industry began to develop their own political voice, one at odds with their employers. Through the early years of the twentieth century, industrial workers in the state supported the Republicans' platform. Many felt that they benefited from the transfer of wealth from the agricultural to the industrial sector and from the South and West to the Northeast that protective tariffs and the gold standard fostered. Except for a brief support for the Greenback-Labor Party in 1880, West Virginians gave little support to insurgent movements that staked claims on the wealth generated in the nation other than the distribution governed by tariffs and currencies. Outside of Wheeling, Charleston, and Huntington, the labor movement was relatively weak.[63]

The men who brought the glass industry to West Virginia unwittingly helped change the political economy that underpinned the development faith. Skilled glassworkers were union members, many of whom had social-democratic traditions, both from their European backgrounds as well as their experiences with the restructuring of the industry. In 1902, they made up one-eighth of the union members in the state. Furthermore, the glass industry was among the most organized in the nation, and it had the highest strike rate at the turn of the century.[64] As the labor movement expanded in the first decade of the new century, glassworkers contributed ideas, organizational skills, militancy, and money to the unionization of numerous West Virginia towns.

In an atmosphere of growing contentiousness between capital and labor, unions placed new and different claims on wealth. The old claims for the gold standard and protective tariffs began to wear thin, as workers observed the widening unequal distribution of the benefits of industrial growth. By 1910, votes for Progressive bolters from the Republican Party and for Socialists were threatening to disrupt the status quo; in 1912, the two groups of insurgents captured between 35 and 40 percent of the votes in the state and national elections. Moreover, the state Democratic platform that year spoke to the sentiments of "Progressivism." It demanded regulation of public utilities, the enactment of a progressive income tax amendment, the direct election of United States senators, and the protection of workers from private company guards, from competition with convict labor, and from judicial injunctions.[65] Nowhere was insurgency consistently more potent than in those towns where the glass industry had located. And the impact was significant; as a result of votes for third parties, Democrats gained control of the state legislature for several years—one of the few times they did so between 1895 and 1932. In 1911, as a result of an untimely death, West Virginia sent two Democrats to the United States Senate. If glass manufacturers failed to exert a direct influence on the political economy of the state, they did so indirectly for a time through the workers they recruited.

———————

The glass industry became an important force in West Virginia as a result of two transformations: first, a restructuring of the industry, and second, a transformation of the political economy of the state. The story of glass manufacturing adds considerably to the picture of the industrialization of the Mountain State. It demonstrates that some of the men who shared the development faith had a vision of economic growth that would include a local manufacturing base to provide diversity and a home market for the state's abundant energy resources. This sort of development might lead to a more modern, urban industrial society that would ultimately generate internally the conditions for further and sustained development: the finances and the will to create new products, open new markets, and reorganize production and the structure of the enterprise, according to regional economist Richard Simon.[66]

But these men confronted several barriers. First, they faced business and political leaders who believed that it was enough to encourage the investment of capital into the state—that money pouring in to exploit the natural resources somehow on its own would bring about the conditions for sustained growth. They failed to grasp that untaxed coal, oil, and gas, flowing out of the state for the benefit and under the control of outside interests, might not necessarily attract enough capital or other sorts of investment to ensure sustained growth. In addition, even some of the industrialists who held the vision of a diversified economy with a strong manufacturing component benefited enough from the political control of coal, oil, and gas developers that they never mounted a serious challenge.

Second, these men faced the demands of militant and organized workers who had their own ideas about economic development. Particularly in the upper Monongahela valley and along the Ohio River, glass manufacturing caused a large influx of skilled industrial workers who brought traditions of culture and politics that contested the path of development charted by the Republican men who shared the development faith. For these workers, the accumulation of capital for additional investment was not meaningful unless labor could share in the benefits through better wages and working conditions. Especially as the ongoing restructuring of the glass industry threatened their status, security, and livelihoods, these industrial workers helped galvanize oppositional political movements in the glass towns of West Virginia. I will now turn to case studies of the transforming effects of the glass industry in Moundsville, Clarksburg and Fairmont. Each of these towns attracted different branches of the industry: glass tableware in Moundsville, window glass in Clarksburg, and glass bottles in Fairmont. Moreover, the character of the industry in each would have an impact on the composition of the workforce, the cultural and political traditions that emerged, and the nature of the challenge to the existing political system.

4 Moundsville: Enterprising Managers
and Upright Citizens

In 1902, when the glassworkers' weekly journal, *Commoner and Glassworker*, recounted the story of the Fostoria Glass Company, it pointed to the ironic twists of circumstance that benefited the town of Moundsville. The incorporators included Wheeling, Wellsburg, and Pittsburgh investors, and they chose two men who learned the trade in Wheeling's innovative Hobbs, Brockunier Company to manage the works. They even took advantage of the generous incorporation law in West Virginia, although their plan involved manufacturing pressed and blown glass tableware in Fostoria, Ohio. Unfortunately for the company, the "boom" that brought natural gas development to western Ohio in 1887 delivered less gas than expected, and in 1891 the Fostoria managers began seeking a new home. Unwilling to again bank everything on the potential of "inexhaustible supplies of natural gas" alone, the managers sought a location that also had coal in abundance to provide an alternative fuel source, if necessary. Their search brought them to Moundsville, just twelve miles south of Wheeling, whence they had fled four years earlier.[1]

Little did Fostoria's investors and managers know that they were part of an exodus of glass factories to West Virginia, one that eventually lifted the state to being the second largest producer in the United States. The success of the Fostoria Company held out a great deal of promise to the promoters of the development faith in the Mountain State. As the state began to tap its tremendous fuel reserves, the industrialists of the north-

Map 3. Moundsville, West Virginia, 1899. This bird's-eye view captures Moundsville during the Fostoria Company's early years. Drawn by A. E. Downs and published by James B. Moyer, Myerstown, Pa., [1899]. Geography and Map Division, Library of Congress.

ern panhandle believed they could attract manufacturing enterprises and investment capital to the state. Such changes would, in turn, enhance the influence of the Republican industrialists in the northern parts of the state. The Fostoria Company represented that promise, particularly since it involved resident investors and drew on the earlier development of the glass industry in the area.[2] In some respects, Fostoria fulfilled this vision. The company forged a largely stable relationship with its workers. As a result, Moundsville grew, and other manufacturing investment followed, turning the town into an extension of the Wheeling industrial zone. Indeed, with excellent railroad connections, inexpensive land and fuel, and access to the Ohio River, there were ingredients for further growth. Ultimately, however, the town could not overcome the barriers of a difficult topography, a small population base, and a late start in the capital sweepstakes. Neither could it stifle the suspicion among some that its inclusion in an area known for its militant and Socialist labor culture made it a less desirable location for additional investment.

Nevertheless, the restructuring of the glass industry complemented a changing political economy that transformed Moundsville. The factory disrupted the normal rhythms of the town, competed for the all-too-few available workers, and forced new uses of the landscape, often involving conflict with local farmers. Development also required new sources of revenue that meant increased taxes for citizens who did not benefit from the changes. At the same time, skilled glassworkers of German and Irish backgrounds flocked into what had been not much more than a village. These workers brought with them a well-developed work culture and union organization, and they competed for housing, recreational opportunities, and political influence in local affairs. Saloons, Catholic churches, and working-class associations challenged the prim, Protestant culture of this predominately agricultural community. The glass industry forever changed Moundsville, even if it was unable to completely transform the state.

Moundsville before the Glass Industry

Moundsville, until the 1880s, was a small town in Marshall County, the southernmost county of the northern panhandle. The Virginia legislature separated Marshall from Ohio County in 1835, and initially named Elizabethtown, a small village abutting Moundsville, as the county seat. The state of West Virginia consolidated the two villages in 1866 under the name of Moundsville, and divided the new county seat into three wards. The same state legislature designated the town as the site of the state penitentiary, and used the convicts then confined in the Ohio County Jail to build the prison. Two other major landmarks drew attention to Moundsville. One was the large Indian burial mound southeast of where Little Grave Creek leaves the Ohio River, just a few blocks from the State Penitentiary. First discovered by Joseph Tomlinson in 1772, the fifty-foot-high mound attracted considerable local and national attention, including several visits from Henry Rowe Schoolcraft, the noted anthropologist and expert on Native American culture. The second was the "camp meeting grounds" about a mile north of town, which began hosting religious revivals in the 1820s and gave a distinct Protestant character to the area. In 1874, the Wheeling District Camp Meeting Association purchased the site and built a 2,500–seat auditorium for the summer revivals.[3]

Situated in a rich and fertile yet narrow valley on the east bank of the Ohio River, Moundsville was primarily an agricultural hinterland to Wheeling during the first two decades of statehood. The county shifted production toward supplying the city with dairy products in the 1860s and 1870s, and the hilly interior proved amenable to raising cattle, swine, and especially sheep. Marshall County produced 207,000 pounds of wool in 1880. What industry existed in the county in 1880 reflected its agrarian character. There were 15 flour and gristmills, 1 broom factory, 6 leather curing and tanning establishments, 13 lumber mills, 2 coopers, and 1 whip company. Moundsville added an iron works and a factory to make plows in the 1870s to make it easier for local farmers to buy farm implements.[4]

Marshall County also began to benefit from the steep rising hills that prevented Wheeling from expanding to its east. As a result, the city's industrial growth followed the narrow shelf of land along the Ohio River to its south. In the 1840s, the manufacturing center of the city shifted south of Wheeling Creek. In the 1850s, new iron, nail, glass, and brick factories began to locate in Ritchietown, a separate incorporated town that became Wheeling's Eighth Ward in the 1860s. By the end of the Civil War, iron mills had ventured as far south as Benwood in the Union Magisterial District of Marshall County. The impact of Wheeling's industrial sprawl changed the district to the immediate north of Moundsville. Although only one of nine districts, the Union District accounted for more than 20 percent of the county's population and 55 percent of its foreign immigrants. Benwood's two iron mills also employed three-fifths of the manufacturing workers in the county in 1880.[5] At least some of the Republican industrialists in Wheeling must have looked longingly at the potential for continued expansion southward. After all, Marshall County had delivered a reliable 57 percent of its vote to Republicans throughout the 1870s and 1880s, despite the statewide dominance of the Democrats.[6]

Still, growth came slowly to Moundsville and Marshall County. During the 1880s, population grew by only 11 percent, to just under 21,000. With the exception of Benwood, Marshall County was a remarkably homogeneous agricultural area. Even including the mills at the northern edge, 95 percent of the county's people were native-born whites, and about 1 percent were blacks. There were some subtle shifts, however. By 1890, 1,825 adult males worked in manufacturing, an increase of 75 percent. In addition, much of the county's growth had occurred in Moundsville, which increased from 1,774 to 2,688 people.[7] Such modest numbers did not begin to catch the attention of the Wheeling and Wellsburg glass men who put together the capital to start the Fostoria Glass Company.

Only a few years later, however, Moundsville began its period of rapid growth. Key was the creation of the Moundsville Mining and Manufacturing Company, a corporation designed to acquire farmland at the northern edge of town and develop an attractive mining and manufacturing site. This corporation was the idea of Charles A. Weaver, president of Weaver and Bardall, the local whip manufacturer. Weaver was born in York, Pennsylvania, in 1845. He began his whip company in 1866 in Allegheny, Pennsylvania, and then moved to Moundsville in 1877. There, he won a contract from the State Penitentiary to operate his factory with convict labor inside the prison walls. Prospering, he began investing in banking and real estate, and also served several terms as the Republican mayor of Moundsville.[8]

Weaver attracted a range of investors to his scheme for a development company. Locally, stock dealer J. B. Hicks, sheriff H. W. Hunter, and merchant W. W. Smith purchased shares. Wheeling investors included Louis Stifel, heir of a textile print works, Gibson Lamb, and Alfred Paull, son of a prominent Ohio County judge and local business executive; and, from Kingwood, lawyer William G. Worley. Among the officers were businessmen from Baltimore and Washington, D.C. Serving as vice-president was John W. Mason, the state's Republican Party chairman, a commissioner of internal revenue, and a close associate of Stephen B. Elkins, who had recently assumed leadership of the state's Republican Party.[9] Consequently, the company seeking to bring industry to this small town involved some promoters of the development faith who had reputations that extended beyond the area.

The emergence of the Moundsville Mining and Manufacturing Company in 1891 was fortuitous for the men who had begun the Fostoria Glass Company. Three of the five founders of Fostoria were from the northern panhandle, and they hired two plant managers, Lucien B. Martin and William S. Brady, who had received their introduction to the industry in Wheeling. In fact, although Wheeling's nickname was "the Nail City," in the Civil War era, it was also home to what glass historian Dennis Zembala calls a remarkable "fraternity of invention" in the glass tableware industry. Beginning with the arrival of John L. Hobbs in 1845, Wheeling became a hub for chemical and technological improvements in the composition of glass and the development of furnaces, molds, and presses. At the Hobbs, Brockunier Company factory in South Wheeling and the Sweeney family's factory in the north end of town, men like Charles Oesterling and the two William Leightons, senior and junior, transformed the pressed and blown glass tableware industry. The elder Leighton, in particular, introduced a critical change when he developed a formula that substituted lime for the lead flint that gave glass tableware its brilliance and distinctive metal ring. Leighton's lime glass closely approximated the look and durability of "flint" glass but was much cheaper to produce. With such innovations, the Wheeling firms were at the nation's forefront of what came to be called, somewhat incorrectly, the flint glass industry.[10]

When the Wheeling and Wellsburg investors in the Fostoria Glass Company chose Martin and Brady to establish the factory in the emerging gas belt of northwestern Ohio, they counted on their ability to apply the knowledge gained in Wheeling. Martin headed the sales department, and Brady was the financial manager, using skills he had learned at Hobbs, Brockunier. To manage the plant, they brought the practical mechanic Henry Humphreville, who had learned his trade in the other center of glass innovation, Pittsburgh.[11] The managers recruited heavily in the Wheeling area for their skilled craftsmen, whom they took to Fostoria, Ohio, in large part because the town promised virtually unlimited supplies of natural gas at low rates. Natural gas was rapidly becoming the fuel of choice in glass manufacture, and the investors hoped to take advantage. Once in operation, Fostoria followed the product lines of tableware, tumblers, and novelties "similar to the old Hobbs plant at Wheeling," according to the *Commoner and Glassworker.* Although successful in Fostoria, the company soon learned that the gas boom in Ohio was not what they had expected.[12]

In 1891, the Fostoria Company packed up its molds, presses, and ware, and moved the operation to Moundsville, West Virginia, where there "were coal mines in abundance, and nearby almost inexhaustible supplies of natural gas." It is likely that the Moundsville Mining and Manufacturing Company had an inside track for recruiting the firm from

Ohio. Two of its officers, Louis Stifel and Alfred Paull, were connected to the glass industry in Wheeling. Stifel was the son-in-law of John Oesterling, who was part of the Hobbs, Brockunier management, and Paull was the secretary of the company. Consequently, the Wheeling connections of the Fostoria managers probably helped bring them back to West Virginia. But they took fewer chances with the promise of natural gas near Moundsville. Their new furnaces relied on artificially produced gas from the burning of coal, a resource they knew was plentiful. The factory located on the new Moundsville Mining and Manufacturing development at the northern edges of town, directly across the railroad tracks from the coal mine and tipple of the developers.[13] Thus, the Fostoria Company was poised to become a major firm in the flint glass industry just at the point when changes in the economy were causing a major industrial restructuring. For the next decade, Fostoria struggled to find its place; in the meantime, it began the transformation of Moundsville.

A Restructured Industry, a Town Transformed

The boosters in the Moundsville Mining and Manufacturing Company praised the newcomers to town as "energetic." They were the kind of people who would build homes and become permanent. Had the boosters been aware of the lives of glassworkers, they might have been less optimistic. Men in the industry, especially those who had served an apprenticeship for one of the trades, were a "tramping" fraternity, a highly mobile group that took their skills on a tour of glasshouses in the country. Moundsville's "flints" were no exception. Shortly after Fostoria moved to town, a photographer took a picture of more than forty craftsmen outside the plant. Thirty years later, the *American Flint* ran a copy of the photo and asked for information about those included (see illus. 5). Letters to the editor painted a portrait of the "tramping artisan." Joe Flaherty wrote of a career that took him to the Belmont, Crystal, and Findley factories in Ohio after leaving Moundsville; Joseph Laurell worked in Wheeling, Moundsville, Cameron, Wellsburg, and Weston in West Virginia before retiring in Ohio. Hillman Crow traveled farther afield; he spent time in Canada and the Midwest after leaving Fostoria.[14]

The arrival of the Fostoria Company should have worried the boosters as well. The company brought nearly its entire complement of craftsmen with them, triggering one of the early confrontations between workers and local townspeople. Some local landowners sought to take advantage of the scarcity of housing for the sixty to seventy flints coming to Moundsville. Renters organized a meeting at the courthouse to protest the

A group of men and boys employed by The Fostoria Glass Company, Moundsville, W. Va., June 5, 1896.

(The American Flint, February, 1927)

1 FRANCIS MURPHY, died at Moundsville.
2 C. C. (COONEY) VAUPEL, died at Moundsville.
3 CHARLES (MOUNTER) KERN, died at Moundsville.
4 WILLIAM (BILLY) PRACHT, now at Bellaire, Ohio.
5 HARRY HUMES, now at Wheeling, W. Va.
6 JOSEPH SCHERTZINGER, working at Indiana, Pa.
7 MICHAEL J. CLARKE, Superintendent Hemingray Glass Company, Muncie, Ind.
8 RICHARD HUMES, died at Moundsville.
9 JESS CRIMMEL, conducting confectionery at Moundsville.
10 JOHN H. CLARKE, with General Electric Company, Bridgeville, Pa.
11 JOSEPH GIBSON, died at Steubenville, Ohio.
12 WILLIAM G. LEONARD, working at Moundsville.
13 MICHAEL COUGHLIN, working at Moundsville.
14 HENRY (HANK) FRETER, now in Florida.
15 THOMAS J. CLARKE, died at Muncie, Ind., Sept. 6, 1911.
16 THOMAS HIGGINS, now at Los Angeles, Calif.
17 C. C. HIGGINS, Night Manager at factory at Los Angeles, Calif.
18 JAMES J. McKAY, President Local Union No. 90, Baltimore, Md.
19 UNKNOWN TO ME.
20 HENRY SEAMON, last heard of he was at Wheeling, W. Va.
21 JOSEPH VOITLE, glass maker for Fostoria Glass Co., Moundsville.
22 WILLIAM P. CLARKE, President American Flint Glass Workers' Union, Toledo.
23 DENNIS J. MURPHY, died at Wilkinsburg, Pa.
24 GEORGE E. BRYSON, died at Moundsville.
25 PHILIP CARNEY, working in factory at San Francisco.
26 PATRICK Mc KAY, working at Paden City, W. Va.
27 HUBERT OMLOR, conducting gents' furnishing house at Waynesburg, Pa.
28 GEORGE PATTERSON, working at Moundsville.
29 WILLIAM FRETER, now in Florida.
30 BERNARD McENTEE, last heard of at Chicago—Installment business.
31 PATRICK MORAN, died at Morgantown, W. Va.
32 JOHN T. McKAY, Night Manager at Paden City, West Virginia.
33 JACOB KERN, was Manager when picture was taken—died at Moundsville.
34 ANDREW WELSCH, died at Moundsville.
35 JAMES MADDEN, Manager of Central plant at Wheeling, W. Va.
36 GEORGE G. ROBERTS, with window and plate glass company at Ballspon, Va.
37 JOHN LEONARD, working at Moundsville.
38 WILLIAM BLACK, now on police force at Moundsville.
39 THOMAS MOCKLAR, died at Stockton, Calif.
40 ALFRED BURK, working at Fairmont, W. Va.
41 JAMES M. O'NEIL, working at Dunkirk, Ind.
42 JOHN PELKEY, working at Moundsville.
43 JOHN F. MULLEN, working at Paden City, W. Va.
44 CHARLES KLEINER, now at Mount Vernon, Ohio.
45 PETER WELSCH, working at Wheeling.
46 UNKNOWN TO ME.
47 CANNOT DISTINGUISH.
48 UNKNOWN TO ME.

Accept this souvenir as an expression of friendship and good will from one who frequently finds pleasure in recalling the days we spent together, and let it be understood that my heart longs for the opportunity to again greet the friends of my youth. I have never forgotten them or allowed my heart or my mind to even suggest that they be set aside.

Those were trying days, yet I have found that the struggles of my youth served a noble purpose—they contributed greatly towards erecting a foundation on which I have firmly stood throughout the years that followed. I would not, if I could, exchange my early hardships for an easier life. My experiences have been my greatest asset.

I express the hope that those companions of my youth who are still among the living are enjoying health and happiness, while I offer my supplications to Almighty God for the repose of the souls of those who have been called to render an account of their stewardship.

William P. Clarke

The American Bank, Toledo, Ohio

"usurious rates" charged by landlords for inadequate accommodations. To the local newspaper, which supported the Democratic Party, this exemplified the sorts of problems that came with industrial development. Nevertheless, the town responded by quickly establishing a building association and cautioning landlords against exorbitant rents.[15] Still, less than 1 in 10 of the skilled craftsmen took advantage of the inexpensive lots offered in town to become homeowners during the 1890s. Because a number of the craftsmen had originally worked in South Wheeling, some chose to live near their former homes and commute the twelve miles on the new interurban trolley line. For example, Charley Morningstar quickly became known as "streetcar Charley" because of his reputation for affability as he rode the trolley to Fostoria daily. Even the local managers stayed closer to Wheeling; William S. Brady built his new home in Glendale, several miles north of Moundsville.[16]

The quest for economic development created other problems. The construction of factories and rail connections caused tensions between the boosters and local farmers. Moundsville Mining and Manufacturing notified the town against trespassing and cattle grazing on the land it acquired at the north end of town, and then impounded cows found on its property. A year later, the boosters introduced stricter ordinances against the commons rights formerly enjoyed by livestock owners, but lost the town council vote.[17]

The developers were more successful at pressuring the town to pass bonds and raise taxes to fund streets, sewers, street lights, and other improvements that served the interests of the corporations. The rapid growth experienced by Moundsville (it doubled in size in the 1890s) required additional taxes for police and fire protection, a source of anxiety for the modest-sized farms in the area. This compounded the farmers' dissatisfaction with high tariffs, which they blamed for the increased prices they paid for all sorts of goods. Moreover, since the glass plant employed significant numbers of women and children, local farmers and families also had to compete for labor. As many former domestics took jobs at

OPPOSITE: *Illus. 5. Fostoria's AFGWU Local 10 produced two union presidents but also a number of future factory managers. This photo was taken in 1896, five years after the Fostoria Company moved to Moundsville. Note the Irish and German surnames, as well as the evidence that glassmaking was a traveling fraternity.* American Flint, *February 1927. Courtesy of United Steelworkers of America, Flint/Glass Industry Conference.*

Fostoria, some complained that they could not "find a girl to do house work."[18] More troubling to the town was the perceived increase in crime and disorder. Much-increased traffic on the trains due to the factories at the north end of town meant a greater potential for outsiders to move around unnoticed. In addition, the influx of transient glassworkers added to the customers of saloons and hotels. The pro-Democrat *Echo* called attention to the rapid growth of saloons in town and the unwillingness of the Republican boosters to enforce local ordinances. It also recommended chasing off the "shanty colony" that emerged near the river, another unfortunate result of business development.[19]

The *Echo*'s editor made numerous appeals to wed the growing industrial working class to local Democrats' antidevelopment, profarmer politics. He had some reasons to feel encouraged. Fostoria's skilled workers were union members attuned to the efforts of big corporations to destroy organized labor. Their union, Local 10 of the AFGWU, raised funds for striking steelworkers in Homestead, boycotted Fairmont Coal and nonunion cigars, and helped develop a local federation of trades to coordinate the activities of various unions. Equally important, many of the members of Local 10 were Irish and German Catholics who frequently supported the Democrats.[20] However, the AFGWU supported the high-tariff, hard money policies of the Republicans for the protection they brought to the glass industry, and Local 10 members objected to the anti-Catholic rantings of the *Echo*. Nor did many flints sympathize with the antisaloon sentiments of the local Democrats, although they accommodated the strong antisaloon politics in the town by organizing private clubs among ethnic groups. Emil Stahl and Frank Callahan, among other former glassworkers, opened clubs to attract the German and Irish flints who worked at Fostoria. Consequently, the neighborhood near the Fostoria plant actually enhanced Republican control of the town in the 1890s; in 1896, for instance, the Third Ward gave 70 percent of its votes to William McKinley, the Republican candidate for president.[21]

In other ways, changes in the industry in the 1890s put a terrible stress on glassworkers' adherence to the Republican development faith. During the 1880s, the flint glass industry had expanded by 75 percent with the availability of cheap fuel. At the same time, the cooperation between the AFGWU and the manufacturers had significantly improved wages, raising labor costs from 47 percent to 55 percent of the cost of production. Fostoria had actually been a part of that expansion.[22] But in 1893, a deep economic depression upset union–management relations. Sixteen firms took advantage of the depression to try and rid the industry of the AFGWU. They formed a combine, the U.S. Glass Company, to coordinate their resources and market power, and immediately broke off negotiations with their union workers. For the next four years, the AFGWU refused to allow union members to work for the companies in the "combine" or handle their ware. The union began an assessment to help the nearly 1,500 members thus locked out, ultimately paying out approximately $1.2 million in benefits and wages. While only twelve of the 1,500 locked-out members abandoned the union, U.S. Glass at first was able to command about one-quarter of the market, paying reduced wages to nonunion workers. As a result, this contest not only taxed the resources of the AFGWU and its members to help locked-out workers but also put pressure on union firms to lower costs in order to compete.[23]

This environment affected labor–management relations during Fostoria's early years in Moundsville. Although Fostoria's management did not join the combine, the fledgling company looked for ways to weather the depression and compete with the nonunion sector of the industry. One concession the AFGWU made to companies was to abandon four weeks of the traditional six-week summer stop. At Fostoria, the day-to-day negotiations became increasingly hostile. To cut costs, the company sought wage cuts, unilaterally increased production quotas (called "moves" in the plant), and reduced numbers of union members. The union men responded by contesting each of these issues, staging brief walkouts, enforcing the union's own rules against members who exceeded the "move," and demanding that the company give all men equal time.[24]

Three issues generated considerable animosity. First, the company sought to implement new rules concerning pot setting, the onerous chore of replacing the pots in which the batch was melted (see illus. 6). Pots weighed several tons, holding between 2,500 and 3,500 pounds of glass. According to one English manufacturer, "the terrible task of setting these pots in the furnace . . . in the teeth of a consuming fire, is perhaps that operation which . . . would most astonish a stranger to such scenes." Craftsmen routinely tried to avoid the task, leaving it to less skilled workers. Seeking efficiency in the process, management's new rules demanded that union members participate, and it fined workers who violated them. On several occasions, Local 10 halted work and demanded meetings with management over the imposition of fines.[25] The second issue involved pay for cracked ware. Craftsmen worked hard to make their production quota, and they felt that they deserved to be paid accordingly. However, on occasion, ware would crack in the process of annealing or as it was carried through the plant. Management began refusing to pay for cracked ware, even though it was not clear who was at fault. Despite several conferences, neither side would budge. Finally, in June 1896, the

Illus. 6. "The Strenuous Task of Setting a Pot." This pen-and-ink drawing captures the removal of the old pot by the workers under the "anxious peer of the foreman." The pots held between 2,500 and 3,500 pounds of glass. Who did the work of setting new pots amid a "consuming fire" proved to be one of the most contentious issues in the factory. National Glass Budget, *June 6, 1903. Courtesy of* National Glass Budget *and the* Glass Factory Directory.

men walked out, effectively choosing to begin the summer stop at that moment. They also resolved not to return unless all the men were "taken back" when the stop ended. A month later, the company capitulated, seeking to restart production as the depression began to ease.[26]

The third issue was the most contentious. During the depression, Fostoria reduced its number of craftsmen and began subcontracting its glass-cutting work to save money. John Heedy, a former AFGWU member, opened his own small glass-cutting firm in Moundsville and began doing work for Fostoria and other firms along the Ohio River. The problem was that Heedy began operating his shop as a nonunion concern. When Local 10 discovered this, it threatened to expel Heedy from the union and to refuse to work on any ware designated for Heedy's shop. For two years the company and the local fought intermittent battles over this issue. The local even fined members whose sons worked for Heedy, and denied relatives of the "scab cutters" admission to the union.[27]

The AFGWU attributed the increased level of conflict with employers to companies' efforts to restructure the industry. Indeed, wages stagnated throughout the 1890s, and the industry grew by only about 25 percent, following a rate in the 1880s of three times that. Flints began to take a hard look at their attachment to the Republican Party. Nathan B. Scott, the prominent Republican leader in Wheeling, came under heavy criticism from the AFGWU when he attached his Central Glass Works to the U.S. Glass combine. Just a few miles north of Wheeling in Wellsburg, the AFGWU ran a candidate for the West Virginia senate on the Democratic ticket against Samuel George, a Republican glass manufacturer who had joined the combine. Even in Moundsville, Local 10 began to question the political norms; in August 1899, the members resolved to invite Socialist leader Eugene V. Debs to give a lecture in town.[28]

Along the Ohio River, the flints had a strong enough presence to effect some change, despite the toll taken by the depression. Scott's ambition for the West Virginia seat in the U.S. Senate eventually forced him to pull his Central Glass Works out of the combine. Likewise, Samuel George reopened negotiations with the AFGWU and returned to the union-shop fold. By 1899, U.S. Glass included only five of the original sixteen factories that had united in 1893.[29] The men who ran Fostoria, Lucien Martin and William S. Brady, briefly forged an alliance with a newly emerging trust, the National Glass Company. The National was a combination of nineteen firms in Indiana, Ohio, Pennsylvania, Maryland, and West Virginia, with an authorized capital of $4 million. But this trust opted to allow each plant to make its own determination about operating union or nonunion. Most of the plants chose the former, and the National Glass Company restored peace and harmony to the industry. In fact, the trust used its relationship with the AFGWU to help regulate competition in the industry and control future growth. Union members benefited as well. In the five years after the emergence of the National, average earnings for male workers in the industry increased by 19 percent.[30]

Association with the National Glass Company ended the involvement of Lucien Martin and William S. Brady with Fostoria. In March 1901, Martin left Moundsville to assume duties as head of the commercial department for the National Glass Company in Pittsburgh. On Martin's last day, the office staff presented him with "a handsome vase." A bit later, he and his son were "decoyed into the factory where they were greeted by a selection from the famous Fostoria Glass Band, after which Charles Morningstar, on behalf of the employees, presented Mr. Martin with a fine gold pen and his son with a diamond stud. The occasion was a memorable one and fully enjoyed by all," according to the *Commoner and Glassworker.*[31] Brady served as director for a brief time until the new management team arrived. Then he, too, left to work at National Glass Company. Despite the contentious relationship that had characterized the 1890s, the union men seemed willing to forgive all grievances, particularly since their future seemed much brighter and they had survived the corporate restructuring of the industry.

Glassworkers could also feel optimism about the growth of the town, as well as pride in their improving local status. Around the time Martin departed, Moundsville was a town of about six thousand people, but already the second leading manufacturing center in the northwestern corner of the state. The United States Stamping Company (which made enameled cooking ware) and the Suburban Brick Company joined Fostoria in the north end of town, giving employment to nearly one thousand workers. Two building and loan associations helped wage earners start the process of becoming homeowners, and the streetcar system carried others to Wheeling every fifteen minutes. Boosters like Charles Weaver called Moundsville "the coming industrial city of West Virginia." His involvement in United States Stamping, the Moundsville Development Company, and several banks was a testament for the development faith.[32] Flints were also major assets to this growth. The 106 members of Local 10 worked nine hours a day for between $4 and $5, significantly above the average industrial wage. Over the ensuing decade, more than 1 of every 3 became homeowners, beginning to fulfill the expectation that Weaver had when he began the Moundsville Mining and Manufacturing Company. Just as important, flints began to appear on the political slates of both parties in local elections.[33] Clearly, Moundsville had become a glass town.

In 1902, when he came to town to take over the reins of Fostoria, W. A. B. Dalzell brought a wealth of experience. Born in Pittsburgh in 1858, Dalzell was the son of a steamboat captain. He grew up at a fortuitous time for a young man with business interests; the Pittsburgh High School started a Commercial Department to train the new middle class in 1868, and Dalzell graduated from the program in 1874. Four years later, he entered the business side of the glass industry in Pittsburgh with Adams and Company. From there, he rose quickly. In 1883, Dalzell and his brothers acquired a glass plant in Wellsburg. Just a year after Fostoria opened in the gas belt of western Ohio, he joined with William Leighton Jr. to start a company in Findlay, Ohio. In 1899, he managed the western department of the National Glass Company, from which he made the move to the Fostoria Company when Lucien Martin moved to Pittsburgh.[34]

The company Dalzell inherited was well positioned for expansion.

In 1896, developers made a big natural gas strike in nearby Cameron, West Virginia, which supplied Fostoria with inexpensive natural gas to complement its coal-fueled gas producers. At the same time, the company added a line of decorated lamps to its manufacture of tableware for the hotel and saloon trade. In 1902, Fostoria added a new fourteen-pot furnace devoted to two new lines of tableware, and a year later added a new factory, increasing the size of the company to 850 workers, making it "the largest independent glass plant in the United States," according to the *National Glass Budget*. From every indication, the future was promising. The *Commoner and Glassworker* noted: "The management has been recognized as a friend of the workmen, and there is no community where there is a larger number of employes in continuous service than at this factory."[35]

Dalzell hoped to cultivate a stability that would prove reliable to his Republican development faith. The manager was a deeply religious and straitlaced man who believed in hard work and discipline. One worker recalled his early experience with Dalzell's sternness. He had gathered a gob at the end of a pipe for a skilled craftsman who was occupied with another task. Eventually, the young gatherer had to throw away the glass because it got too cold to work. When Dalzell saw this, he took the young man aside and told him to collect his wages at the end of the day and not return.[36] But Dalzell's stern demeanor did not prevent him from cultivating a loyal following. He became a fixture in a number of local groups that enabled him to develop a close relationship with a key segment of his employees. He was a Mason, a Knight Templar, and a member of the First Methodist Episcopal Church in Moundsville. From these associations, Dalzell recruited his most trusted circle of plant supervisors.

Craftsmen against the Development Faith

During the first decade of the twentieth century, the skilled glassworkers expanded the influence of their union in Moundsville. Part of the town's acceptance of organized labor had to do with the nature of skilled work in glass tableware. Membership in the AFGWU was much less restrictive than in the bottle or window-glass unions. The development of presses and molds in the nineteenth century had reduced the skill level needed to do much of the work, and made the flints the lowest paid glass craftsmen. The AFGWU responded to this low pay situation by reducing the length of the apprenticeship to one year. The AFGWU also did not have the rules limiting apprenticeships to relatives of members that characterized the window and bottle-making unions. Thus, as Fostoria grew to more than eight hundred workers, it opened opportunities for locally born boys (and a few girls) to learn a trade. By 1910, less than half of the boys apprenticing for a trade had a father in the industry. One result was that Fostoria's workers began to integrate into and more closely resemble the rest of Moundsville's population. While 3 of 8 Fostoria workers were immigrants or children of immigrants, in 1900, only 1 in 5 were by 1910, and 1 in 6 by 1920.[37]

The structure of the factory ensured that the skilled craftsmen, who made up roughly 30 percent of the workforce, ruled the workplace. The largest part of the shop floor consisted of numerous small teams of workers led by a blower, a presser, or a finisher who directed the labor of gatherers (who were, in effect, apprentices) and helpers who had such job titles as rougher, smoother, carry-in or carry-out boy, snap-up boy, and warm-in boy. Separate departments housed mold-making shops, etching and decorating shops, coopers, machine repairers, and the workers who touched up, selected, tested, and packed the ware. The factory layout reflected gender and age divisions. Actual ware production was almost exclusively male. Blowers, pressers, cutters, and finishers (AFGWU members) were men in their twenties or older and those most likely to be foreign born or their children; gatherers were males in their late teens or early twenties preparing for one of the trades; and the helpers were men and boys ranging from age eleven upward who did the monotonous unskilled work around the furnaces or in the warehouses. The decorating and etching department was equally divided along gender lines, as was the selecting, testing, and packing department. The main difference was that decorators and etchers were better paid and more likely to be foreign born. The average age of workers in each was early to midtwenties. Touch-up was solidly a young female department; all the girls were native born and in their late teens or early twenties (see table 4.1).[38]

The influence of skilled craftsmen in the factory continued on the outside. As they purchased homes and established neighborhoods near the factory, flints dominated much of Moundsville's social life. When Local 10 of the AFGWU held its annual entertainments, they were important community events. The local newspaper advised: "It is due the glassworkers that they be greeted by a packed house." These entertainments included recitals, vaudeville skits, "blackface antics" and music from the Fostoria Glass Works Brass Band, reflecting both local tastes as well as the prevailing racial attitudes. The Band, in particular, was famous in the area, giving free open-air concerts to large crowds, and organizing annual camping outings on the banks of the Ohio River when the plant reinstated the longer summer stop in 1902. Together with the

Table 4.1: Workforce Composition: Fostoria, 1910

Category	Male	Female	Native born/ Native parent	Native born/ Foreign parent	Foreign born
Foremen (n=16)	100.0	0.0	56.3	18.8	25.0
White collar (21)	47.6	52.4	90.5	9.5	0.0
Craftsmen (116)	100.0	0.0	66.4	24.1	9.5
Mold shop (20)	95.0	5.0	55.0	25.0	20.0
Gatherers (41)	100.0	0.0	85.4	15.6	0.0
Decorators (55)	50.9	49.1	72.7	9.1	18.2
Skilled, non-glass (16)	100.0	0.0	75.0	18.8	6.2
Unskilled men (41)	100.0	0.0	95.1	4.9	0.0
Children (73)	97.3	2.7	93.2	6.8	0.0
Select, test, pack (33)	57.6	42.4	93.9	6.1	0.0
Touch up (24)	0.0	100.0	100.0	0.0	0.0
Totals (n = 456)	83.0	17.0	79.8	13.1	7.1

Source: Manuscript Census schedules, 1910, Marshall County.

glassworkers' Seldom Seen Fishing Club, the flints entertained "hundreds of visitors during the camping season and their fame as entertainers . . . spread throughout the state."[39]

Flints were at the center of the local sporting scene. In addition to their fishing clubs, glassworkers established the Fostoria Pleasure Club, dedicated to family camping trips. Craftsmen Jake Crimmel and J. W. Gallagher organized a local baseball team in 1896 that they ran out of Crimmel's private club. Flints followed the exploits of several members who eventually played in the major leagues, including Harry Morgan, who pitched for the Red Sox, and New York Giants catcher Tommy Needham. In 1902, Crimmel, who by then had left Fostoria to open his own restaurant, was behind the formation of the Moundsville Athletic Association and was subsequently the proprietor of the local bowling alley. Football was another sport of choice for Moundsville flints (see illus. 7). They even recruited glassworkers from Wheeling to join the team, whose success was a source of pride for Fostoria's workers.[40]

Fraternal orders and churches further integrated glassworker families into the community. For example, when local flint Joseph Martin died at the young age of twenty-seven in 1908, Local 10, the Fraternal Order of Elks, the Knights of the Golden Eagles, and the Calvary Methodist Church memorialized him. Martin was hardly an exception. In 1902, three of the seven officers of the local Knights of Pythias were Local 10 members, as were four of the Ancient Order of United Workmen's nine officers. The Odd Fellows, the Knights of Pythias, and the Knights of Columbus were other organizations attracting glassworkers. Wives of

Illus. 7. The 1913 Moundsville football team, made up mostly of glass-workers. Football became a popular sport among Moundsville's glass-workers in the early twentieth century. The team even recruited players from Wheeling. Photograph courtesy of Paul W. Myers, former business agent for the American Flint Glass Workers' Union.

the flints contributed to these connections in female auxiliaries like the Ladies of the Golden Eagles. But women had an even greater presence in the churches. The Catholic Church choir contained the wives and daughters of several glassworkers, as did the Epworth League of the Methodist Church. Moreover, as the town grew in the years before World War I, so did the churches, increasing their membership at a rate more than double that of population growth.[41]

The fraternalism of the glassworkers meshed easily with their commitment to the AFGWU. In fact, the flints kept a number of rituals that dated back to the Knights of Labor, which thrived through its connection to fraternal orders. Jake Crimmel remembered his ritualistic initiation into the union: "I answered all the questions that the Black Robed man requested." Like fraternal orders, the AFGWU offered benefits and insurance, and took great pains to teach members discipline and respect for their union brothers. Using abusive language against a brother, drinking intoxicating liquors at union meetings, or starting rumors against either the union's interest or another flint were all grounds for fines.[42] Wives supported this union culture, often through participation in the Women's Label League, which encouraged consumers to look for the union label on the products (especially glassware) that they bought. Nowhere was the fraternalism of the flints more evident than in the elaborate and comic activities of the "Gazams" at the annual conventions. With robes and pointed hats, the Gazams organized the social outings that cemented the craft unity through celebrations that included "songs, story telling, recitations and toasts galore."[43]

Flints often explored solidarity with other craftsmen. Local 10 joined the Ohio Valley Trades and Labor Assembly, which united unions in the greater Wheeling area, as well as the fledgling West Virginia Federation of Labor, which spoke for organized labor in West Virginia's statehouse. Moundsville flints boycotted prison-made clothing, nonunion barbers and newspapers, and merchants who sold nonunion fruit jars. They also responded to requests from railroad workers, iron and steel workers, and miners for assistance during strikes. But on one issue, they consistently opposed the advice of organized labor in the state and the nation—child labor. Flints felt that making their "moves" would be impossible without the assistance of young boys who could maneuver easily through a shop floor cluttered with presses, molds, ware, and numerous small teams of workers. Consequently, they lobbied for years against proposed child labor laws in the state.[44]

The flints' extensive craft culture aimed for an exclusively white solidarity. Although entry into the AFGWU was not nearly as limited as entry into the other unions in glass, the flints still relied on controlling the labor market. One way to achieve this was through racial exclusion. In 1903, the AFGWU took notice of the use of black and Italian strikebreakers in Virginia and Pennsylvania. Just a year later in Moundsville, glassworkers on several occasions emphasized their hostility to blacks and support of the emerging regime of Jim Crow in West Virginia. The flints' football team refused to play a game against Waynesburg College because the Pennsylvania school had African Americans on its team. Six weeks later, the team fought a pitched battle with blacks who were drinking and annoying fans at one of their home games.[45] These racial sentiments preceded black strikebreaking. Glassworker entertainments featured "blackface" parodies as early as 1898, and a portion of Local 10 gravitated easily to the race-baiting Democrats in town. The Democratic newspaper, *Echo,* routinely attributed increased crime to the arrival of African Americans, and lamented the fact that the town had grown up around the State Penitentiary. Egged on by such sentiments, in the summer of 1907, a local crowd even chased a black revival from the local camp meeting grounds. The *Echo*'s repeated calls for a "white man's government" in the state resonated with an exclusionary craft-union culture.[46]

Women and children, who made up better than one-fourth of Fostoria's workers, found only somewhat better support from Local 10's members.

When the company tried to break the strike of the "girls" in the selecting department in March 1904 by bringing in replacements from McMechen, the flints not only walked out in sympathy but also gathered to menace the potential scabs. However, when boys struck to improve their wages, they won little support from the men under whose supervision they worked, and the company denied their demands.[47] On more than one occasion, flints abused their young helpers. William Fish had to appear in court for striking a boy with a "carrying-in fork" after the boy chipped some ware, and John Carney caused his helper to "run off" due to constant physical tormenting. In another instance, a fight erupted at the factory gate when two coal miners appeared at the end of a shift to get revenge on Dan Henkle for assaulting their fifteen-year-old relative. Many glass-workers also had unpleasant memories of their youthful introduction to the tyranny of the glass craftsmen. Guy Alexander remembered that the first thing he got at work was "a kick in the ass." He dropped a tumbler, and "the presser cracked me over the head with his scissors."[48]

Certainly, there never was only one craft-union culture. While they might be united on issues of craft control, wages, and working conditions, glassworkers divided over many other issues. For example, the plant manager laid off John Carney until Carney could recruit a boy to replace the one he ran off. This triggered a debate in Local 10 over whether to support a union brother or object to his abusive behavior. The same day, local members disagreed about the need to enforce fines against men who had been drinking before the meeting.[49] In fact, the AFGWU's code of the craft, ranging from the antics of the Gazams to the partisan preferences in the political arena, caused a significant amount of conflict within Local 10, which was the only organized voice for workers at Fostoria.

One of the principal divisions among the flints was ethnoreligious in character. The glass industry contributed to the dramatic growth of the Catholic Church in Moundsville and Marshall County. While the vast majority of less skilled workers grew up in the rural Protestant area around Moundsville, over one-third of the workers in the skilled production departments had at least one foreign-born parent. The town experienced an influx of newcomers of German, Irish, and French heritage, most of whom were Catholic. Religion thus not only tended to separate skilled from unskilled but also the craftsmen themselves.[50] This, at times, caused resentment, particularly since Catholics, especially Irish Catholics, dominated the leadership of the exclusionary AFGWU. The *National Glass Budget* frequently resorted to slurs when discussing union leaders:

One would think that at least the fine fed and high salaried Irish gentle-
men who hold official positions in the A.F.G.W.U., none of whom are
less than lineal descendents from the hog-trotters of Allen and the swine-
herds of Connamara and Sligo, would have appreciated their transference
hither much higher, and thanked their lucky stars that their mugs and
lugs appear as often in the "Commoner" [the prounion journal] as did
those of their ancestors in the rogues galleries of the auld Dart.

In short, the *Budget* hoped to fuel antiunion, ethnoreligious resentment against the Irish men who filled the leadership positions of the
AFGWU.[51]

To the *Budget*, this leadership helped explain the growing militancy
of the AFGWU. In 1903, the union ousted President Charles Voitle, a
former Fostoria worker and original member of Local 10. Voitle, an Ohio-
born Methodist, was a moderate who ran afoul of some locals because
they thought he was too close to the employers. He had allowed several
companies to continue operating during a dispute, and he undermined
the AFGWU convention's demand for a wage increase he thought too
high. Voitle quickly found employment in management, suggesting that
his critics may have been correct.[52]

His replacement was Thomas Rowe, an Irish Catholic with Socialist leanings. Rowe feared the threat posed by semiautomatic technology,
already in use on wide-mouth jars and containers and lamp chimneys.
Employers using new semiautomatic machines frequently chose to operate nonunion. In response, Rowe attempted to implement an AFGWU
program of cooperative production and a more confrontational attitude
toward management, particularly as the economy went into recession
following the Panic of 1907. On Labor Day, 1909, Rowe tore into the
industry: "The numerous demands for wage reductions; the many decla-
rations for the 'open shop' by corporate greed; the shameless corruption
of the legislatures; the debauching of courts and the reinforcements of a
subsidized press is stirring the mighty hosts of labor and quickening the
heart-beats of collective protest." By 1910, Rowe was advocating support
for the Socialist Party as the only solution to the continued degradation
of the trade.[53]

Opposition to the leftward drift of the AFGWU on both the national
and the local level appealed to anti-Catholic and anti-Irish prejudices.
While the *National Glass Budget* lampooned Rowe and that "same old
Irish bunch," Fostoria's management aggressively worked to divide Local
10. Company president Dalzell recruited a team of moderates to run the
plant, beginning with Calvin B. Roe, an Ohio farm boy who entered the

industry at Dalzell's Findlay, Ohio, factory and rose through the personal attention of his boss. Dalzell understood the importance of including Local 10 members as well. For the company's managerial positions, he handpicked men like Joseph Voitle, the brother of the ousted AFGWU president; A. C. Scroggins, whose son worked in the nonunion mold shop of John Heedy; Jacob Kerns; and Scott Littleton. These former union men were all born in the 1850s and 1860s in either Ohio or West Virginia. More important to Dalzell and Roe, they shared many of their employers' connections. Unlike most glassworkers, Kerns, Scroggins, Voitle, and Littleton were Masons, as were Dalzell and Roe. These managers were also Methodists, temperance advocates, homeowners, and Republicans, making them ideal for Dalzell's team.[54]

Fostoria's Protestant managers took their Republican politics into the factory. Guy Alexander, who began working in the plant in 1906, recalled that the management was openly and unapologetically Republican. They routinely gave party candidates permission to lobby in the factory. Not surprisingly, the best jobs and the greatest security went to men who shared those beliefs. Meanwhile, Local 10's leadership was increasingly in the hands of Catholics, who began voting with the Democrats. John Mullen, James McKay, Pat Sullivan, Frank Carney, John McKay, Conrad Vaupel, and C. J. Barth—mostly of Irish and German ancestry—assumed leadership of the union, as well as prominence in the Marshall County Democratic Party. William P. Clarke, who became AFGWU secretary treasurer in 1907 and president in 1916, "took exception" to Fostoria's Protestant Republican management, and "had to leave the city of Moundsville" because he could no longer work there.[55] Instead, he joined the pro-Socialist administration of AFGWU president Thomas Rowe. Indeed, Fostoria's Protestant managers worked to systematically eliminate the Irish presence in the factory (see table 4.2).

Table 4.2: Ethnicity of Moundsville's Immigrant Craftsmen in 1900 and 1910, by percentage

Group	1900	1910
German	36.7	44.6
Irish	36.7	16.2
British	16.3	9.5
French	6.1	10.8
Other*	4.1	18.9

Note: *Includes Belgian, Swiss, Bohemian, Austrian, and Canadian.
Source: Manuscript Census schedules, 1900, 1910, Marshall County.

The hostility did not stop at the plant gates. Fostoria's managers became integral to the antisaloon agitation that swept the town in the first decade of the century. Again, this was an issue that divided the craft culture of the flints. Some members of Local 10, like their employers, believed that alcohol destroyed the honor and dignity of the craftsmen; others felt that drinking cemented the bonds of manly solidarity. But when the local Protestant community, which included Dalzell, Scroggins, Roe, Voitle, and Kerns, mobilized to put the weight of law behind their values, Irish and German glassworkers felt the effects. On numerous occasions, local police raided the clubs and saloons of former flints Emil Stahl, Frank Callahan, and James Higgins for selling liquor on Sundays. When the antisaloon interests succeeded in ridding the town of bars in 1907, Stahl and Callahan had to open private "social clubs" to avoid prosecution (see illus. 8). Protestants also sought to prohibit Sunday baseball and football games, another important outlet for glassworker recreation.[56]

To many flints, this crackdown on their leisure went hand in hand with the company's abandonment of the summer stop and efforts to reduce wages when the economic recession hit in 1908. Meanwhile, the Ohio Valley labor movement exposed the machinations of Republican U.S. senator Nathan B. Scott, who secretly opposed labor reform measures—such as employer liability and laws limiting the length of the workday on federally funded contracts—while claiming to support trade unions. Growing fears about the potential impact of mechanization only

Illus. 8. Former flint Emil Stahl (standing in the doorway) had to convert his saloon into a private club in response to the campaign of Moundsville's antisaloon politicians in 1907. The saloon's proximity to the Fostoria factory made it a favorite spot for glassworkers. Francis Bonar Collection. Courtesy of the West Virginia State Archives.

worsened the situation. Support for protective tariffs no longer seemed enough to keep glassworkers loyal to the Republican Party.[57]

At the end of the decade, the most militant members of Local 10 followed the lead of AFGWU president Rowe and helped establish a local branch of the Socialist Party. The most prominent flints on the Left were Ross Leidy, a thirty-year-old glassblower born in Ohio; Nicholas Rhinehart, a German-born decorator in his fifties; William Cullum, a local boy working as a gatherer; and Charles Scroggins, who must have been at odds with his brother, the Fostoria manager and local Republican activist. For these men, the Democratic Party offered a weak alternative to the development faith of Republicans. The Democrats' platform called for reducing the costs of government and better roads to help farmers, hardly issues of burning importance to glassworkers who feared further technological and managerial restructuring of their industry.[58]

Nicholas Rhinehart, who served on the executive committee of the state's Socialist Party, explained the cause to Moundsville's citizens:

> Today the machinery and the land used for industrial purposes are owned by a rapidly decreasing minority. . . . The fact that a few capitalists are permitted to control all the country's industrial resources and social tools for their individual profit, and to make the production of the necessaries of life the object of competitive private enterprise and speculation is at the bottom of all the social evils of our time.

Glassworkers needed to fight against the "capitalist class," which "in its mad race for profits, is bound to exploit the workers to the very limit of their endurance and to sacrifice their physical, moral and mental welfare to its own insatiable greed."[59] At a time when violent labor conflicts in Los Angeles, Philadelphia, the copper region of Michigan, and the coal fields of southern West Virginia grabbed the headlines of the newspapers, Rhinehart's plea for socialism elicited growing support. It helped that Fostoria, in the midst of an economic downturn, was only offering part-time employment to its skilled workers, while the *National Glass Budget* gloated that new machines would soon put the glass unions out of business. Moreover, just fifteen miles to the north, a federal judge issued a restraining order against AFGWU organizing, and Nathan Scott's Central Glass Works was in the midst of a battle to deny union recognition to its workers.[60]

The Socialist Party surprised local observers when it won 15 percent of the votes in Moundsville in the 1910 election for U.S. Congress and the state legislature. Reducing Republican margins, this election was a severe jolt to the development faith. John W. Davis, the Clarksburg Democrat, won election to the U.S. House of Representatives, and G. B. Slemaker won election to the state senate, the first Democrat from Marshall County to win in decades. The significance of Slemaker's election was magnified because the West Virginia legislature would choose two U.S. senators in its 1911 session. Slemaker helped the Democrats gain control in the State House, sending coal operator Clarence Watson and William Chilton, both Democrats, to the Senate. To the Socialists, however, this only proved that there "was really no political difference between" the two dominant parties. "The end and aim of each of them [was] to serve Capital."[61]

The party improved on its showing in the local elections in March 1911. The local party appealed to voters on a range of issues, including replacing the contract system for city work with public employees paid a minimum wage of $2.00 per day for eight hours of work; the municipal ownership of utilities; the opening of public school halls for social and educational purposes free of charge; the improvement of streets and lights for those living in the suburbs ("the land of mud and darkness"); and the procurement of proper grounds for a city park and public restrooms. There was also an air of civic morality in the party's program. The platform promised to enforce ordinances against spitting on sidewalks, the fast driving of horses or automobiles on city streets, and the selling of intoxicating liquors to minors. In short, "to stand for and work for the interest of the working class," to the Socialist Party, meant pledging to deliver "a better moral, social and intellectual environment for our youth and people."[62]

In the First and Second wards, neighborhoods that were dominated by glassworkers, the Socialists ran James Ryan and Mel Higgs, both glass cutters at Fostoria. Higgs won 21 percent of the vote, and Ryan captured 31.7 percent, enough to tip the First Ward into the Democrats' win column, and almost enough to demand a recall in the three-way race. Citywide, the party's mayoral candidate polled 203 votes out of 1,667 cast (12 percent), enough to elect a Democrat mayor in this former Republican stronghold.[63] Such local insurgency led to defections within the Republican ranks, as the Progressives also put a reform-oriented ticket in the field for the 1912 presidential election. The Progressives appealed to many who were unhappy with the development faith but uncomfortable with the Socialist alternative; the party's portion of the vote dropped to about 8 percent of the total in November 1912, but the combination of the reform tickets meant that Marshall County had two Democratic state senators. In the city elections four months later, the Socialists claimed a respectable 11 percent, and Moundsville elected a Progressive Party mayor and councilman in the First Ward.[64]

The flirtation with socialism was short-lived, however. Amid the constant attention focused on radicalism and violent labor conflict, many in Moundsville looked for a more moderate solution. Particularly damaging to the Socialist cause was the admission by the McNamara brothers, leaders of the Structural Iron Workers union, that they were guilty of a series of bombings, including the bombing of the *Los Angeles Times* building. The Ohio Valley Socialists had been vocal supporters of the union, accusing prosecutors of a conspiracy to blame organized labor for the violence.[65] Pat Sullivan of Local 10 tried to claim a middle ground for many of the flints and most of organized labor, suggesting that they felt that strikes and violence were things of the past. Too, the weight of routine defeats, despite their best efforts, must have sent some in the direction of parties that had the potential for success. James Ryan, who had run such a strong race for the Socialists in the First Ward in 1911, finally won his seat on the city council as a Democrat in 1915. Of course, changes in the state Democratic Party made this shift less abrupt. In 1912, West Virginia Democrats passed a platform that included regulation of public utilities, the endorsement of a progressive income tax, and protection for unions against the use of judicial injunctions and company guards during strikes. In 1914, the platform demanded a workman's compensation act, the prohibition of martial law during labor disputes, and a ban on corporate campaign contributions. The fledgling reform elements of the state Democrats proclaimed that the "wealth of the country is required to contribute a fair share" to the common good.[66]

Despite these progressive platforms, when glassworkers helped defeat the Republicans, it represented a Pyrrhic victory at best. The West Virginia congressional delegation, which included Democrats Davis, Chilton, and Watson, was tied to coal and railroad interests that hardly amounted to a rejection of the development faith. Control of the party by factions that had dominated through the late nineteenth century kept the Democrats firmly in the grasp of a group of men who could stifle elements of the platform that ran counter to business interests.[67] Consequently, as socialism diminished, there were few options for a labor movement in the state that hoped to enact a new set of claims on the distribution of wealth or protection for working people. Locally, the Republican Party began its own newspaper in town to emphasize its perspective and tout the party's past achievements. By 1916, the Republicans were back in control of politics in Moundsville and Marshall County.[68]

Fostoria's managers survived the radical ferment within the company's ranks with only minor incidents. Dalzell and his team reinforced the social and cultural divisions among the flints to keep at least a portion of

Local 10 loyal to the company. They also expanded the plant to add more workers and provide fairly reliable employment in a tight labor market. Howard Denoon, for one, recalled his family arriving in Moundsville in 1910, in response to the opportunities at Fostoria. He and his brother, aged twelve and fourteen, found work at $5 a week to help their impoverished working-class family. Both found it relatively easy to get a gathering job and learn a trade if you showed any interest at all. Eventually, they realized that the trade paid enough for their family to live better than they had previously.[69] But Dalzell and Roe kept alive the threat to shut the plant down if they did not get what they wanted. In May 1914, AFGWU member John B. Cullum complained: "Things at the old Fostoria plant are not as good as they have been in the past." Two months later, Dalzell closed the plant during a dispute with the union.[70]

The combination of good jobs in a tight labor market and the knowledge that management had the ability to take them away served to discipline the union. However, the company stopped short of trying to completely rid itself of Local 10. Instead, Fostoria used the AFGWU to train new skilled workers and maintain a relatively peaceful mechanism for resolving disputes that arose in the plant. The flints also helped supervise the nonunion production helpers. Finally, because they were paid by the piece with strict output quotas, the AFGWU served to help regulate competition in the industry. Without some new machinery that could eliminate the need for skilled workers altogether, the glass tableware industry settled into a stable relationship with the union by World War I.[71]

But, unfortunately for the boosters who had held such high hopes for the town in 1900, the infusion of new jobs and people after 1910 slowed to a trickle. Marshall County, which promised a fertile area for the industrial expansion of Wheeling, grew by a disappointing 1,500 people between 1910 and 1920, less than 4 percent. Moundsville did only slightly better, expanding from about 11,000 to 12,300. Certainly, the area generally seemed less attractive to investors. Wheeling was one of the most heavily unionized cities in the country. The tin plate workers had fought a protracted battle against the steel industry in 1910 and again in World War I, and the city's Ohio Valley Trades and Labor Assembly had a strong Socialist leadership that supported militant labor actions.[72] The presence of the AFGWU and the rise of a Socialist bloc in Moundsville proved no more inviting to capitalists looking for a safe environment for investment. Absent local sources of capital, of which there were few, Moundsville's claim to be "the coming industrial city of West Virginia" had a hollow ring.

Conservative Craftsmen in the Mound City

By the time Guy Alexander and Howard Denoon obtained their apprenticeships at Fostoria in the years around World War I, the company had
begun to shift its emphasis from lines for the hotel and bar trade to
tableware for home use. The decision was fortuitous for Fostoria. The
prohibition movement was gaining ground, winning in West Virginia in
1913 and nationally in 1919. The change brought some hardship, however. Alexander recalled that there were no raises between 1913 and
1916, as the industry felt the brunt of Democratic tariff reductions, and
that there was a good deal of conflict on the shop floor. Adding to the
old contentious issues of pot setting and cracked ware, the company
tried to increase the number of apprentices and to force each shop to
work four-and-a-half-hour moves (shifts) without stopping, regardless
of whether or not they had made their quota. But the militancy of a few
years earlier had declined, and most of the issues were negotiated within
the plant. Neither Denoon nor Alexander could remember a strike during those years.[73]

Fostoria's situation, like the glass industry in West Virginia generally,
improved during the United States' involvement in the war. By 1919,
the value of the state's glass production had grown dramatically, due in
part to inflation and in part to the virtual elimination of imports. The
value of window and bottle production increased by 245 percent; pressed
and blown glassware by a more modest 106 percent. Fostoria began paying dividends to stockholders again in 1916, and gave its employees a
"voluntary wage increase of 15 percent" in April 1917. To avoid the
government's rationing of natural gas, the company put another coal
gas producer in operation that fall.[74] The war did temporarily disrupt
the workforce, however. The company and the union cooperated with
government needs, and sent some of Fostoria's workers to Steubenville
and Cambridge, Ohio, to make light bulbs or other items deemed more
necessary by the federal government, typically at an increase in pay.
Workers had little say in the matter; Denoon recalled that if glassworkers refused, they were never rehired.[75]

The war not only boosted earnings and job opportunities but also
eliminated the lingering remnants of socialism. Local 10's members en-
thusiastically participated in local patriotic demonstrations and raised
funds to send tobacco and other items to the "boys at the front." In the
spring of 1917, glassworkers of German heritage, many of whom had
supported the Socialists, pledged a "Declaration of Loyalty to the United
States" through the front page of the *Echo*. Dalzell headed up the local

Liberty Loan drive and printed full-page ads in the local papers decrying "German Savagery." Rumors of German sabotage included reports of glass being found in local foodstuffs. In April 1918, a mob attacked two Benwood immigrants for arguing with a soldier at the railroad station. Ironically, at just this time, the town learned that America's most eminent Socialist, Eugene V. Debs, would begin his prison term in Moundsville for his antiwar speeches.[76]

The immediate postwar years only intensified the antilabor atmosphere, amid leftist uprisings in Europe and labor unrest in the United States. In West Virginia, state Democratic and Republican leaders joined together to enact laws mandating loyalty oaths and creating a state constabulary, while the federal government used the war and the postwar social turmoil to increase surveillance of immigrants and labor activists. Between 1919 and 1922, the West Virginia government relied on these tools to quash working-class militancy, from the steel mills of Weirton to the coal fields of Logan and Mingo Counties.[77]

In this chilling atmosphere, the German and Irish members of Local 10 took pains to emphasize their allegiance to America (see illus. 9). Longtime local officer Charles Morningstar presented a motion to have the local buy and dedicate a service flag. At the dedication, Morningstar offered a prayer, other members sang patriotic songs, and Victor Myers gave a speech in which he praised all of Fostoria's employees currently serving in the armed forces. Throughout the country's involvement, the local granted union cards to apprentices who were drafted before completing their training. In early 1919, Morningstar again led the local's involvement in creating a memorial and holding a banquet for all returning soldiers.[78] The postwar years also revived the fortunes of the local Republicans, due largely to their claim to be the party of prosperity and to their rejection of Wilsonian liberalism. Between 1915 and 1929, Democrats won only two of twenty-eight races for the West Virginia legislature in Marshall County. Republicans also swept city elections by wide margins in 1917 and 1919. Only in the glassworker neighborhoods in the north end of town did the Democrats manage to hold their own.[79]

The immediate postwar years brought layoffs and wage reductions as the glass industry readjusted to the economic downturn and the resumption of foreign competition. Wage rates and union density in the glass tableware industry had benefited greatly from the war. The AFGWU's membership peaked in 1920, at 9,813 in 108 locals. But the recession of the early 1920s reduced employment in the industry by more than one-fifth. West Virginia and Fostoria suffered much less than most, but Local 10's members had to share work in 1920 and 1921.[80] Glass manu-

Illus. 9. On November 11, 1918, Fostoria glassworkers participated in a mock funeral for Kaiser Wilhelm, celebrating the defeat of Germany in World War I. Popular patriotism helped diminish the leftist politics of Local 10. Photograph courtesy of Paul W. Myers, former business agent for the American Flint Glass Workers' Union.

facturers used the hard times, combined with the prevailing anticommunist sentiments, to foster antiunionism. The *National Glass Budget* warned: "It is for the 40,000,000 independent workmen of this country to decide whether the leaders of the organized and enchained 3,000,000 are to impose English conditions which will soon mean Russian conditions." Under the assault, AFGWU membership declined by one-third by 1925.[81]

William P. Clarke, who had left Fostoria in 1907 to join Thomas Rowe's progressive administration in the AFGWU, rose to union president in 1916. But the declining fortunes of the flints tempered his radicalism after the war. Addressing the National Association of Manufacturers in April 1920, Clarke hoped employers would follow the "golden rule" in their treatment of workers. He hoped to distance organized labor from "the so-called radicals and Bolsheviks" but asserted that "those who are at the foundation of unrest from the employers' side cannot be so easily detected." The challenge for "loyal, patriotic citizens of America" was "to find some definite method of segregating the disloyal employer and disloyal employe from our patriotic citizens." Clarke left office in 1932 without being able to achieve such an accommodation; AFGWU membership when he was finally defeated was under six thousand.[82]

Diminishing opportunities for skilled union craftsmen in the glass tableware industry made a job at Fostoria increasingly attractive to men like Howard Denoon and Guy Alexander. When they finished their apprenticeships they moved into decent-paying jobs with a union-protected voice at the workplace. The company's management extracted as many concessions from Local 10 as it could, but it made no effort to operate nonunion. The company's growing national reputation for quality tableware placed a premium on its ability to retain skilled workers and maintain a stable working relationship with them. Indeed, Dalzell's son, William F., joined the firm in the 1920s and created a special design department that ensured the company's success in high-quality tableware. The younger Dalzell understood the importance of his employees' welfare, and "he was instrumental in developing new, progressive labor policies." He won over many supporters from Local 10.[83]

Fostoria was a desirable employer to workers outside the skilled trades as well. The company employed between 600 and 650 workers through the 1920s, supplying roughly 40 percent of the manufacturing jobs in Moundsville. Furthermore, although real annual earnings had dipped between 1914 and 1918, they rebounded by 1920, and less skilled glassworkers actually recovered more quickly than did those in the crafts.[84] Thus Fostoria offered well-paying industrial jobs to more than 400 workers who were not union members in a town that offered limited opportunities. However, most of the laborers and semiskilled workers were young; if the company did not tap them for the opportunity to learn one of the trades, they were not likely to stay. Only 1 in 5 was working at Fostoria five years later, only 1 in 9 after ten years. Those who demonstrated "encouragement" and obtained an apprenticeship showed a strong loyalty to the company. Nearly three-fourths of the gatherers were still at Fostoria a decade later. In fact, when Fostoria hosted a service recognition dinner for employees in 1949, it celebrated eighty-three men and women who had worked for the company for more than thirty years and fifty who had exceeded forty years of service.[85]

In the 1920s, then, the factory took on a remarkable stability, especially in the ranks of the skilled, and looked much as it had a decade earlier. About one-sixth of the workers were female, primarily young, unmarried women still concentrated in the decorating, etching, selecting, and packing departments, although by 1920, women made up one-third of the office staff. Another one-twelfth of the workforce was made up of boys under the age of seventeen performing the monotonous tasks of the mold boy or the "carry-in" boys who darted from furnace to shop to lehr, carrying the ware. Most of the production work remained uniformly male. Moreover, the vast majority of people in the factory were born in West Virginia or Ohio; only 1 in 6 Fostoria workers in the 1920s was an immigrant or the child of an immigrant. And they tended to be committed to the area. Three of every eight household heads owned their homes.[86]

But the stability achieved by Fostoria did little to improve the attractiveness of Moundsville for further development. The only other plants in town, the U.S. Stamping Company (enameled metalware) and the United Zinc works, together combined to employ the same number of workers as Fostoria, but no other new companies located in the town. Moundsville's population numbered only about 12,500 by 1930. In fact, Marshall County lagged well behind the growth rate of the state as a whole between 1910 and 1930.[87] Only part of Moundsville's stagnation could be attributed to its militant labor past. The rising hills that abut the east end of town meant there was little flat land for the development of modern industrial factories, a factor that also inhibited the growth of Wheeling to the north. The small population base and lack of capital also hampered additional development, which shifted to the densely packed counties to the north of Wheeling. These counties were directly across the Ohio River from Steubenville and East Liverpool, Ohio, two urban manufacturing areas that enhanced economic growth on the West Virginia side as well.[88]

At the same time, the more moderate politics of Local 10 continued to demonstrate an obstinate rejection of the development faith even after socialism faded. The glassworker neighborhoods near the Fostoria plant routinely supported the Democrats at election time, stubbornly resisting the trend in what became a reliably Republican area through the 1920s. In municipal elections, the flints helped occasionally elect a Democrat as mayor and often sent a Democrat to represent them on the city council. But these working-class neighborhoods were often more defiant than progressive; they voted against levies for schools as well as improved firefighting and garbage disposal equipment. By the end of the 1920s, Local 10 had retreated even from most of its obligations to the labor movement.[89] The proud craftsmen of Fostoria had achieved an accommodation with the company, if not the development faith.

5 Clarksburg:
A Craftsman's Paradise

In the fall of 1901, the *National Glass Budget* noted a disturbing trend in the window-glass industry, the rapid spread of worker-owned cooperatives. "The most energetic co-operators are the French and Belgian blowers and gatherers," the *Budget* complained, "because they are as a rule, closer students of economics than the average American workman." They "evidence a fraternity, a spirit of equity, and an absence of selfishness which is decidedly exceptional among skilled workmen."[1] As the emergence of new technologies, corporate organizations, and global competition began to threaten the cozy relationship between employers and craftsmen in window glass, skilled immigrants turned to strategies they brought with them from Europe to sustain their craft privileges and workplace control. Since they earned high wages and the cost of starting a window-glass plant was still modest, cooperative production was a promising enterprise, particularly if the cooperative could obtain inexpensive fuel and cheap land.

Clarksburg, a small, north-central West Virginia town of fewer than six thousand people in 1900, offered an ideal location to French and Belgian window-glass workers seeking a site for a cooperative factory. Soon to be dubbed "the fuel city of the fuel state" by the *Manufacturers' Record*, Clarksburg offered cooperators plentiful supplies of natural gas and low-cost land for development adjacent to newly improved railroad facilities. The Lafayette Window Glass Company, a cooperative controlled by French window-glass workers, began the process of making Clarksburg a

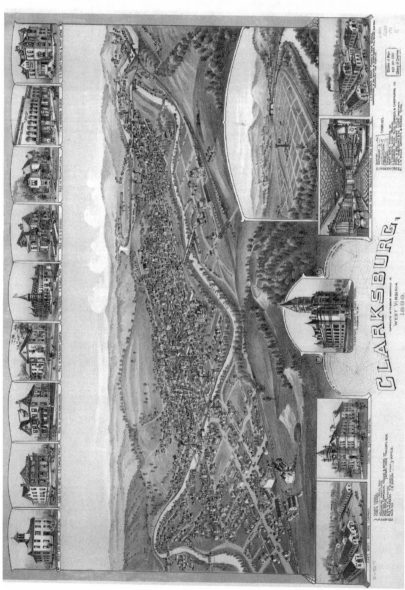

Map 4. Clarksburg, West Virginia, 1898. Note the projected development of North View (inset), which became home to the Lafayette Cooperative Window Glass Company in 1899. Drawn by T. M. Fowler and published by T. M. Fowler and James B. Moyer, Morrisville, Pa., [1898]. Geography and Map Division, Library of Congress.

glass town when it began producing in 1899. Within a decade, the town had five window-glass plants employing more than one thousand workers, many of them skilled French and Belgian immigrants.[2]

For a generation, Clarksburg was a craftsman's paradise, not only because it was a haven for cooperative and independent companies that maintained craft modes of window-glass production but also as a result of the town's spatial development, which segregated glass plants outside Clarksburg's corporation limits in independent communities. Not only did skilled glassworkers have control of the workplace but also they exerted considerable influence over community politics and social life. At first, the glass communities meshed smoothly with the business interests that dominated the ascendant Republican Party in the town, but by 1910, conflicts were surfacing that encouraged Clarksburg city officials to explore ways to subsume and curb the immigrant craftsmen's independence. In the process, glassworkers contested Clarksburg's geography, politics, and social relations. Ultimately, technology and a powerful corporation eliminated this craftsman's paradise, but it left a legacy of worker action that complemented New Deal liberalism.

Emergence of the Fuel City

Until the end of the nineteenth century, Harrison County hardly qualified as a promising enterprise zone. The population had grown by less than 9 percent during the 1880s, and manufacturing employment in 1890 totaled just slightly more than three hundred persons. The vast majority of the population relied on raising cattle, hogs, and sheep on small farms. While 274 adult men worked in manufacturing, 2,198 operated farms, seven-eighths of which were owner-run. In the 1870s and early 1880s, Harrison County farmers supported the agrarian-oriented wing of the Democratic Party and sent its favorite son, lawyer John J. Davis, to the U.S. Congress. Davis, a staunch opponent of Radical Reconstruction and black equality, thwarted the political ambitions of local Republican leader Nathan Goff Jr. and helped the Democrats control West Virginia for a generation. Davis's program advanced the interests of white farmers and wage earners, associating his Republican opponents with big business, increased taxes, and high tariffs. He railed against "the compact forces of the organized, unscrupulous and desperate money power" that undermined the independence of the producing classes.[3]

Goff's promises of prosperity through enterprise slowly tipped the balance in Harrison County in favor of the Republican Party's emphasis on economic development. Goff, a Union army officer and Civil War hero, had labored long and hard to make the link between the party's new probusiness ideology and its earlier Unionism. He almost single-handedly revived the party's fortunes by successfully winning and defending a seat in Congress in the 1880s when Democrats controlled the state. In 1884, Harrison County registered a majority of its votes for Republican James G. Blaine; in the 1890s, it would fall ever more reliably in the GOP column.[4] But Goff also made numerous enemies in the party due to his handling of patronage and party funds, as well as his behind-the-scenes manipulation of party nominations. As the party's fortunes improved, a new generation of Republican activists was ready to put leadership in the hands of Stephen B. Elkins, a well-connected industrialist who could bring outside funds to Republican coffers.[5]

Elkins had his eyes set on the U.S. Senate seat from West Virginia, and thus encouraged Goff to run for governor. Goff made a surprisingly strong run in a state that the Democrats had dominated for a generation. In a letter to the *Toledo Blade*, he laid out the Republicans' development faith. Goff wanted to shift the source of government revenues from internal taxes to high protective tariffs on manufactured goods and on coal, oil, and gas. He asserted that such tariffs would "give employment to the labor and capital of this country," and he worried little about the Democrats' fears of creating a huge surplus of government revenues. Goff wrote that the government could easily get rid of any surplus by increasing spending on coastal defenses, internal improvements, and education, the social capital that would lead to further development.[6]

From the letters written to Goff during the 1888 campaign, these arguments were beginning to change politics in the state, especially among the growing numbers of industrial workers. Miners in southern West Virginia, potters in the northern panhandle, and iron workers in Wheeling, among others, felt that tariff reductions would "force us to accept what is nearly the English standard of wages," which was below the American standard of living. Indeed, Goff's opponent, A. B. Fleming of Fairmont, was reluctant to debate in Wheeling, where a vibrant manufacturing economy existed.[7] Although Goff actually won the election by 110 votes, the Democratic Party contested the outcome. Backroom maneuverings by the Democratic-controlled state House of Delegates eventually denied Goff his election, and he failed in a separate bid to gain the U.S. Senate seat that Elkins coveted. By 1890, Elkins had managed to ease Goff out of the party's leadership at a propitious time. The Republican party was on the verge of recapturing control of the state and injecting it with a strong booster philosophy that emphasized economic development, especially railroad building and the exploitation of the state's abundant fuel resources in coal, oil, and natural gas. Goff's defeat in the gubernatorial contest and his ouster as party leader forced him to turn his energies to local economic activities.[8]

Goff's exit from the Republican leadership did not mean that he rejected its faith in economic development. He brought the party's pro-development ideas to Clarksburg with a renewed vigor. The chief heir of both his father's and his uncle's estates, Goff was president of the Merchants National Bank and owner of "choice real estate" in Clarksburg. By the end of the 1880s, he and his associates owned both the gas company and the electric company, eventually merging the two in 1903. His development activities were wide-ranging. Goff invested in the development of several coal and coke companies, as well as the West Virginia and Pittsburgh Railroad, to connect his coal lands to Pittsburgh markets. In addition, he leased the coal rights on his 645–acre Elk Hill farm to the Fairmont Coal Company, which paid him handsomely. To take full advantage of his coal property holdings, Goff negotiated with the Baltimore and Ohio Railroad to move its station from the east end of town to his Elk Hill farm, on the north side of Elk Creek, which he was in the process of dividing into lots. He then asked the town of Clarksburg to build a bridge to connect his development, soon to be renamed Glen Elk, to the town's central business district. Failing to convince the town to foot the bill, he and his partners built the bridge privately and then charged a toll.[9]

Equally important was Goff's connection to Richard Tasker Lowndes, who married Goff's sister in 1896. Lowndes, the son of local merchant Lloyd Lowndes, was a local businessman with an uncanny knack for investments. At the age of twenty-eight, he won a forty-year franchise from the town to produce gas for streetlights and incorporated the Clarksburg Gas Company. Five years later, in 1876, he purchased a failing sawmill; he operated it profitably for the next quarter century. He also ran the best clothing store in Clarksburg, a woolen mill that made blankets, and several banks. In the 1890s, he and Goff were partners in a variety of highly successful business ventures involving coal, oil, and natural gas that attracted the attention of such major investors as Carnegie Steel and Standard Oil to Harrison County. By the turn of the century, Clarksburg was at the hub of a flood of investment into the rich fuel resources of the county. To promote their ventures, Lowndes and Goff headed a syndicate of prominent local Republicans who purchased the *Clarksburg Telegram* and turned it into the voice of capitalist economic development.[10]

The partnership of Lowndes and Goff sparked a dramatic period of industrial growth. Coal production jumped from 113,000 tons in 1891 to over a million tons a decade later, and over three million tons by 1906.

On May 5, 1899, Goff's efforts at drilling for oil also finally began to pay off when he hit a gusher, and he drilled twenty-five more wells in the ensuing two years. By 1907, his earnings from oil sales alone amounted to $1,077,991. The 1890s also witnessed the development of several natural gas companies in the area involving many of the same local Republican businessmen.[11] These men began to invest in the development of Clarksburg, adding banks and commercial enterprises to handle the business activity, and planning neighborhoods to house workers and attract factories to the city. Indeed, Clarksburg's development spearheaded the transformation of Harrison County that began to take off in the 1890s. The decade witnessed a modest growth in the town's population from 4,305 to 5,758 (34 percent), slightly higher than the rate for the county as a whole.

Such change was not without opposition. Clarksburg and Harrison County had not yet completely broken with the "Old Dominion"-style politics inherited from Virginia. The red brick Victorian courthouse continued to harbor political cliques in a town where hitching posts still lined the streets, according to historian William Harbaugh. In 1897, when John W. Davis, son of John J., returned to his hometown after a brief tenure as a professor at Washington and Lee University, he revived Democrat fortunes in town. The United Mine Workers (UMW) was in the middle of a struggle to gain recognition from the operators of the rapidly expanding coal mines in the upper Monongahela valley. The UMW faced entrenched opposition. Judge John Jay Jackson of the U.S. District Court issued a broad injunction that prevented the miners "from doing pretty nearly everything except carry food home for their babies," according to Davis.[12] Miners defied the order, and federal marshals arrested twenty-seven for trespassing on county roads.

The UMW retained the Davises (father and son) to represent them, and the younger John W. Davis argued the case against A. B. Fleming (the former governor) in front of Nathan Goff Jr. (his father's former political foe). Fleming and Goff, although in opposing parties, were both heavily invested in coal and staunch enemies of the UMW. Nevertheless, Davis combated the influential Fleming well, and won light sentences for the strikers, which was considered a moral victory under the circumstances.[13] For the young lawyer, this experience gave him credentials as a politician sympathetic to the interests of labor and the working class. It helped catapult him into his career in the local Democratic Party and eventually into national prominence. It also forecast his considerable legal talents. Over the next two decades, Davis would serve in the United States House of Representatives, as solicitor general of the United States, as the U.S. ambassador to Great Britain, and finally as the Democratic presidential candidate in 1924.[14]

For those in town who felt that Goff, Lowndes, and the Republicans carried entirely too much influence, the younger Davis provided a rallying point. Rural farmers, as well as workers sympathetic to the rights of the miners, felt that government was becoming too subservient to the B&O Railroad and the coal operators. Already, the local Republicans were scheming to have the town buy from Goff the bridge that connected Clarksburg to the new railroad station on Goff's property on the north side of Elk Creek. In the fall of 1898, the Republicans also wanted the county to pay the B&O $150,000, although the railroad had failed to fulfill its contract. The Republicans then made the mistake of nominating Richard T. Lowndes, whose family was closely associated with the B&O, for the seat in the House of Delegates. Democrats denounced Lowndes as a "plutocrat and capitalist," opposed to the interests of farmers and workingmen, and nominated Davis to oppose him. Even more important, Davis received assistance from a group of dissident Republicans, who opposed the tax increase they expected to come from Lowndes's election. Thus, Davis won election to the state House of Delegates, the first Democrat to do so in fourteen years.[15]

The Democrats, however, were certainly not the party of a broad coalition of farmers and workers. The party in West Virginia had rejected the Populist insurgency in 1892 and the producerist politics of the Democrats' 1896 presidential candidate, William Jennings Bryan. It was extremely racist and anti-immigrant. Furthermore, men like A. B. Fleming and Johnson Newlon Camden were ready to make alliances with any politician or judge who would protect the investments of coal, oil, and gas companies. Nor was John W. Davis averse to working for big business. By the end of the century, Davis handled the legal affairs of Standard Oil and its Short Line Railroad in Harrison County. When the B&O bought the Short Line, it retained the services of the younger Davis, much to the dismay of his father.[16] Both parties spoke a language of class while secretly sharing hopes for the state's continued economic development, which they associated with a safe environment for capitalist investment. The Republicans emphasized the benefits of high tariffs for the working man and the investors; the Democrats countered with the advantages for producers in a politics of limited government, low taxes, and low prices resulting from free trade. Mix in issues like the prohibition of alcohol, the rise in crime, and attitudes toward black and immigrant labor, and it becomes possible to construct a rough geography of politics in Clarksburg and Harrison County at the end of the nineteenth century, a period of intense partisan conflict.[17]

Despite the victories of John W. Davis in the courtroom and in politics, the Republicans were on the ascendance. In Clarksburg, they generally carried Wards 2, 3, and 5 (the more heavily populated commercial center of town), leaving only the more sparsely populated First and Fourth wards (at the eastern and northwestern fringes of town) to the Democrats. The more rural sections of the county traced their party allegiances back to the Civil War. Steady Republican successes in the county and in Clarksburg meant a politics of the development faith. Between 1900 and 1910, the Clark and Coal magisterial districts, which contained Clarksburg and its neighboring communities, nearly tripled in population, from 8,605 to 23,419. Clarksburg became a solidly Republican boom town, with a tin plate mill, a zinc factory, brick ovens, and a variety of other manufacturing enterprises.[18] But at the center of the industrial expansion in the town was the window-glass industry.

The Arrival of the Glassworkers

The restructuring of the window-glass industry in the 1890s had been particularly disruptive. As already mentioned, the shift to gas-fueled continuous tank furnaces for melting the batch dispersed the industry, which had previously been concentrated in the Pittsburgh area. The process began in earnest in 1887, when James Chambers, the Pittsburgh glass manufacturer, began pursuing his idea for a huge new factory in Jeannette, Pennsylvania. Chambers's plant had a capacity to employ about four times the number of skilled craftsmen than the average American window-glass factory of the time.[19] Manufacturers viewed the technological developments occurring in window glass as a tremendous opportunity. They began the 1890s with control of less than half of the enormous American market. Consequently, there was plenty of room for growth, so they worried little about drastically increasing the amount of competition in the industry. Moreover, they enjoyed the considerable protection of the high tariffs dating back to the 1870s.[20]

Over the ensuing decade, there was a flurry of window-glass factory building in the gas belts of rural southwestern and northern Pennsylvania and in Indiana. The pot capacity of the American window-glass industry nearly tripled between 1880 and 1900. The restructuring created an industry that looked very different. Pittsburgh, which had served as the headquarters of LA 300 of the Knights of Labor—the labor organization representing skilled window-glass craftsmen—saw its place in the industry decline. Meanwhile, Indiana garnered nearly 40 percent of the industry's total capacity. Other evidence of restructuring comes from the average firm size and the percent of the total capacity in tanks. Chambers's Jeannette factory set the trend. Between 1886 and 1898, the pot capacity per firm nearly doubled, from fifteen to twenty-nine. At the same time, the share of the total capacity in tanks, as opposed to the earlier clay pots, grew from 0 to 68 percent.[21]

To accomplish this growth and restructuring, as mentioned earlier, glass manufacturers set out to attract an ample supply of skilled labor, primarily from the European centers of window-glass manufacturing—England, Germany, France, and especially Belgium, which was the largest producer in the world. Belgium had pioneered most of the advances in window-glass manufacture, but the Belgian industry had fallen upon hard times in the 1880s. A rapid expansion in the number of factories and their capacity had collided with the high tariffs in Europe and the United States. Thus, Belgian manufacturers could not sell their entire product, despite reducing their prices and slashing wages. Belgian craftsmen saw their annual earnings drop to less than half of those of their counterparts in other countries, but a repressive government prevented workers from establishing effective unions. Between 1885 and 1887, a series of strikes wracked the Belgian industry, leading to a massive emigration of skilled glassworkers, just as the American industry began to expand.[22]

Employers anxiously welcomed skilled Belgian glassworkers fleeing the tumultuous conditions in Belgium. Their numbers facilitated manufacturers' efforts to expand and capture a larger share of the huge American market, as well as the relocation of the industry to the natural gas belt. The *National Glass Budget* commented that they were "a social, jolly, jovial and sunny-souled set of people" whose sociability was "marked with fine touches of a high spirit."[23] Unions were less sanguine; some union members worried that the influx of immigrants was an entering wedge that could destroy the tightly regulated control that LA 300 had achieved in concert with the manufacturers. Several preceptories (local unions) proposed raising initiation fees for immigrants and limiting apprenticeships to the sons and brothers of native-born craftsmen, even as they admitted that there were not enough skilled workers to fill the void in the new glass plants. The Knights of Labor also experimented with a multinational union structure, opening local assemblies in Belgium, France, and England, hoping to regulate the labor market on both sides of the Atlantic. In 1889, LA 300 recognized its inability to continue to restrict membership in the face of such demand, and decided that it was safer to admit the Belgians than to risk losing control of the new plants.[24]

The tensions accompanying the assimilation of Belgian window-glass workers became uncontrollable with the depression of the 1890s and the ensuing restructuring of the industry. Because American firms had expanded so dramatically, the depression caused a crisis; by 1898 American plants were operating at only 36 percent of capacity. This crisis hurt the older firms, where American-born and earlier waves of immigrant craftsmen were located, more severely than the newer gas-belt firms. Thus, the German, English, and American union members, who had integrated a large influx of Belgians, began to complain of shrinking opportunities. However, because LA 300 had accepted the Belgians, their children were eligible for apprenticeships, and the concentration of Belgians in the newest plants gave their sons advantages over other groups, particularly in the most lucrative crafts of blowing and gathering.[25]

Industry reorganization worsened the tensions. At the turn of the century, at the same time that some of the largest firms formed the American Window Glass Company marketing trust in an attempt to gain control of the industry, a tight labor market led to conflicts between the separate crafts in LA 300, which eventually shattered the union's control and resulted in bitter competition. Again, Belgians played a central role in the conflict. Beginning with the 1894 election of officers, the large Belgian-controlled preceptories began an alliance with Simon Burns to wrest control of LA 300 from the Pittsburgh clique that had built the union. Upon achieving victory, Burns rewarded his Belgian allies with a number of key positions.[26] Faced with the growing power of new corporate organizations on the one hand and hostility from different factions within the union on the other, Belgians used their strength in LA 300 to revive earlier traditions to sustain their families as well as to maintain their livelihoods.

Of particular importance for the Belgian window-glass workers was a new emphasis on cooperatives. Cooperative stores had played an important role in militant glass communities in Belgium. In the United States, the threat of technological displacement forced glassworkers to think about cooperatives in new ways. Taking advantage of the high wages, the relatively low cost of entering the glass manufacturing business, and the openness of American industry, Belgian immigrants launched a cooperative factory movement to preserve craft jobs and the hand-blown production process. The additional productive capacity represented by the cooperatives, however, hindered the regulatory control of the market that employers and the union had jointly established. But because Belgians had provided the backbone of the victorious faction of LA 300, they demanded the union's support for worker-owned cooperatives. By

1900, LA 300 had loaned $29,000 to seven separate cooperative factories; by 1902, cooperatives controlled about 20 percent of the capacity in the United States plants.[27]

The first window-glass plant to appear in Clarksburg resulted from this foray into cooperative production. Ironically, however, the proprietors of the Lafayette Window Glass Company were French, not Belgian. Eugene Kopp, Leopold Castieaux, Nicholas Folora, Emil Castieaux, John J. Trunick, Julien Caussin, and Henry Trunick, mostly from Belle Vernon and Pittsburgh, Pennsylvania, raised over $17,000 from their own savings to build a factory on a five-acre plot donated by Richard Lowndes and Nathan Goff Jr. (see illus. 10). Lowndes also offered the cooperators a contract for gas at the "cheap" rate of 4 cents per 1,000 cubic feet.[28] Lowndes and Goff were anxious to attract an industry and residents for their newly opened development of North View, just outside city limits to the northwest of Clarksburg's central area. North View was on the north side of Elk Creek, close to Goff's gas fields and the new B&O Railroad station. On August 28, 1899, the state of West Virginia chartered the modest-sized twenty-four-pot company, with an authorized capital of $50,000.[29]

The arrival of the Lafayette Company triggered further glass development. In January 1900, John Koblegard, a local merchant and banker, incorporated the West Fork Oil and Natural Gas Company, which immediately began seeking a company to use its natural gas. In April, Koblegard deeded lands at the east end of town to the Republic Glass Company, on

Illus. 10. Board of directors of the Lafayette Cooperative Window Glass Company of Clarksburg in 1913. Front row, left to right: Hippolyte Leuliette, Eugene Rolland, Charles Moine, and Adrian DeMeester. Rear: Louis Schmidt, Paul Kopp, and Julien Caussin. Elizabeth Armistead Collection. Courtesy of the West Virginia State Archives.

condition that Republic would build a factory and contract to use the West Fork Company's gas. By January 1901, Koblegard and Lowndes were trumpeting Clarksburg as "the City of Big Factories." The same month, Belgian workers in Dunkirk, Indiana, frustrated with the declining supply of gas there, purchased a five-acre site in Adamston, just on the other side of the West Fork River from the Lafayette Company. They built the Clarksburg Cooperative Window Glass Company, which opened in April with twenty-four pots. By the end of 1901, the Clarksburg Cooperative Company provided work for 75 craftsmen and an additional 100 workers; Lafayette's workforce totaled 125, of whom about 50 were skilled; and the Republic Glass Company, which made wide-mouth bottles and jars, employed nearly 250.[30]

Over the next decade, the glass industry became the economic life blood of Clarksburg and Harrison County. By 1910, the Lafayette Company in North View was joined by the Peerless Window Glass Company (incorporated in July 1905), a Belgian-run cooperative. At the opposite end of town, the window-glass plants were small, privately owned firms, independent of the American Window Glass Company trust. They included the West Fork Glass Company (June 1905) and the Tuna Glass Company (1907), both of which made windows in the new neighborhood of Industrial, just outside the corporation limits to the southeast. Ten miles to the west, in the small community of Salem, the Belgians added two more window-glass companies, Salem Cooperative Window Glass (July 1908) and the Modern Window Glass Company (July 1910), both cooperatives. Glass factories employed over 1,200 workers in Clarksburg alone, with another 350 in Salem and more in Bridgeport and Mannington. The French-speaking community in the county included more than 1,400 people, and made up over 40 percent of the skilled glassworkers.[31]

Clarksburg, after 1900, increasingly adapted to the rhythms and the needs of the glass industry. One of the first imperatives of the town was the building of new housing. The developers of North View offered free water to anyone who purchased a lot to build a house. But glassworkers were still a highly mobile group, routinely moving to a new factory every

Table 5.1: National Origins of Clarksburg's Immigrant Craftsmen, 1910

Belgian	36.3%	German	12.5%
French	33.9	British	17.3

Source: Manuscript Census schedules, 1910, Harrison County.

other blast. For example, Francois Gregoire, who emigrated from Belgium with his wife and three children in 1887, moved yearly until they settled permanently in Adamston in 1909.[32] Consequently, glassworker neighborhoods were also sites of a transient subculture that included hastily built hotels, boarding houses, saloons, and pool halls.[33] For a decade, the home ownership rates for window-glass craftsmen fell far short of the rates for the locally born semiskilled and unskilled workers who toiled in the factories. In fact, two-thirds of craftsmen were no longer in Clarksburg five years later. Blowers, gatherers, flatteners, and cutters were slightly older and much better paid than others in the industry, but only 1 out of 8 was in the process of owning a home in 1910. Less skilled workers were two to three times more likely to purchase a home.[34]

Consequently, each spring, newspapers carried rumors and speculations about when local factories would "go out of blast," or shut down for the hot summer months. Landlords had to wonder how many were likely to return. Glassworkers enjoyed summer excursions available to few other industrial workers. Local newspapers responded by advertising excursions to places like Deer Park, Maryland, but many craftsmen made known their plans to return to Belgium or France for the summer. Then, every autumn, glassworkers returned and placed the city at great pains to deal with the housing crunch that ensued. Rents skyrocketed. Well-paid skilled workers with cash in their pockets bribed landlords for the best places. Crime and disorder always seemed to worsen, although much more was inflicted against glassworkers than was created by them.[35]

Nevertheless, their transiency created problems. In 1906, for example, one craftsman disappeared from his residence in the Glen Elk Hotel near the end of the blast, deserting his wife, who spoke no English. Early in the following blast, five French glassworkers were arrested in a local crackdown on houses of prostitution, which seemed to be a growing problem in the town. More persistently, critics of the development faith pointed to the "brazen" violation of Sunday saloon closing laws and the free flow of beer and wine in the French and Belgian social clubs that grew up near the glass factories. Citizens in Adamston, which existed prior to the glass industry, were particularly upset about the ways their incorporated village changed once the glass plants arrived. Leading citizens even appealed to Clarksburg authorities to annex the village so that the deleterious effects of industrialization might be controlled.[36]

Although local boosters welcomed the factories, the benefits to many Clarksburg residents seemed much less clear. Unlike the Fostoria factory in Moundsville, window-glass plants created few skilled jobs for native West Virginians. Not more than 1 in 20 was born in the Mountain State.

Six out of ten, on the other hand, were immigrants or their children, contributing to an increase in the foreign-born population of the county from 3 to 11 percent (see table 5.2). At the other end, young men born in West Virginia accounted for two-thirds of the laborers and other unskilled workers.[37] Meanwhile, the need for schools, streets, sewers, and other services increased. The influx of new voters helped repeal the prohibition ordinance and led to thirty-five new liquor licenses in 1905 alone. Opponents of industrialization complained that gambling joints and corruption flourished, and that Clarksburgers needed to "redeem themselves [from] the stigma of shame" for their lax enforcement of the law.[38]

The changes in Clarksburg triggered an insurgent movement that divided those who imbibed the development faith. Attorney Harvey Harmer, a reform Republican from Shinnston who moved to the town in 1890, was a devout Methodist, troubled by both the burgeoning local vice trade and the fact that his party "favored the corporations" over average citizens. Harmer served in the state senate from 1901 to 1905, but his support for a tax on natural gas and his opposition to race track gambling put him on the wrong side of the Harrison County Republican Committee. The party allowed Democrats to vote in its primary to ensure that Harmer would not return to the state legislature. Harmer then decided to run for mayor to clean up "the immoral conditions of the city." He won a surprising victory without the full endorsement of either party, a testament to local disgust with both vice and the excesses of a rapidly expanding town. "It was said one hundred girls left town the night before he took charge," Harmer wrote in his autobiographical sketch. He also closed saloons on Sunday. However, the Republican-dominated city council opposed much of what Harmer attempted to accomplish, and succeeded in removing him a year later.[39]

As the cooperatives began to demonstrate some economic success, local boosters pointed more confidently to the benefits of the development faith. Those glassworkers who invested in the cooperatives began

Table 5.2: Origins of Clarksburg's Glassworkers, 1910

Category	Native born/ Native parent	Native born/ Foreign parent	Foreign born
Skilled glass trades	40.0%	17.5%	42.5%
Non-glass skilled	93.8	6.3	0.0
Semiskilled	85.3	8.8	5.9
Unskilled	90.2	3.3	6.6

Source: Manuscript Census schedules, 1910, Harrison County.

to settle in. Newspapers began referring to the "French colony" of North View and the Belgian neighborhood of Adamston. Many built their own homes on lots near the factories. Paul Kopp, one of the original founders of the Lafayette Company, "built one of the finest residences in Northview [*sic*]," but he was not alone. The Rolland brothers, the Bertiaux brothers, and Jules Malfregeot were among the glassworkers contributing to the building boom in the area.[40]

Glassworker neighborhoods created a rich, yet somewhat insular, vibrancy. Because glassworkers mostly migrated in family groups, they could at times seem clannish, forming self-contained "colonies." Immigrant craftsmen emphasized the annual summer carnivals (ducases) that punctuated the end of the "blast" and brought together extended families that worked in the cooperatives. As mentioned earlier, the carnivals included cooking competitions featuring Belgian treats, pigeon races, handball contests, and music provided by ethnic bands and orchestras. George DelForge recalled that they were "just like a county fair" but

Illus. 11. The Lafayette and Peerless window-glass factories dominated the edge of the North View section of Clarksburg in 1906. Note the apparently isolated setting of the neighborhood. Harrison County Historical Society Collection. Courtesy of the West Virginia State Archives.

that they were "only for the Belgians."[41] The sociability of window-glass community was gender inclusive. The clubs, the ducases, and even their camping trips were family affairs that included women. The weekly dances that took place at the two-story Lafayette Club encouraged dating, socializing, and marriage within the ethnic group, although they also attracted local girls who wanted to dance with the "French boys." The winter hiatus provided the setting for the New Year's celebration, which involved the youngest couple in the community calling on the next youngest for drinks, a process that continued until a complete circle of couples in the neighborhood was completed.[42]

Glassworker neighborhoods demonstrated that they were conservative and self-reliant defenders of the craftsmen's empire. The managers of the Lafayette Company made it a priority to find the glassworker who deserted his wife, and to take responsibility for the workers arrested in a brothel. However, they defined this responsibility narrowly. Few made any effort to build alliances with other workers, and the craftsmen were hostile to other wage earners who intruded into their neighborhoods. Indeed, North View was in turmoil in 1904 over an interracial romance, and a near riot occurred when an African American man yelled at a young French-speaking girl.[43] Window-glass craftsmen worked hard to distance themselves from the hostility directed toward other immigrants. Mindful of the growing unrest that local newspapers complained about, North View glassworkers tried to prevent a zinc works from being built in their village, asserting that it would bring Italians and Poles into their peaceful neighborhood.[44]

Still, glassworkers wanted their presence to be accepted and to become assets to the town, contributing to the tax base, to the increased value of local property, and to the prosperity of local merchants. In addition, they created industrial jobs for local young men, even if the majority were in lower paid positions. Before the glass plants, there had been far fewer options. Outside the factory, glassworkers added to the cultural life of the community. The French colony of North View started a drama club and used the proceeds it generated from performances to create a park in the neighborhood. Many Belgian glassworkers were famous for their musical skills, and for years they offered those talents to the local orchestras and marching bands in Clarksburg and Salem. Adrian De-Meester, a Belgian glassworker who arrived in 1906, recalled: "I did more god darn parading around this town than you can shake a stick at." Other window-glass workers were noted for their ability to make glass canes or glass eggs for decorative and ornamental purposes.[45] In general, the glass industry brought a more cosmopolitan feel to these communities.

Craftsmen and their families created benevolent associations to protect families from disaster, strong craft unions to regulate wages and working conditions, and clubs to skirt local ordinances against enjoying a "Continental Sunday." During the first decade of the twentieth century, at least, the immigrant glassworker neighborhoods surrounding Clarksburg looked to many like a "craftsman's paradise."

Labor Conflict and Political Change

The growing numbers of glassworkers, with their attachment to a European style of craft-based socialist production, at first caused little concern to the men who promoted the Republican development faith in Clarksburg. Although the French and Belgian glassworkers had a warm spot in their hearts for Socialist Party leader Eugene Debs, the son of an Alsatian immigrant, for a decade after the arrival of the Lafayette Company, glassworkers supported the high-tariff, development-oriented politics of the Republicans.[46] During the first years after the arrival of the glass factories, Republican majorities increased in the city, although glassworkers probably only contributed marginally to those increases. High rates of mobility and some immigrants' lack of citizenship papers limited their opportunities to vote.

However, as the ownership groups of the cooperatives began to settle in, their participation increased. Moreover, the geography of the industry in Clarksburg enhanced the influence of glassworkers. In contrast with Moundsville, Clarksburg's glass plants located outside the city limits in villages that were not yet or only recently incorporated. The influx of large numbers of workers gave them an immediate influence in elections. As early as 1907, the Republican ticket in Adamston included two glass craftsmen competing for the five town council positions; another glassworker ran on the People's ticket. North View incorporated later in the decade, but the French and Belgian glassworkers there already carried considerable weight on local issues.[47] Still, through the 1908 elections, the Republican Party's development faith could count on dependable support from the glassworkers. The president of the National Window Glass Workers, A. L. Faulkner, encouraged his members to support William H. Taft for president, and in Clarksburg, they turned out in large numbers for Taft parades.[48]

This Republican orthodoxy was about to change as a result of conflict in the window-glass industry. As a result of the growth of cooperatives, the voice of the manufacturers, the *National Glass Budget,* lambasted them for disrupting the careful regulation of window-glass output, which had involved the union and the companies. The cooperatives, however, were more willing to operate under prevailing price lists because they were less concerned about paying dividends to stockholders. In fact, the cooperatives agreed to the union's wage scale so that they could begin production, while the other firms procrastinated. This strategy infuriated the voice of the manufacturers. Since the *Budget* associated cooperatives with Belgians (and rightly so), it reversed its portrayal of the group. Previously, it welcomed Belgians as hardworking, cheerful craftsmen, thankful for the opportunity to earn high wages and willing to fill the newer, larger factories. But the steady growth of the cooperatives caused the *Budget* to target the Belgians as "infidels" who were excluding American boys from the trade and illegally bringing their countrymen to work in the cooperatives. In fact, the *Budget* claimed that a typical Belgian window-glass worker frequently held more than one job, bouncing back and forth between firms. When one factory closes, "he nimbly vaults into a place prepared for him and kept wide open by his 'comrades' in some co-operative factory. He never gets left." To business interests fearing competition, Belgians were "clannish" workers who learned economics "at the hands of the *Partie Ouvrier.*"[49]

The *Budget* instead supported the larger firms that had joined together to form the American Window Glass Company. Often called "the trust" by glassworkers, it controlled about half of the total industry capacity; the cooperatives and a loose federation of independent companies divided the remainder. Then, in 1903, the firms that had formed the trust introduced a cylinder blowing machine, the Lubbers machine, which gradually eliminated the need for blowers and gatherers, the two largest crafts. These machines, once improved, also enabled the trust factories to increase productivity by as much as 90 percent, and thus make glass at a significantly lower cost.[50] In window factories, much more than in tableware, technology was a real factor undercutting labor, not just a looming threat. The craftsmen who had remained united in LA 300 splintered; separate organizations of flatteners and cutters negotiated with the American Window Glass Company, while other unions emerged to try to represent the diverse segments of the industry. The *Budget* crowed: "some window glass workers are beginning to lose faith in the protecting power of the tariff, and . . . the trades union, large defense fund, and absence of non-union factories . . . are not such a safe anchorage and sure shield as they were once deemed to be."[51]

The Lubbers machine enabled the trust to put a good deal more glass on the market and also slash prices. Increasingly, the only way for the independent firms to compete with the American Window Glass Company was to reduce wages. By 1907, the situation was building to a confrontation. One Clarksburg glassworker wrote that the trust, "judging from its unwarranted price cutting on or about March 30, is the common enemy of both the workmen and the hand manufacturers, and we think the efforts of both of these factions should be directed against that concern and quit quarreling among themselves."[52] Unfortunately, the advice went unheeded. That summer, the independent firms in West Virginia formed an association directed by Clarksburg investor John Koblegard. When Koblegard attempted to cut wages, workers at the independent firms in Clarksburg went on strike. Throughout the winter, Clarksburg area plants, except for the cooperatives (Lafayette, Peerless, Clarksburg Cooperative, and Salem Window Glass), were idle. Fistfights erupted whenever the Tuna or the West Fork companies made preparations to

Illus. 12. The Tuna Hotel, 1910. This hotel in the Industrial neighborhood of Clarksburg housed some of the seasonal window-glass craftsmen who worked at the Tuna Window Glass Company. In 1907 and 1908, labor conflict erupted whenever the factory tried to employ strikebreakers. Harrison County Historical Society Collection. Courtesy of the West Virginia State Archives.

reopen. Tensions also erupted between strikers and French and Belgian craftsmen, who some blamed for the overproduction in the industry, especially since the cooperatives continued to operate during the strike.[53]

To the dismay of the American Window Glass Company and the *Budget*, the independent Clarksburg glass companies and their workers came to a settlement—but not one that significantly improved the outlook for either the workers or the independent companies. The Clarksburg letter to the *Commoner and Glassworker* noted that a number of skilled workers were leaving their trade, "as there is not very much encouragement in the window glass business any more." Frustrated with deteriorating conditions in the industry, some glassworkers began to explore opportunities outside glassmaking. Edgar Castiaux opened a grocery, Jules Jauquet and Emile Loriaux were "busy making cement pavements," and William Gray went into the ice cream business.[54]

Others chose a different path. Those committed to maintaining the industry as one in which craftsmen could aspire to workplace control and a decent standard of living set in motion forces that would push the glassworkers away from the Republican Party. The strike of 1907–8 helped reunite the four crafts under the banner of a new union, the National Window Glass Workers (NWGW). At the same time, it also united many of the cooperative factories to improve their bargaining power in the glass trade.[55] Leaders of this movement in the Clarksburg area included Aristide J. Rolland, chief preceptor (local union president) in North View, Leon Quinet, a blower in North View, and Samuel Powell, an Adamston flattener. Rolland was one of five brothers who had come to Clarksburg from Pittsburgh as part of the Lafayette cooperative in 1898. Born in France in 1883, Aristide boarded with his brother Charles, a North View homeowner. Quinet was a Belgian immigrant who had worked in Indiana and Pennsylvania before joining the North View community. In 1908, at age 30, he became one of the leaders of the Belgian group that bought the Salem Window Glass Company; three years later, he was a leader of the Harrison County Socialist Party. Powell was an English-born worker in his early thirties who was already a homeowner in Adamston. These three were leaders of a crescendo of disaffection for the development faith, but they were also representative of the glassworker communities that built an alternative political movement.[56] Belgian, French, and English immigrants had social-democratic traditions forged in their homelands. In the case of the Belgian and French glassworkers, those traditions included cooperative production and a fierce defense of the craft.[57]

The glassworkers' growing disenchantment with the Republicans centered on John Koblegard, who directed the West Virginia independents. Koblegard, a Danish immigrant, was, like Richard T. Lowndes, an exemplar of the Republican development faith. He began as a grocer, but later invested in real estate, oil, and gas development, and eventually both the pottery and the glass industries. His West Fork Window Glass Company was located at the opposite end of town from the cooperatives. It was Koblegard's desire to cut wages and remain competitive with the American Window Glass Company that precipitated the strike. The glassworkers did not forget. Although the union president, A. L. Faulkner, continued to advocate for the Republicans, many NWGW members in Clarksburg began to argue for independent politics. Shortly after the strike, one local glassworker wrote that the economic problems facing the industry resulted from the millionaires who were representing them in Congress. By the fall of 1908, a report of the political debate in one Clarksburg local concluded: "Socialism was ably defended by W. H. Gebhard, while M. J. Clarke espoused the cause of Bryan and Democracy . . . but poor Bro. Taft was without a defender."[58]

The winter of 1909 brought another strike against the factories that were part of Koblegard's organization. This time, however, the French and Belgian union members working in the cooperative plants held a grand ball, raising funds to benefit the strikers. Aristide Rolland's Lafayette preceptory as well as Leon Quinet's Salem group contributed to the efforts. One Clarksburg worker urged window-glass manufacturers to improve conditions "instead of forever trying to browbeat the workmen (on whom they depend for the turning out of their product)." When Koblegard attempted to reopen the West Fork plant, NWGW members gathered to prevent workers from entering. After months of threats, the West Virginia independent plants finally agreed to the union scale.[59]

Glassworkers took their grievances against Koblegard and the Republicans into the political arena. In February 1909, the city rejected the bond issue promoted by the Merchants Association (of which Koblegard was an officer) to improve the water works and sewage system and encourage further development. Then, in the January 1910 local elections, Adamston ran glassworker Grant Miller for mayor on the People's ticket. In the Clarksburg elections that April, the Fourth and Fifth wards, which were home to many glassworkers who worked at the cooperatives on the west end of town, rejected the Republican ticket for reformers in the Citizens' League.[60] The most dramatic evidence of the declining hold that Republicans had over glassworkers came that fall; the city of Clarksburg voted for John W. Davis to represent the district in the U.S. Congress. Davis, the first Democrat elected from the district since 1894, won, despite running on a platform that called for a reduction in the tariff. Two other signs from the 1910 elections pointed to glassworker disaffection. First, the Socialist congressional candidate garnered about one-fourth of the vote in Adamston and better than 10 percent of the vote in North View, the two neighborhoods with high percentages of French and Belgian craftsmen. Second, although the Clarksburg labor movement endorsed Nathan B. Scott for the Senate, the glassworkers repudiated the labor council's endorsement.[61]

The power of high tariffs and the development faith to keep glass-workers in the Republican fold was waning, a casualty of the diminished regulation of the industry by the dual monopoly of employers and labor unions that had bolstered the craftsman's paradise. In 1911, "Harold" wrote to the *Commoner and Glassworker* from Clarksburg, with more than a bit of hyperbole, that window-glass workers were now the poor-est paid of skilled workers; "the factories are closed during the fall and winter when the weather is pleasant for their work. Now we are asked to work in summer for the poorest wages ever paid and when we buy a few lights of glass we pay a higher price than ever. Who is getting the profit?"[62] Other political parties began to look more attractive. For in-stance, Davis backed a workers' compensation law in Congress and won popularity in Clarksburg as he accommodated himself to the liberalism of President Woodrow Wilson's administration. However, the Democrats lost glassworker support when they passed the Underwood tariff, which lowered rates on imported glass by one-third to one-half.[63] Similarly, the Progressive Party attracted support from Clarksburg glassworkers be-cause it raised the possibility of regulating the sort of trusts that seemed to be taking complete control of the glass industry. In North View, the Progressive ticket in the 1912 election included two glassworkers; in 1913, it triumphed, with glassworkers filling three of the seven elected positions.[64]

In the years preceding World War I, a significant portion of window-glass workers chose to vote Socialist. Demography was partly respon-sible. Worsening conditions in the Belgian glass industry added to the concentration of Belgians in the North View, Adamston, and Industrial neighborhoods in Clarksburg. Between 1910 and 1920, immigrants actu-ally increased their share of the skilled positions in the industry; together with their children, they accounted for between 46 percent (cutters) and 71 percent (gatherers) of the four glass trades. Craftsmen of Belgian heri-tage alone made up roughly one-third of the union members in the area. Moreover, they continued a transnational connection to Belgium, which was experiencing a period of rapid growth in socialism, cooperative en-terprises, and militant trade unionism. These workers integrated easily into the cooperative factories and politically Left communities that were growing in Salem, Adamston, and North View. Smaller groups of French, German, and English glassworkers, each with their own socialist traditions, supplemented these numbers. The influx of these immigrants added to the number of cooperative factories in the area, as well as co-operative stores, and they made up much of the audience for Socialist lectures and the readership of the local Socialist newspaper.[65]

Between 1911 and 1915, glassworkers demonstrated their impact at the polls. The local elections in January 1911 alarmed the county's Republican Party, which had relied on glassworker support as late as 1908. The Socialists and the Progressives split the seats in Adamston, and the Progressive ticket swept the field in North View. The Socialists, led by Samuel Powell, and Citizens Progressive tickets, headed by Lafayette worker Harry Leuliette, continued strong showings in these areas for the next four years. In Salem, Leon Quinet led an energetic Socialist movement that captured nearly 40 percent of the local vote. The national elections of 1912 brought Republicans little relief. In the glassworker neighborhoods in Harrison County, either Eugene Debs (Socialist) or Theodore Roosevelt (Progressive) carried the day over Woodrow Wilson (Democrat) or William H. Taft (Republican). This sentiment undercut Republican dominance of county and state politics and helped lead to the presence of Democrats in the West Virginia congressional delegation. In 1914, the Socialists again carried about 12 percent of the vote in the congressional and state elections. The Republicans temporarily lost their plurality in the county.[66]

Socialist glassworkers did not leave complete statements of their political program or how they planned to remake their society. However, it is possible to get glimpses into the issues that motivated their politics. One issue was the regulation of big corporations. The American Window Glass Company routinely dumped excess production on the market, driving down prices and wages. The wage scale that the NWGW negotiated with the hand plants in 1912 provided for 30 percent reductions in wages to enable this segment of the industry to compete. Clarksburg glassworkers felt that corporations should not have such power over their employees or in an industry.[67] To Republicans and even some Democrats steeped in the development faith, such sentiments must have seemed ominous for the future. Certainly, one local entrepreneur thought so. Ernest T. Weir, owner of a local tin plate mill, began making plans to move his operations to a more hospitable environment where organized labor would be less oppositional. His Finnish immigrant tin plate workers had joined the glassworkers in the local Socialist movement and even built a hall that served as a club, dance floor, and meeting room for the Clarksburg Left. Weir, disturbed by the politics of Clarksburg that spilled over to his tin plate workers, ultimately built his own company town, named Weirton, in the northern panhandle.[68]

Socialists were especially perplexed that governments used their authority to help companies defeat strikes. Glassworkers in West Virginia witnessed firsthand what happened to workers who fought corporations. The use of martial law against the UMW in the upper Monongahela valley and in the southern part of the state roused window-glass craftsmen from their lethargy toward broader working-class struggles. Closer to home, they saw Weir successfully obtain injunctions to crush a strike at the tin plate mill in 1913. The NWGW preceptories in the state raised money for the strikers and protested the actions of state officials. During an age of industrial violence, glassworkers were increasingly vocal about the use of private and state police forces against strikers. One of the advantages that glassworker enclaves had in Clarksburg was their ability to control local police forces. In North View, for example, former Lafayette glassworker Henry Trunick was the police chief. Likewise, Adamston's local government prevented police from helping corporations control strikers.[69]

Another complaint that glassworkers hoped socialism might address concerned the positive help that government might provide for workers. Certainly protective tariffs were a part of that, and were one reason that the NWGW had only slowly deserted the Republicans. But Socialists also wanted protection against poverty resulting from injuries on the job or unemployment, and they felt that government should protect workers' right to join unions and negotiate the terms and conditions of their employment.[70] To many glassworkers, socialism promised an opportunity for working people to wrest control of government from the capitalists and use it to serve the entire society. In Adamston, the Socialist administration accomplished basic improvements: a water works, paved streets, and sewer lines—hardly revolutionary changes. However, such changes led to debates about public financing and taxes. Socialists felt it was unfair for government to tax real estate and glass factories but exempt the coal, oil, gas, and timber owned by outside corporations. Glassworkers, in particular, worried that the lack of a tax policy on natural gas, according to the state Public Service Commission, meant that "in ten years the gas will be gone." Certainly a Socialist administration could do better. They also objected to the insufficient government regulation of railroads that charged glass plants higher rates or refused to allot them enough cars for their shipping. In short, glassworkers sought a government that would help them improve on what the cooperative factories were trying to do, to free workers "from the yoke of capitalism."[71]

For the glassworkers, however, the turn toward Socialism did not mean a movement of revolutionary mass politics. Within their trade, they continued to follow an exclusive craft consciousness that limited access to window-glass crafts and excluded semiskilled and unskilled workers from union membership, despite regular appeals from some of these workers.[72] Although Clarksburg NWGW preceptories raised money to help the struggles of union members in other trades, they refused to join the American Federation of Labor or the local federation of labor organizations in the city. Moreover, glassworkers felt little solidarity with other immigrant workers in the area, frequently denying them access to their neighborhoods and routinely resorting to racial and ethnic slurs in the pages of their magazine. Thus, for skilled window-glass workers, throwing off the yoke of capitalism revolved around the insular world of their cooperatives, union, benevolent societies, and enclaves. Their most consistent expression of a broad working-class solidarity was a vote on Election Day.[73]

World War and the Paradise in Decline

In June 1914, Harrison County Socialists hosted speakers urging workers to keep the United States out of the escalating tensions engulfing Europe. In Salem and Clarksburg, the glass plants were preparing to go out of blast for the summer. Although the wages of window-glass workers were declining and the long-term future of the cooperatives and independent firms was in doubt, many Belgian and French families were packing for a trip to their homelands. There were some positive signs for these families. The five Rolland brothers were in the process of buying out the interests of the cooperative owners of the Lafayette and Peerless companies. The Rollands, born in France, had arrived in Clarksburg as part of the Lafayette investors in 1898. They had been ardent cooperators, and Aristide was even a leader of the NWGW and the local Socialist movement. Thus, many workers felt they had little to fear from the change in ownership. Unknown to most, however, the Rollands planned to modernize the plants to make them more competitive. Meanwhile, rumors were circulating that the giant Pittsburgh Plate Glass Company was planning to build a plant in town, an alarming sign of corporate capitalism in the industry.[74]

Clarksburg and Harrison County were still thriving with glass manufacturing. Despite the pockets of socialism that threatened the development faith, the Republican boosters could take some encouragement from the increase in the value added through manufacturing in the county. There were at that time eleven glass firms operating in Clarksburg, and three more in Salem, just ten miles to the west. In Clarksburg alone, glass manufacturing represented capital investment of more than $2 million and provided work for more than two thousand in a growing town of more than twenty thousand. In addition to the eight window-glass plants, the large Hazel-Atlas Company made tumblers at the west end of town, and the Travis Company and the innovative Owens West Virginia Bottle Company made bottles and wide-mouth jars. Three other small specialty firms made mirrors and optical glass.[75] In fact, that summer and fall triggered a chain of events that restored local boosters to a comfortable control of Clarksburg and Harrison County.

Because of the high proportion of immigrants who filled the skilled positions in the industry, as well as the threat from European imports, window glass had always been sensitive to international events. The outbreak of world war dramatically intensified that sensitivity in the summer of 1914. Many of the Belgian families who had gone to Europe that summer were trapped there and unable to secure permission to leave. Authorities gave some of the men notice that they had only twenty-four hours to turn themselves over for military duty; women and children found it difficult to secure travel visas. Adding to the personal tragedies affecting many families separated by the outbreak of war were the rumors of terrible hardships in Belgium. One glassworker wrote from Jumet that the factories were closed, and the cooperative stores were already limiting the distribution of food in August. The *National Glass Budget* said that the refugees who fled Belgium "bring terrible stories of the devastation of the land. From end to end of the little kingdom is nothing but misery, suffering and starvation." Most of the industries had been unable to pay wages for weeks.[76]

Glassworker neighborhoods and sympathetic townspeople sprang into action. Newspapers listed the names of families trapped in Europe; glassworkers who had either stayed at home that summer or had managed to escape began raising money to assist others to get out of Belgium. North View, Adamston, and Salem were abuzz with tag days, picnics, benefit concerts, theater performances and basketball games, food drives, sewing circles, and bake sales, anything to contribute to Belgian relief and reunite families. Groups of glassworkers contacted the Belgian consul or pressured the Red Cross to intercede on behalf of these Belgian American citizens. Others made sacrifices even more personal; Andre Hermaux, Leon Dandoi, and Aime Henry left in June 1915 to join the Allied forces in Belgium. Over the ensuing two years, the NWGW loaned thousands of dollars to the Belgian window-glass union and contributed scores of members to the armed services.[77]

Concern for European homelands and separated families gradually diminished support for socialism among the immigrant glassworkers. By January 1916, neither North View nor Adamston had Socialist tickets in local elections. That fall, the Socialists received only about 4 percent of the vote in the county. Salem's Left also slowly lost much of the momentum it had been building. Men like Leon Quinet, who had provided so much of the Socialist Party's energy, devoted most of their attention to relief for Belgium. When Governor Hatfield visited the town in July 1915, a crowd gathered to demand that George King remove the red flag from his restaurant, which also served as the Socialist Party headquarters. No Belgian glassworkers came to King's defense. Although the Belgians had opened a cooperative store, a Socialist newspaper, and another cooperative factory in town during the war, after 1916 they did not run any candidates on the Socialist ticket. In March and again in May 1917, Salem held large patriotic meetings to pledge loyalty to the United States government. The local paper editorialized against "half-baked pacifism."[78]

A second factor undermining the Socialist inclinations of Belgians in north-central West Virginia involved changes associated with the consolidation of Clarksburg. The city absorbed the formerly independent townships of Adamston and North View, limiting the ability of the skilled French and Belgian glassworkers to exert influence as part of a much larger administrative unit. The consolidated local government also cracked down on labor and Socialist activities during the patriotic upsurge generated by the war. Leading citizens sponsored superpatriotic America First Day celebrations targeting immigrant labor organizations as un-American. City officials undertook a more vigorous enforcement of the law, bolstering the police force and increasing surveillance. The U.S. Marshall used undercover agents to spy on anyone suspected of radical sympathies in the county, creating a chilling atmosphere for remnants of the Left. Then, in 1921, Clarksburg adopted the city manager form of government and changed procedures to elect the council from a city-wide vote, further diminishing the glassworkers' ability to have a distinct voice in city politics. Neither North View nor Adamston were able to elect a glassworker to represent their wards in the early 1920s.[79]

Interestingly, support for socialism decreased as the economic underpinnings of the craftsman's paradise temporarily improved. The devastation of Belgium's window-glass industry significantly improved prospects for even the less efficient hand-blown glass factories. Despite increased production in the American plants, window-glass manufacturers reported less stock on hand. The value of window glass produced in West Virginia grew by 245 percent during the war years. Fuel costs also benefited the West Virginia plants; the price of gas in the state was less than half that of Pennsylvania and about one-third of Ohio's. Wages began climbing again, and steady employment meant that annual earnings were double what they had been in 1914, although inflation diminished some of that improvement. Cooperatives in Salem and Clarksburg anticipated expansion or new factories to meet the demand. Even government rationing of fuel could not dampen the hopefulness of the small independent and cooperative firms in Harrison County. The regulations of the U.S. Fuel Administration allotted gas on a ratio of past use, not factory efficiency. Thus, the less productive hand plants received fuel at the same rate as the more technologically advanced machine plants.[80]

This regulated protection disappeared quickly at the end of the war. More important, the impact was compounded by the emergence of new technologies in window-glass manufacture. During the war, both Pittsburgh Plate Glass and the Libbey-Owens-Ford Company introduced processes and machines that could draw glass in continuous sheets, eliminating all the skilled laborers except the cutters. These processes enabled mechanized window-glass companies to easily surpass the productivity of previous plants and drastically cut the cost of glass. Equally challenging, both of these companies located factories in West Virginia, right in the center of the hand-blown window-glass industry. Pittsburgh Plate Glass's modern, new factory opened for business in Clarksburg in 1916 (see illus. 13); Libbey-Owens-Ford began producing sheet-drawn window glass in Charleston in 1917.[81]

Once the government lifted its rationing of fuel, these new sheet-drawing plants shifted into high gear. The small independents and cooperatives, and even the American Window Glass Company, found it increasingly difficult to compete. Together with the union, they attempted to keep glass prices high by strictly regulating the number of factories operating during the year. Workers found that they were getting only about six months' employment per year, at wages that forced most of them to obtain other jobs for at least part of the year. This solution did not last. Ironically, one of the hand plants that had a steady market for its product, the Buckeye Company in Ohio, filed an antitrust suit against the collusion of the industry and the union that limited its right to make glass. The Buckeye Company asserted that attempts to restrict production were futile without the cooperation of Pittsburgh Plate Glass and Libbey-Owens-Ford. Ultimately, the federal judge agreed, but he refused

Illus. 13. When Pittsburgh Plate Glass built a plant in Clarksburg in 1916, it located in a rural area several miles to the southeast of the city. Theodor Horydczak Collection. Courtesy of the Library of Congress.

to rule against the union and the other companies because by 1923, the hand plants were already an insignificant part of the industry.[82]

Confronted with all of these setbacks, the skilled glassworkers recoiled into a defensive posture. The declining position of the union encouraged some craftsmen to propose accepting some semiskilled workers, particularly the snappers. Snappers had first emerged in the nineteenth century as general helpers to the blower. However, as the continuous tank reorganized the factory, snappers took on more duties. Young boys were no longer able to fulfill the tasks; by 1910, snappers were men who made a career out of the job. They had asked to be included in the NWGW several times, but union members worried that snappers might then expect to move into one of the glass trades. With membership declining, the issue resurfaced in 1919 and again in 1923. Both times, the NWGW rejected admitting snappers to the union, a sign that the socialism of skilled glassworkers had always had its limits.[83]

By the middle of the 1920s, the NWGW had only a shadowy presence in Clarksburg. Window-glass manufacturing continued in the area, but now under the control of private interests that introduced the new technologies and processes. At the west end of town, the Adamston Flat Glass Company and Rolland Brothers mass-produced glass in the neighborhoods that had once been dominated by the cooperatives. To the southeast of the city, the huge Pittsburgh Plate Glass factory picked up many of the glassworkers who had formerly worked at the old West

Fork and Tuna plants. Total window-glass employment was down in the late 1920s, but it still accounted for approximately one-fourth of the manufacturing jobs in the city, as the population approached thirty thousand.[84] The nature of employment, however, changed significantly. The workers, except for a small group of glass cutters, were semiskilled machine operators, no longer highly skilled craftsmen. As late as 1914, nearly half of Clarksburg's labor force worked in factories owned by individuals, partnerships, or cooperatives; by 1920, 95.5 percent worked for corporations, a sea change that reflected the ongoing restructuring of window glass.[85]

When asked, many former craftsmen claimed they would look for other types of work rather than take jobs in the mechanized factories. The U.S. Department of Labor surveyed the prospects of hand plant workers in 1929 and found that only 68 of 605 former NWGW members had obtained employment in the mechanized factories. Years of part-time or seasonal employment in other occupations due to the policies of the union in regulating output had prepared some for the decline. George Villian became a barber; Omar Lambiotte became a pipe fitter; Eugene DeCamp sold meat; others opened restaurants, groceries, and flower shops. Many of the immigrants who had been reluctant to purchase homes in the first decade had become entrenched in their comfortable neighborhoods. In 1920, almost four out of ten window-glass craftsmen were homeowners, a rate that surpassed that of most industrial workers in the city. Nearly seven out of ten of those homeowners were still in Clarksburg fifteen years later. The glassworkers, nearly all of whom had come from elsewhere, had not only changed the town but also made it home. Not only did they stay but also, in contrast to the Department of Labor's findings, three-fifths of them continued to work in the window-glass industry.[86] Despite a distaste for the regimen of the mechanized plants, movement into less skilled work entailed little hardship for most. Because of the irregular operation of the hand plants, NWGW members were earning between $1,100 and $1,400 per year in 1922; the average wage of Harrison County window-glass workers in 1929 was about $1,400. Even considering that hand plant workers had been able to make additional money during the months when the factories were out of blast, total earnings were at least respectably close.[87]

For their part, the glass companies were surprisingly willing to hire the men who had been stalwart union members. By the mid-1920s, Pittsburgh Plate Glass and the other glass companies felt they had little to fear from the prolabor sentiments of the former craftsmen. Moreover, the companies understood that many of these men had knowledge of glass that gave them an advantage in monitoring conditions at the tank, the drawing chamber, the flattening table, or the annealing lehr that were part of the newer processes. In addition, their skills in handling glass helped prevent breakage. Fortunately for some of the glassworkers, the Rollands also had strong community connections in North View that encouraged them to keep on the French and Belgian glassworkers who had joined with them in the NWGW and in neighborhood politics.[88]

Clarksburg after Paradise

The window-glass industry had transformed Clarksburg in the three decades after its arrival. With the incorporation of the Adamston, North View, and Industrial neighborhoods, it stretched along an east-west axis growing to 4.9 square miles. The town had grown from a small county seat of four thousand to a city of just under thirty thousand. Although the abundance of coal, oil, and natural gas had activated the growth of Clarksburg and Harrison County, it quickly became noted more for its growth of manufacturing than its resource extraction. In 1930, manufacturing occupied 41 percent of its male workforce; mineral extraction employed only 6.4 percent. Even county-wide, manufacturing employed five workers for every three in mining.[89] The rural homogeneity of the population was another casualty of Clarksburg's transformation. By 1930, 1 out of 6 residents of Harrison County was an immigrant or the child of immigrants. In the immediate vicinity of Clarksburg, where almost half of the county's population lived, that ratio increased to better than 1 in 5. The French and Belgian glassworkers also contributed to a different religious composition. In 1926, Catholics made up 37 percent of Clarksburg churchgoers, more than the Baptists and Methodists (the next two largest denominations) combined. The Catholic share of religious congregants had more than doubled since 1906.[90]

For those who had touted the development faith, Clarksburg seemed to have fulfilled the promise. In addition to its glass factories, there was a tin plate mill, a pottery, a chemical company, a zinc plant, several brickworks, and a modern bottle factory. The county was producing coal, oil, and natural gas in sufficient quantities to provide inexpensive fuel to any industrial enterprise that wished to locate in the area. Other indicators of a workforce primed for economic development, such as literacy and annual earnings, seemed to forecast a bright future.[91] The city also had excellent rail connections, an interurban trolley line that not only spanned the city but also offered service to Fairmont in the next county, and the efficient city manager form of government, directed by Harrison G. Otis from 1921 to 1927. Otis's leadership left the city with playgrounds, an updated sewer system, a health service, modern police and fire protection, and a host of other improvements. Finally, the boosters must have been pleased that the Republican Party seemed comfortably ensconced in both city and county offices.[92]

But the 1920s represented the high-water mark for Clarksburg. City population had, in fact, begun to level off at around thirty thousand, a figure it reached shortly after 1920. Manufacturing employment in the county actually peaked in 1919 and declined until 1940. The Adamston Flat Glass Company and Rolland Brothers merged in the 1930s to form Fourco Glass and, together with Pittsburgh Plate Glass, helped West Virginia remain the second leading state in the country in glass manufacturing, but the industry never exceeded its 1920 employment figures. The nature of the employment relationship had also changed. In 1914, just 56 percent of the city's wage earners worked for corporations; five years later, 96 percent did, in larger factories with more modern technology.[93] Clarksburg had attracted large factories, but, with the exception of Rolland Brothers, nonresidents owned them and managed their affairs from outside the state.

The hopes of the turn-of-the-century boosters like Nathan Goff Jr., Richard T. Lowndes, and John Koblegard that attracting manufacturing enterprises to use the area's fuel resources would lead to self-sustaining economic development were ultimately dashed. Until 1919, the rate of increase in the number of wage earners in the value-adding industrial establishments actually outpaced the rate for the nation. Likewise, the wages they earned surpassed the national average. After 1919, however, that pattern ceased. In Clarksburg, much of the change involved a new restructuring of the window-glass industry, which reduced its share of the local workforce and paid its workers lower wages.[94] No other industry stepped in to take up the slack.

The glassworkers—men like Aristide Rolland, Samuel Powell, and Leon Quinet—who had been so active in building an alternative politics in the city retreated in the 1920s. They had no union to support them at the workplace and no political organization to sustain a distinctively working-class voice. However, their neighborhoods remained, and individuals showed up as representatives of Adamston and North View on the local Democratic and Republican committees. John Caussin and Minnie Schmitz represented former Lafayette Company families among the local Democrats, while some familiar glassworker names—Cox, Nicholson, and Trunick—appeared on the Republican Committee from Adamston and North View.[95] Some others, like Arthur LaChapelle and Réne Zabeau, held onto their reminiscences of the craftsman's paradise as they submitted to the supervision and lack of freedom in the machine plants, waiting for the opportunity to once again assert their right to bargain over the terms and conditions of their labor.[96]

6 Fairmont: A Cutting Edge
of Mass Production

In May 1910, a worker using the pseudonym "Regalia" wrote to the *Commoner and Glassworker* that the new Owens West Virginia Bottle Company plant being built on the east side of Fairmont, West Virginia, was "one of the marvels of the glass world." The huge complex covered fifteen acres, but the company planned to employ few skilled workers. When the factory opened in the fall of that year, company officer and inventor Michael Owens claimed that the factory could operate "without the necessity for human hands."[1] Although it was not quite as automatic as Owens claimed, the plant did help complete a cycle of technological transformation in the glass container industry, eliminating the highly paid, skilled bottle blowers. Ironically, Owens had begun his career as a union glassworker at the innovative Hobbs, Brockunier glass factory in South Wheeling, where his father still lived, and where he continued to have connections with glass craftsmen. In fact, his fondness for his home state was one of the reasons he chose to build his modern marvel in Fairmont.

Despite his fascination with the new factory, "Regalia" probably had a less sanguine view of Owens's energies on behalf of the Mountain State. Within months of the factory's opening, Owens doubled the size of his Fairmont plant and equipped a new factory in Clarksburg, just fifteen miles to the south. Regalia was hardly baffled by innovation. At the Monongah Glass Company, where Regalia likely worked, production lines already operated with semiautomatic machines mass-producing

Map 5. Fairmont and Palatine, West Virginia, 1897. Palatine (foreground), which became East Fairmont shortly after this map appeared, became home to the Owens West Virginia Bottle Company plant in 1910. Note the glass plants on the west side of the river in the neighborhood known as the South Side. Drawn by T. M. Fowler and published by T. M. Fowler and James B. Moyer, Morrisville, Pa. [1897]. Geography and Map Division, Library of Congress.

containers for its new contract with the Beechnut Packing Company.[2] Such changes altered the labor relations climate of the town. The Johns Brothers bottle factory soon went out of business, as did the Fairmont Window Glass Company, slowly reducing the numbers of union members on the industrial South Side of Fairmont. German, English, Belgian, and French craftsmen fled Fairmont during the next five years; Italian immigrants and African American migrants from the South grabbed their places. By the end of World War I, the majority of Regalia's fellow glassworkers were strangers to him.

The decisive shift to mass production technologies around 1910 bolstered the prevailing antiunion attitudes of employers in Fairmont. The town's major capitalists—men like James O. Watson, Clarence Watson, and A. B. Fleming—were predominately coal operators who sought to keep production costs as low as possible by using nonunion labor. Although they briefly flirted with investing in a manufacturing base to complement their development of coal, oil, and natural gas, their heavy investment in providing coal to the Great Lakes market made them more concerned with defeating organized labor than with fostering high-wage industrial employment in the county. The drive for political and social control, not local economic development, guided their decisions. Although Fleming and the Watsons surely felt more at ease with the mechanized factories that dominated the local glass industry after 1910, the new industrial workers proved to be more troublesome than the coal barons could have imagined.

Awakening from a "Rip Van Winkle Sleep"

Fairmont dates its official existence to an 1820 act of the Virginia General Assembly that created the town of Middletown on a 254–acre tract of land owned by Boaz Fleming. In 1842, it became the county seat of the newly formed Marion County, carved out of Monongalia County to the north and Harrison County to the south. Early the following year, residents rechristened the town Fairmont to avoid confusion with a town in Frederick County, Maryland. Already a trading center for the surrounding hinterlands, Fairmont gained increased local importance with the completion of the county courthouse in 1844 and the arrival of the B&O Railroad, which ran through the town en route to Wheeling in 1852. That same year, the father of the West Virginia coal industry, James O. Watson, and the "father of West Virginia," Virginia's Unionist governor in the Civil War, Francis Pierpont, opened a coal mine in Palatine, just on the other side of the Monongahela River, and began shipping coal to

Baltimore via the B&O. A year later, Fairmont obtained a charter for its first bank, which began accumulating capital for further investments.[3]

Despite the town's location in the Pittsburgh Seam, one of the nation's richest bituminous coal deposits, these promising early developments did not result in an economic takeoff for more than three decades. Because the B&O was so important to the Union efforts during the Civil War, Confederate units repeatedly raided and disrupted normal traffic, making shipments uncertain, according to historian Michael E. Workman. Although local mining rebounded somewhat in the late 1860s, the Panic of 1873 and the ensuing economic depression again halted development and destroyed the Watson-Pierpont partnership. Watson, however, was not deterred. In 1874, he began a new partnership with his son-in-law, Aretas Brooks Fleming, a lawyer with extensive family connections in Fairmont, which made him a valuable political ally. His knowledge of the state's archaic land law and ability to command local kin allegiance were critical to the coal interests. Both Fleming and Watson were pro-Union but also Democrats. Thus, when the party returned to power in the state in the early 1870s, Fleming was well positioned. He joined the business development wing of the party, building alliances with U.S. senators Henry Gassaway Davis and Johnson Newlon Camden.[4]

Political control did not translate into immediate economic success for the Watson-Fleming partnership. In the 1870s and 1880s, the upper Monongahela valley was an insignificant home market for coal, since there was little manufacturing activity and the population was relatively small. Although the valley was connected to a major trunk line—the B&O Railroad—the railroad's discriminatory rates against shipping by local companies discouraged the development of markets elsewhere. As Fleming later recalled, "for many years but little consideration was shown local shippers, or the communities through which the [B&O] ran. When quite young I remember hearing it said that it did not pay the railroad to bother with local freights. . . . This policy of the railroad . . . retarded the growth and development of that part of our state served by the B&O—then the only railroad in the state."[5] Moreover, Fairmont's location on the Monongahela River did not offer an alternative. Little had been done to add the locks and dams that would have opened the river to coal barge transportation. Thus, despite its location just seventy miles to the south of Pittsburgh, Fairmont coal could not break into that market. By the time investors made sufficient navigation improvements on the Monongahela (late 1890s), other areas were adequately supplying the steel city with coal.[6]

Fairmont faced yet another impediment to early development. On

April 2, 1876, a fire destroyed most of its business section. Without local fire engines, only bucket brigades of all available citizens and a fortunate shift of wind prevented the ruin of the entire town. The losses to most of the principal businesses in Fairmont, which totaled over $75,000, hardly seem catastrophic, but it is important to note that as late as 1891, the deposits of all the banks in the entire state of West Virginia amounted to only $8.3 million. Without an infusion of capital from outside the state, any loss was significant.[7] As a result, in 1890 the combined population of Fairmont and Palatine (which became Fairmont's east side in 1899) was only slightly above 3,000. During the decade of the 1880s, the entire county grew by just 20 percent to a mere 20,721 people. Only three hundred people found employment in manufacturing enterprises.[8]

The disappointing growth of Fairmont and Marion County until 1890 masked forces that were about to change the situation. Fleming's strong support for Camden began to pay off in the late 1880s. In particular, Camden threatened the stranglehold that the B&O exerted over West Virginia both through his plans for a competing rail network and through his seat in the U.S. Senate, where he could cooperate with social groups clamoring for railroad rate regulation. In the Senate, Camden attached an amendment to the Interstate Commerce Act (1887) forbidding practices that allowed railroads to charge higher rates to companies shipping freight short distances than to those engaged in long-distance shipping. Such practices had prevented the development of West Virginia, according to Camden. Equally important, Camden organized the construction of several rail lines connecting the rich coal fields of north-central West Virginia to the B&O's main stem. Taking advantage of these developments, Fleming and Watson opened the Montana Coal and Coke Company in 1886, which produced 46,724 short tons of coke for industrial fuel for the Chicago and western markets in 1890. At the same time, Fleming and Camden united in a venture to acquire some sixty thousand acres of coal lands in the state. By 1890, the region was poised to become a major center of coal and coke production, with the Fairmont operators in leadership positions.[9]

As Fleming and the Watsons expanded their economic influence, their political clout peaked. Marion County voted Democratic throughout the 1870s and 1880s. Fleming won election to the state legislature and the Constitutional Convention of 1872, and then served as judge of West Virginia's Second Judicial Circuit from 1878 to 1888. In the winter of 1887, however, Democratic president Grover Cleveland committed the party to a drastic reduction in the tariff schedules, a position that rankled state party leader Henry Gassaway Davis. The tariff issue further divided the West Virginia Democrats, who had just finished a factional battle that had resulted in the replacement of the probusiness Camden in the U.S. Senate by the conservative agrarian and ex-Confederate Charles James Faulkner. As Democrats approached the 1888 gubernatorial race, several of its major figures—Camden and Davis in particular—were either too disgruntled or too controversial to heal party divisions.[10]

Factionalism thus cleared a path to the Democratic gubernatorial nomination for A. B. Fleming. According to his biographer, Jeffery Cook, Fleming was a hybrid political character. Born in 1839, he was partly a conservative "of the old southern states' rights variety" who supported a limited government involvement in the economy and partly a proponent of regional economic development. Consequently, Fleming appealed to both wings of the West Virginia Democracy. Even though he was a business partner of Camden and shared the development faith, he was careful to cultivate an image of independence, since Camden's name conjured up an image of control by outside corporations in the eyes of many agrarians. Moreover, Fleming appealed to the agrarian wing because of his stance on tariffs. He opposed protectionism, in contrast to Davis, who, along with Camden, led the development wing of the party. Davis supported protective tariffs as the means by which West Virginia coal could compete for markets in the Great Lakes region. Fleming felt that tariffs should exist solely for government revenue; West Virginia coal operators could compete for markets by keeping their production costs lower, mainly by repelling the demands of labor.[11]

As mentioned in chapter 5, Fleming gained the governor's chair in the controversial election of 1888, despite the fact that his opponent captured a narrow majority of the votes. Still, the closeness of the contest signaled the resurgence of Republicanism in the state at a point when the Democrats were divided. Fleming worked hard to unify his party, not only with appointments to state jobs but also with his own private patronage machine in the north-central West Virginia coal companies. He cherished the state's inclusion as part of the South, but he promoted the "New South" of "economic regeneration" and national reconciliation. Critical to fostering a modern industrial economy, according to Fleming, was attracting outside capital. Consequently, he worked to keep taxes low and property safe. He became West Virginia's most active booster, advocating the state's participation in the 1893 World's Columbian Exposition in Chicago and writing articles touting the state's resources in such New South publications as the *Manufacturers' Record.*[12]

At the same time, the office of governor enhanced Fleming's personal fortune. While in office, he acquired iron-ore lands in the eastern

panhandle, timber lands in Boone County, and coal and oil lands in various locations in the state. Credit financed nearly all of his acquisitions,
obtained in part because of the prestige he brought to investment groups
and in part as a result of his close relationship with Joseph Sands of the
First National Bank of Fairmont.[13] Such investments gave him an abiding
interest in thwarting the miners' efforts to unionize the coal industry, as
well as the means to do so. The first organizing campaign occurred while
Fleming was still in office. In 1892, the United Mine Workers (UMW)
entered the Fairmont field hoping to "do away with the company store,"
to initiate regular wage payments, and to have a union member monitor
the weighing of the coal. The union established locals at the Monongah and Montana mines, in which Fleming was a partner. Fleming's
brother-in-law, J. E. Watson, squelched the drive by threatening to close
the mines if the UMW struck. The governor, who viewed the UMW as
part of a conspiracy to prevent West Virginia coal from competing with
the unionized northern coal fields, delighted in Watson's news that the
proposed strike "bursted completely."[14] This established a pattern of
antiunionism that Fleming followed for the next three decades.

While still governor, Fleming also explored the idea of developing a
local market for the coal, oil, and natural gas his companies produced.
With Joseph Sands of the Fairmont National Bank, Owen McKinney and
C. S. Smith (publishers of the local Democratic newspaper), and several
of the Watsons, Fleming helped organize the Fairmont Development
Company, with capital authorized at $600,000. These boosters began to
promote the south end of town along the Monongahela River as an industrial zone, offering low-cost sites and inexpensive contracts for coal
or gas to companies that would locate there. The Fairmont Development
Company also built a connecting "belt line" that attached this industrial
zone to the main stem of the B&O Railroad.[15]

Fleming's name lent the air of importance to the enterprise, and
McKinney promoted the venture in a special edition of the *Fairmont
Times*. By the time McKinney's special industrial edition appeared in
April 1892, the developers had commitments from two glass companies
and a machine works to move into the town's South Side. McKinney
praised the developers as "public-spirited men who invest their capital
lavishly and succeed in attracting foreign capital." One new industrialist
proclaimed: "I located here [from Pittsburgh] because I think Fairmont
has the very best advantages for coal, location, shipping facilities, lime-
stone deposits—and it has no tax to pay."[16]

Consequently, as Fleming left office in early 1893, he felt proud of
his accomplishments. He had kept state government small and taxes low

while protecting private property. In his hometown, men who shared the development faith viewed him as a local hero, someone who promoted a modern industrial economy and who was able to bring resources to the state to accomplish those goals. That he greatly increased his own personal fortune from the capitalist development of the state and his region did not trouble too many. Fleming's party swept to victories in the county and the state in 1892. In fact, the industrial wing, not the agrarians, seemed to be in the ascendancy.[17]

Ultimately, however, Fleming failed to completely unify the party and guarantee its future. His opposition to high protective tariffs left him unable to bring Henry Gassaway Davis back into the Democratic fold in a meaningful way. The party managed to hang on to the state in 1892, but a growing number of swing counties and mining counties began moving into the Republican column, largely on the strength of that party's support of the protective tariff and hard currency. Then the Panic of 1893 devastated the Democratic fortunes in the state and the nation. Just two years after Fleming left office, the Republicans, led by Davis's son-in-law Stephen B. Elkins, took control of West Virginia politics and remained in power for most of the next three decades. Even Marion County rejected the party of Fleming in 1894 and 1896.[18]

Glass and Coal in the Fairmont Field

Fairmont appeared ready to welcome a diversified industrial development in the fall of 1892. Although coal continued to be the economic engine of the county, the boosters in Fairmont felt there was plenty of room to support a manufacturing base to complement resource extraction. Indeed, local manufacturing might help even out the peaks and valleys of an export economy based on coal. Marion County's oil and gas boom helped. State geologist I. C. White discovered oil and natural gas in the northwestern part of the county, and by 1892 there were two hundred producing wells. In March of that year, three brothers originally from Baltimore, Duncan, Matthew, and Alexander Sloan, agreed to establish a glass bottle plant in Fairmont. Less than a month later, two sets of brothers—E. J. and John Beebe and Robert and John Johns—contracted to move their glass bottle factory from Findlay, Ohio, to Fairmont. The normally farmer-oriented *Fairmont Free Press* confessed to a bit of sheepish amazement. It acknowledged that many had "hooted" at the idea of attracting factories less than a year earlier, "but the progressive [men] went after them with their cash and brought them in, and here they are."[19]

Expectations of benefits from the belt line industrial hub on the

South Side were considerable. The Fairmont Development Company offered two hundred inexpensive housing lots in two public auctions, the second of which sold one hundred lots in three hours. The *Free Press* advised local residents "with capital" that they could make a killing in new homes. It praised the new industries as "the kind we can appreciate, for they mean dollars and cents to the people of this community." The *Fairmont Times* noted that the town had awakened from its "Rip Van Winkle sleep." In addition to the glass plants, Fairmont housed a brick works, two planing mills, a foundry and machine shop, and the B&O Railroad's repair shops. Just outside the town boundaries was the Barnesville Manufacturing Company's textile mill.[20]

Not all went smoothly, however. The slow progress on the Belt Line Railway made it difficult for the glass factories to obtain the required sand. Likewise, the gas and sewer lines moved more slowly than expected, leaving the factories without the necessary utilities to operate at full blast. More troublesome was the contest between the factories and the town's residents over water. Local citizens complained that usage by the glass plants drained the supply. By January 1893, the town sergeant responded to public pressure by enforcing rules against leaving water running at night to avoid freezing. Thus, just months after the opening of factories, the Fairmont town council faced pressure to erect new water tanks, improve sewer and gas lines, and pave the streets of the rapidly developing South Side. Boosters also encouraged the town to invest in modern firefighting equipment, particularly with the memory of the devastating 1876 fire still in their consciousness.[21] Beginning early in 1893, the men who championed the development faith floated the idea that Fairmont needed to incorporate as a city. Such a move would unite the town with West Fairmont and Palatine, which lay on the opposite side of the Monongahela River. It could also enhance the resources and the tax base of Fairmont, enabling the boosters to distribute the burdens of the new expenses resulting from development.

Immediately, farmers and "country people" objected. Some complained of the added inconvenience of mail service; others worried about the higher property taxes that would inevitably follow. For many, however, resistance to the idea was rooted in cultural issues. The dearth of housing attracted young workers without families to the glass factories. Particularly distressing was the lack of adequate boarding facilities for the single women who gained employment. Within weeks of the opening of the plants, citizens demanded that town police crack down on a new South Side speakeasy. At the same time, the local police had to hold Belgian glassworkers while immigration officials investigated whether they had been illegally imported under contract. In January 1893, local carpenters took advantage of the building boom to initiate a strike for higher wages. In March, the town of Fairmont just barely maintained its "dry" status in local elections by a vote of 119 to 116. The *Free Press* asserted that the arrival of factories would doom the antiliquor laws; already it noted the increased presence of speakeasies, as well as rowdy entertainments, such as a boxing match on the Watsons' land in Palatine.[22]

The optimism of the fall of 1892 turned sour just a year later. When the Panic of 1893 struck, the fledgling glass plants, like the local coal industry, struggled to survive. Then, during 1894, the Fairmont Glass Company burned to the ground, ending the involvement of the Sloans in the city. The *Free Press*, which had been so approving of the development faith in 1892–93, turned against the local corporate interests. Its columns complained about the "rule or ruin" policies that the Monongah Coal and Coke Company used against its employees. When the town of Monongah elected miner R. U. Myers as mayor, company manager A. J. Ruckman fired him. The *Free Press* lauded the mayor and claimed that the company was "unwise, un-American, unlawful." In the spring of 1895, the paper tackled the state's tax policies, which exempted coal companies from taxes, and the gold standard, which prevented miners from obtaining full-time work. Increasingly, the paper contrasted the "industrious, sober and honest citizens" in trade unions with the selfish behavior of the corporations.[23]

To men like A. B. Fleming, Owen McKinney, and the Watsons, the diversified development of Fairmont began to seem like a mixed blessing to the coal interests. The skilled bottle makers at the Johns Brothers factory were members of the Glass Bottle Blowers Association as well as a local labor movement that hoped the protective tariff of the Republicans would create an "economy of high wages."[24] The Fairmont coal operators had the opposite interests. They had fought off UMW organizing drives in 1892 and 1894, and Fleming's lobbyists helped defeat legislation introduced by Marion County Republican Jesse Sturm that would benefit the miners. But the Democrats had lost the state by 1896. When the UMW returned to the Fairmont field in 1897, Fleming quickly turned to the courts, applying for an injunction against union organizers led by Eugene V. Debs. Although the Republican special judge John W. Mason issued the injunction, the reform-oriented Republican governor, George Atkinson, appeared less reliable. Democratic Party chair and Fleming lobbyist W. A. Ohley complained that the labor organizers "are all here [in Charleston] trying to get Atkinson to give them some sort of a free-dom-of-the-State order that will knock out your injunctions, but while the Governor is a pretty big fool I doubt if he will attempt to supercede [sic] the courts in this matter."[25]

The injunctions gave the operators a reprieve. Fleming personally prosecuted twenty-eight strikers arrested for violating the injunction, in front of his old adversary, Judge Nathan Goff Jr. The heavy hand of the law broke the backbone of the strikers in the fall of 1897. But elections the following year sent mixed messages to the local developers. Fleming's supporter Owen McKinney won election to the House of Delegates, but Jesse Sturm captured the state senate seat in a district that included Marshall and Wetzel counties.[26] Since men involved in the coal industry belonged to both parties, it is difficult to detect clear class-oriented patterns in the voting. However, many industrial workers, especially in glass, supported the protective-tariff, high-wage policies of the Republicans. Local farmers, nonunion miners, and the Fairmont coal operators were more likely to support the Democrats, although for different reasons.

Because the Fleming-Watson interests viewed the state Republican administration as less reliable in the wake of the union activity, their desire to attract manufacturing firms waned in the 1890s. As the profits of Fairmont coal improved as a result of the operators' ability to remain nonunion, the owners invested increasingly in coal and less in diverse industrial enterprises. A variety of glass companies contacted Fleming and the Board of Trade in the 1890s, but few received encouragement. Alex Humphrey rebuilt the old Sloan glass factory but went bankrupt shortly thereafter. Owen McKinney lent his support to a group of local investors to try and restart it in 1898, but despite their presence, the company generated insufficient investment to survive.[27] At the start of 1902, McKinney complained to Fleming about the demise of the Fairmont Development Company. He asserted that, with just one exception, "there has been no new industry, giving permanent employment to any considerable number of people, established in Fairmont for the past six years." Such a condition was "ominous" for local real estate interests. McKinney hoped he could revive Fleming's interest in arousing the community "to the necessity of doing something along this line to keep Fairmont in her place at the head of the growing cities of West Virginia."[28] Fleming declined to respond.

Although four different glass companies had made attempts to operate in Fairmont during the 1890s, only the Johns Brothers Company, run by three Welsh-born craftsmen, existed when the census takers canvassed the town in 1900. Fairmont's population stood at 5,655, but only a small portion of the 32,000 people in the entire county worked in manufacturing. There were fewer than forty skilled glassworkers, mostly of German and British backgrounds. They made up the membership of GBBA Branch 77, and earned good wages (between $5 and $6 a day) making beer and mineral water bottles. Like skilled glassworkers elsewhere, they were a privileged, lively group, enjoying camping trips, musical entertainments, sporting contests, and elaborate ceremonies at which they initiated new members and solidified the brotherhood of the craft.[29]

Despite the availability of plentiful supplies of natural gas and the existence of four local banks with increasing sums of investment capital, however, the manufacturing base of the town stagnated during the 1890s. The political economy of the Fairmont coal operators was a major reason. After 1900, as West Virginia's natural gas reserves made it a more attractive destination for the glass industry, glass manufacturers relocated in Fairmont even without local encouragement. Like Clarksburg to the south, the first decade of the twentieth century brought an expansion of industry to Fairmont, and glass manufacturing had an important role to play.

Making a Glass Community on the South Side

In 1901, the South Side finally began to attract companies that created a glassworking community. That year, a group of skilled window-glass workers began the Crown Window Glass Company as a producer cooperative employing seventy-five men. This company joined the Johns Brothers bottle factory, the lone survivor from the 1890s. In 1902, the glass tableware trust, the National Glass Company, reopened the old Humphrey plant, employing 132 men and 22 women under the direction of Thomas Owens, the brother of the prominent glass industry inventor Michael J. Owens. These three plants supplied approximately one-third of the five hundred union members in the town. In an area where the powerful coal operators worried about organized labor's influence in establishing a high-wage economy, the arrival of factories paying skilled workers more than $5 per day must have made them uneasy. In fact, the AFGWU had only recently gained union representation for all the skilled workers at the nineteen National Glass plants.[30]

The growth of a union presence in Fairmont had immediate repercussions for the coal industry. In 1902, the UMW again sent organizers into Marion County, this time led by the fiery Mary Harris "Mother" Jones and Thomas Haggerty. Again, the courts performed splendidly for the company; Judge John Jay Jackson issued a wide-ranging injunction that led to numerous arrests. But the resentments were not so easily contained. That fall, the Fleming-Watson interests ran Owen McKinney for Congress from West Virginia's First District on the Democratic ticket. McKinney, the editor of the *Fairmont Times*, was also a lobbyist for Fleming and the newly formed Fairmont Coal Company. Not only did he lose the race, with a poor showing in the manufacturing counties of the panhandle and neighboring Harrison County, but also he lost in his own home town and county. In Fairmont, the glassworker neighborhoods on the South Side gave his opponent 55 percent of their votes. The spillover was significant as well; Marion County sent Republicans to the state senate and the House of Delegates, a legislature that eventually reformed the state's tax code in ways that infuriated Fleming.[31] Just two months later, Fairmont's first "organized labor" ticket appeared in city elections. Its leaders included two railroad engineers, two carpenters, a bricklayer, a cigar maker, and two glassworkers from the Fourth Ward. In a heavy turnout (88 percent of the registered voters participated), the labor ticket won between 25 and 45 percent of the vote in the city's five wards, despite running at least one candidate who was "a stranger almost to the city."[32]

Organized labor's political mobilization was short-lived. In the surrounding coal fields, the Fairmont Coal Company, soon to be merged into the giant Consolidation Coal Company, began implementing a program of welfare capitalism and paying decent wages that resulted in generally peaceful labor relations in the Fairmont field for the remainder of the decade. Behind the scenes, Fleming kept his lobbyists busy at the State House in Charleston, working against any "vicious legislation" introduced by legislators sympathetic to organized labor, despite the fact that Marion County sent Republicans to the House and Senate until 1909.[33] But organized labor maintained its presence in the town. In Fairmont, unions represented barbers, electricians, carpenters, painters, musicians, sheet metal workers, tailors, stogie makers, railroad employees, and glassworkers. In fact, outside the coal mines, nearly half of the town's wage earners enjoyed the benefits of union wages and working conditions.[34] Politically, the problem for the labor movement in Marion County was that the mines employed more than twice as many workers as manufacturing firms did.

Fairmont grew rapidly between 1900 and 1910, expanding from 5,655 to 9,711 people. The steady construction of housing for the growing numbers of miners in the rich coal deposits around Fairmont kept employment high in the building trades. Skyrocketing shipments of coal made the town increasingly important as a railroad center, adding not only operating employees but also union men to work in the local railroad repair shops. Meanwhile, improvements to the Belt Line on the South

Side made the area attractive to glass manufacturers, who employed well over one-third of the industrial wage earners in Fairmont by 1910.[35]

Despite the improvements to the South Side, there was no guarantee that glass companies would thrive in Fairmont. For example, the Humphrey Glass Company had flourished only briefly in the 1890s. A team of local investors made an attempt to restart the factory at the end of the century but failed. Then the National Glass Company operated a Fairmont plant there, but it closed in 1907. According to the *National Glass Budget*, the shutdown "was hastened owing to labor troubles which were suddenly terminated by the National's new general superintendent."[36] Likewise, the Crown Window Glass Company failed in 1904 and reopened under new management in 1905, and the Johns Brothers bottle works eventually ran into financial difficulties in 1906, requiring a financial reorganization. Robert Johns stayed on the board of directors but lost control of the company.[37]

The most important arrival in the glass community on the South Side was the Monongah Glass Company, headed by William Moulds. Born in Ireland in 1843, Moulds had immigrated in 1850 to Steubenville, Ohio, where he apprenticed as a glass mold maker. In 1864, he volunteered in the 150th Ohio Volunteers. At the end of the war, he moved to Pittsburgh, and in 1872 to Rochester, Pennsylvania, where he eventually rose to the position of general manager of the Rochester Tumbler Company, one of the largest tumbler manufacturing firms in the country. In 1901, a fire destroyed that plant, forcing Moulds to look for a new opportunity. In 1903, he negotiated with the Fairmont Board of Trade for property at the far west end of the South Side. In 1904, he opened the Monongah Glass Company with 160 employees, many of whom were boys (see illus. 14).[38]

Moulds was an innovator. While at Rochester, he had installed the most advanced tumbler machine, developed by Michael Owens. By 1908, the Monongah plant was equipped with two regenerative continuous tanks and five gas engines, and contained its own machine shop, cooperage shop, and box factory. It had doubled its size in 1906, and then acquired the factory formerly occupied by the Humphrey Glass Company and the National Glass Company's Fairmont plant. Moulds also added semiautomatic machinery to increase the company's production, now well known for its "pressed and blown tumblers and stem ware, needle etched, engraved, sand blasted, and decorated for family and bar trade."[39] Although technologically advanced, Moulds operated a union shop, negotiating with Local 49 of the AFGWU. He did, however, demand production concessions from his workers. Local 49 feared protesting too much; after all, the National Glass Company's Fairmont plant had closed

Illus. 14. In his caption, Lewis Hine identified these boys as headed home at 5 P.M. from the Monongah Glass Works, Fairmont, West Virginia, October 1908: "A native remarked 'De place is lousey wid kids.'" Photograph by Lewis Hine. National Child Labor Committee Collection. Courtesy of the Library of Congress.

abruptly during labor turmoil in 1907. Furthermore, Local 49 members, like those of Branch 77 of the GBBA, which represented workers at the Fairmont Bottle Company, read repeated warnings, both in the glass trade journals and in the local newspaper, about the potential of new machinery to eliminate skilled workers from the bottle and the tumbler production processes.[40] Thus, so long as the companies provided good wages and steady employment, glassworkers on the South Side were happy not to make waves.

The South Side glass community of 1910 in many respects resembled aspects of those of both Moundsville and Clarksburg. The Fairmont Bottle Company and the Monongah Glass Company brought in many craftsmen who were either born in Germany, England, and Ireland or were the children of such immigrants. Meanwhile, the Fairmont Window Glass Company employed a core of Belgian and French craftsmen. Of the 208 skilled glassworkers in Fairmont in 1910, 47.6 percent were immigrants or their children. For the less skilled jobs, the town's glass factories relied on locally born young men and women (54.7 percent West Virginia born) or, increasingly, on the influx of Italian immigrants, who made up almost 30 percent of glassworkers born abroad.[41]

The fact that three different unions represented skilled glassworkers on the South Side did not inhibit the development of community identity. Even the rivalry between the AFGWU and the GBBA for control of the glass container industry did not appear to spill over into the neighborhood. Bottle blowers played friendly baseball games against the flints, and they shared entertainments, as well as outings for fishing, hunting, and camping. Only the window-glass workers did not fit easily into the craft culture of the South Side, but that was largely the result of language barriers. However, even they shared the Catholic Church with many of the German and Irish craftsmen who made bottles, tumblers, and stemware. In addition, they all agreed that the growing temperance crusade in Fairmont was a menace to their enjoyment of their leisure time.[42]

The unsteady performance of Fairmont's glass companies during the 1890s and the early twentieth century had some ramifications, however, one of which was the transient nature of the South Side glass community. As late as 1910, despite the efforts to offer house lots at reasonable prices ($250), few glassworkers had made permanent commitments to the area. Less than 4 percent of Fairmont's glassworkers were homeowners; only 5 percent of the skilled workers who were heads of households owned their homes.[43] Many local citizens griped about the rough nature of the industrial parts of the city, pressuring police to crack down on saloons, "gambling joints," and other breeding grounds of rowdy behavior. Agitation escalated until Fairmont adopted an antisaloon license law, effectively banning alcohol from the town in 1909.[44]

The transiency of glassworkers limited their influence in local politics. After the brief appearance of a union labor ticket in 1902–3, glassworkers had little presence on tickets and were only foot soldiers at election time during the decade. Those who had been in town long enough

Table 6.1: Origins of Fairmont's Glassworkers, 1910

Category	Native born/ Native parent	Native born/ Foreign parent	Foreign born
Skilled workers	52.4%	21.6%	26.0%
Unskilled workers	73.6	2.7	23.6
Management	60.9	21.7	17.4

Source: Manuscript Census schedules, 1910, Marion County.

to qualify to vote generally supported the Republicans in the presidential elections of 1900 and 1904, but bottle, window, and tableware workers began to grow disenchanted with the party in 1908. The growing threat of mechanization increasingly outweighed that of foreign competition. The well-deserved reputation of Republican judges for issuing injunctions against labor actions made even the conservative GBBA president Denis Hayes question his loyalty to the Republicans.[45]

Republican antipathy to labor encouraged union members to look elsewhere. As in Moundsville and Clarksburg, some of Fairmont's glassworkers looked toward socialism; but more in Fairmont initially chose the Democrats. In the spring of 1908, as several local unions, including the railroad brotherhoods and the window-glass workers, were locked in confrontation with their employers, Fairmont's working class broke with the Republicans. In March, a young Democratic political maverick, Matthew M. Neely, surprised local citizens by winning the election for mayor with votes from the Second, Fourth, and Fifth wards, the parts of town dominated by glassworkers and railroad workers. Neely was hardly a labor candidate in 1908. Born in Doddridge County, West Virginia, in 1874, he had worked as a schoolteacher and had served in the Spanish-American War before graduating from West Virginia University's law school in 1902. Setting up practice in Fairmont, Neely also garnered popularity as an officer in the local National Guard unit. In 1904, he rose to prominence as an opponent of the state's tax reform, and in 1908, his platform emphasized opposition to Republican taxes and inefficiency. Neely also rejected the premises of the local prohibition movement, which endeared him to many glassworkers.[46] Although support for Neely did not amount to a labor program, the ambitious young mayor quickly learned how to appeal to his base of support; over the next decade, he became a better friend to those organized workers who had the power to return him to office.

The shift to the Democrats carried beyond Neely's victory. In the fall, Marion County elected three Democrats to the state House of Delegates, including William B. Ice, a stonemason who supported progressive reform measures. Then, in the spring of 1909, the Democrats captured two more city council seats in local elections, amid a new round of injunctions issued by Republican judges against union organizers in the surrounding coal fields.[47] The following year was even more devastating for the Republicans. The Socialist vote on the South Side rose to 8.5 percent. More significantly, Marion County Democrats, with overwhelming votes in Fairmont, won all three House of Delegates seats, both state senate seats, and the race for United States Congress. Just a few months later, these legislators helped elect two Democratic U.S. senators to represent West Virginia, including Fairmont's own Clarence Watson.[48]

Aside from their votes, Fairmont's glassworkers appeared to contribute little to the revolt against the Republican party. It is certainly debatable whether electing John W. Davis to the U.S. House of Representatives or putting Clarence Watson in the Senate amounted to much of a triumph. For the most powerful antiunion men in the city, the Watson-Fleming interests, the revolt was an unexpected boon. Nor is it likely that they would have trembled at the 1 of every 12 voters in the glassworker neighborhoods who voted for the Socialist Party. Unlike their counterparts in Clarksburg and Moundsville, Fairmont's glassworkers did not build a neighborhood political organization that enabled their members to compete for office in city and state elections. In fact, the most important political issue noted by "Regalia," the Fairmont correspondent to the *Commoner and Glassworker*, was that the revolt against the Republicans reopened the local saloons after two years as a "dry zone." After all, the local plants were "running full," the summer shutdown approached, allowing many to go camping along the Ohio River, and the pressers beat the blowers in baseball at the South Side Park.[49] The impending changes to be brought by modern, mass-production factories were still in the future.

A Marvel of the Glass World

Companies based in Connecticut and Ohio increasingly shaped Fairmont's glass industry in the twentieth century's second decade. On the South Side, the Monongah Glass Company entered into an agreement with the Beechnut Packing Company and a Hartford, Connecticut, engineering firm to develop technology that could "make automatically glass jars suitable for the vacuum-packing process" recently developed by Beechnut. By 1915, the company had ballooned to 784 workers, operating in several South Side factories that had formerly housed independent companies. Furthermore, although the Monongah Glass Company continued with a fine line of "engraved, needle etched, and rich or brilliant cut" tumblers, an increasing share of its business involved the mass production of jars for Beechnut. According to the historian of technological innovations in the glass industry, Warren C. Scoville, Monongah began using the "Hartford feeder" first for jars, but then found it adaptable to bottle machines as well.[50]

Just as important were the changes on Fairmont's east end. On the other side of the Monongahela River, in what had once been the separate town of Palatine, the inventive genius of the glass industry, Michael J. Owens, decided to build his company's first completely mechanized bottle factory. Owens, born along the Ohio River in what became West Virginia on January 1, 1859, was the son of an Irish immigrant coal miner. At age ten, he entered the innovative Hobbs, Brockunier factory in Wheeling and rapidly progressed through the ranks to become a blower by age 15. Immersed in the glassworker culture of Wheeling, Owens joined a debating society and became active in the AFGWU. In the early 1880s, he helped organize a cooperative glass tableware factory in Martin's Ferry, Ohio, and was active in organizing for the flints and their weekly, the *Ohio Valley Boycotter*. In 1888, Owens participated in a union drive that forced Edward D. Libbey to close his New England plant and move to Toledo, Ohio. Ironically, later that year, Owens went to work for Libbey's new plant. Within three months, Owens was foreman of the blowing department; within two years, he was superintendent of the factory. Moreover, he had won Libbey's confidence, gaining financial backing for his wide-ranging experiments in glassmaking technology.[51]

Over the next two decades, Libbey and Owens developed a partnership that transformed the workplace and the business structure of the glass industry. After introducing a machine to make light bulbs for the Libbey Glass Company, in 1895, Libbey and Owens formed the Toledo Glass Company to promote and market the technology for other products. Toledo Glass was less interested in making glass than in developing and licensing glassmaking technology. At the turn of the century, Libbey and Owens sold patent rights to machines that made tumblers to the National Glass Company, and then negotiated an agreement for the preferred stock of the Macbeth-Evans Glass Company in exchange for exclusive rights to technology for making lamp chimneys. Meanwhile, Owens used these resources to bankroll the development of an automatic machine for making bottles (see illus. 15). To license domestic users of this new machine, the partners and their backers incorporated the Owens Bottle Machine Company in 1903. Despite these innovations, only three companies had purchased licenses for the bottle machines as late as 1909. Although five new companies applied for licenses for specific types of glass containers that year and the company would acquire a number of companies through horizontal integration by 1914, Owens decided that the company could reap more benefits by actually engaging in production. Consequently, in 1909, the Toledo entrepreneurs incorporated the Owens West Virginia Bottle Company and immediately began to build its first modern marvel in Fairmont.[52]

Despite his union background, by 1910 Owens had a reputation for

Illus. 15. The 10-arm Owens automatic bottle machine, ca. 1910. Six-teen of these machines were in operation at the Owens Bottle Machine Company factory in Fairmont in 1913. National Child Labor Committee Collection. Courtesy of the Library of Congress.

"extravagant egotism and intellectual arrogance," even among other industrialists, according to Scoville. He infuriated both union members and his company directors with his insistence on control. As a factory manager, he refused to negotiate with the GBBA or employ experienced bottle blowers on the machines, despite the fact that union president Denis Hayes advised his men to do nothing to restrict output. At the same time, he still presumed to lecture Hayes on the proper policies that the GBBA should pursue as late as 1912.[53] Meanwhile, he insisted on locating his factories in places that defied the counsel of company officers and stockholders. For example, he built his Fairmont factory in a narrow river valley in which wind gusts and spring floods frequently disrupted production, and in a town with a high percentage of union members. Yet, after two years, Owens decided to expand production there in the face of such inconveniences rather than admit that his advisors might have been correct in recommending another site for the plant.[54]

Union members, in particular, had good reason to dread Owens's influence. The bottle machines made anywhere from 16 to 30 times more bottles per hour than hand producers. In 1907, however, there were only 22 in operation. By 1910, that number had increased to 71, by 1912 to 133, and by 1914 to 187. Meanwhile, GBBA membership felt the impact. At its 1906 convention, the union represented 6,397 journeymen and 1,523 apprentices; in 1912, membership had declined to 5,528 journeymen and 764 apprentices. Conditions were actually far worse; 1,717 journeymen and 289 apprentices were unemployed. Union officer Harry Jenkins complained: "We can't fight this new thing. When the linotype came to the printers, and when a great many other trades introduced mechanical devices, it did not hurt the workmen. . . . But the glass blowers have met a different kind of mechanism. It doesn't take any one to run it. . . . We can't make any real fight against it."[55]

On Fairmont's east side, where the Owens West Virginia Bottle Company erected its plant, a very different sort of glass neighborhood emerged (see illus. 16). Of the 355 glassworkers who lived east of the Monongahela

Owen's Bottle Works, Fairmont, W. Va.

Illus. 16. When it opened in 1910, the Owens Bottle Machine Company factory in Fairmont, West Virginia, was a modern marvel. Postcard. From the collections of the Corning Museum of Glass.

River, 244 (68.7 percent) were classified as unskilled laborers by the 1920 U.S. census taker. Adding in the neighborhood west of the river that was closer to the Owens plant than the South Side factories increases that to 69 percent. Fifty-seven of the east end glassworkers had been born in Italy, and 22 were African American migrants from the South. Another 193 (54.4 percent) were born in West Virginia of West Virginia parents. In short, the glass community near the Owens Company was predominately unskilled, mixing Italian, African American, and locally born whites. The vast majority of the workers had no previous experience in the glass industry. This composition was not unlike the "judicious mixture" that West Virginia coal operators used to maintain a nonunion workforce.[56]

Although the family background of Fairmont's glassworkers appears somewhat similar across neighborhoods, that is not really the case. The national origins of the immigrant groups making up each neighborhood suggest an important difference. Since the Owens factory required few skilled workers, the majority of its immigrants were Italians with limited experience in the glass industry. East of the river, immigrants found themselves limited to the lower rungs of the glass industry occupational ladder, a significant change from what had been the norm for glassmaking before 1910. The Monongah Glass Company, however, still recruited some immigrants for its skilled workforce. By 1920, most of the Belgian, German, British, and Irish glassworkers lived on the South Side (see table 6.3). Near the Owens plant, 57 of the 62 immigrants (91.9 percent) came from Italy. While Italians also made up the largest single group on the West and South Side, they accounted for only 44.8 percent of the 125 foreign-stock glassworkers.

Table 6.2: Comparison of Glassworker Neighborhoods, Fairmont, 1920

Workforce composition	East End wards 1–3	West & South Side wards 4–8
Management/White collar/Foremen	11.2%	9.9%
Skilled craftsmen	10.1	41.8
Semiskilled	9.5	18.0
Unskilled	69.2	30.3
Glassworker family background		
Native-born White/Native parent	70.0%	61.0%
Native born/Foreign parent	6.3	10.5
Foreign born	16.9	22.9
African American	6.8	5.6
(Number)	(367)	(323)

Source: Data compiled from Manuscript Census schedules, 1920, Marion County.

Table 6.3: Nationality of Fairmont's Foreign-Born
Glassworkers, 1910, 1920

Country of origin	1910 %	1920 %
Belgium	29.1	7.5
Germany	24.8	14.4
Italy	18.4	60.4
England/Scotland/Wales	9.2	7.0
Ireland	9.2	6.4
France	8.5	1.0
Other	0.7	3.2

Source: Data compiled from Manuscript Census schedules,
1910 and 1920, Marion County.

Despite the concentration of unskilled Italian, African American, and West Virginia–born males on Fairmont's East Side, in one area they surpassed the glassworkers congregating on the other side of the Monongahela River. In Wards 1, 2, and 3, of the 174 glassworkers who were heads of households, 69 (39.7 percent) either owned their home or were in the process of buying it. In contrast, in the wards where a much larger percentage of glassworkers were in skilled jobs, less than 1 in 6 (16.2 percent) were homeowners. In fact, the lowest ratio of home ownership was in the Seventh Ward (the old Fourth Ward), which housed the largest number, by far, of glass craftsmen. It almost appears as though the skilled workers of Fairmont could anticipate the complete elimination of their jobs in the city's mass-production factories.[57]

If the Fleming-Watson interests at Consolidation Coal Company believed that by undermining the union interests in the glass industry they were helping to rid Fairmont of political opposition, they were mistaken. In fact, as the population expanded around the Owens plant, the east end of town became a political hotbed. In the spring of 1912, the UMW launched yet another organizing drive in the West Virginia coal fields. Many of the Italian, African American and native-born unskilled workers at Owens had sympathies with the miners; after all, some had probably worked in Marion County mines or had family members there, since the mines hired from the same groups. There was also an ethnic hostility that was intertwined with labor–management conflict. When the Republican judges and the Democratic local authorities combined to issue and enforce injunctions against the UMW, the workers on the east side of the river flocked to the Socialist Party. In city elections in March, Socialist plumber Bazil Layman won 28.9 percent of the vote there. The northern end of town, where many miners resided, gave 26.9 percent of its votes to the Socialists. By contrast, in the heavily union South Side, only 1 of 10 voters chose the Socialist ticket.[58]

That fall, the Socialists named a "strong ticket" for all the Marion County offices. Just before election time, however, the Committee of 100, a local reform group headed by businessmen and coal operators, hosted a revival led by Billy Sunday, the evangelist. Sunday, renowned as a spokesman for prohibition and conservative politics, attracted hundreds to his revivals, where he advocated the state's prohibition amendment, which was on the ballot. Sunday's revivals also gave energy to efforts to resurrect anti-immigrant sentiment in the area, since many Protestant churchgoers blamed immigrants for the flourishing saloon traffic.[59] The combination of Protestant inspiration, nativism, and the antiliquor amendment deflated the Socialist support in the First Ward, although the Socialists claimed between 8 and 9 percent of the votes county-wide. This time, however, it was the South Side glassworkers who led the way, giving the ticket 15 percent of its votes.[60]

The brief challenge offered by the Socialists was enough to galvanize the dominant business interests of the town. As class warfare erupted in the southern West Virginia coal fields, coal operators in the northern parts of the state worried about the impact. They had a staunch ally in U.S. district court judge Alston Dayton, who issued sweeping injunctions against the UMW, upholding the "yellow dog" contracts that the companies required of their miners. These contracts, according to Dayton, in the case of *Hitchman Coal & Coke Co. v. Mitchell*, restrained the miners from joining the union and banned UMW organizers from attempting to recruit members who worked for such companies. Organizers who defied the injunction could be arrested. After it was first used in 1907, Fairmont's A. B. Fleming quickly sought advice about obtaining a similar injunction to head off any efforts on the part of the UMW to expand its organizing to the Fairmont field. By the summer of 1913, the Consolidation Coal Company employed private "guards" to routinely arrest and hold UMW organizers, with judicial sanction, in a "reign of terrorism," according to the *Wheeling Majority*.[61]

Fairmont's coal operators also moved to solidify their influence over local authorities. In February 1913, Marion County delegates in the state legislature proposed a new charter for Fairmont, implementing the commission form of government. The "expressed object" of the reform was "non-partisan government," but even the highly partisan *Fairmont Times* recognized that the new charter would likely disfranchise voters who did not support the two dominant parties. The election process for city council spots for the eight wards (up from five) would choose candidates from a nonpartisan primary and then prevent other names from appearing on the general election ballot. Meanwhile, most of the normal administrative functions of city government would be turned over to professional commissioners. Although legislators tempered the final bill, the *Times* wondered if the Socialists realized that the charter had "put over" a government guaranteed to silence them.[62] In the first city election under the new charter in November 1913, the Socialists nevertheless managed to place a ticket in the field. Only in the glassworker neighborhoods in the First Ward (near the Owens plant) and the Sixth and Seventh wards (the South Side) did the Democrats fail to completely dominate. In the First Ward, Socialist Bazil Layman captured 25 percent of the votes, enabling Progressive C. E. Swisher to defeat the Democrat; in the Sixth, many union glassworkers clung to the Republican Party, while in the Seventh, Socialist glassworker Fred A. Kelley took 12 percent.[63]

In Fairmont, in contrast with Clarksburg and Moundsville, few union glassworkers ran for office, even when they grew frustrated with the two major parties. Their low levels of home ownership hint at a more transient group, perhaps as a result of the frequent failures experienced by some of the city's glass companies. Those few who put themselves forward on labor tickets exemplify this problem. The glassworker who ran on the labor ticket in 1902, George Kerns, was a relative stranger in town at the time. He was gone from Fairmont when the Socialists began running tickets at the end of the decade. W. H. Gebhard, who ran on the Socialist ticket for the city council position from the Sixth Ward in 1913, had worked in Clarksburg as late as 1910, and was gone from Fairmont by 1920. This was also the case for Fred A. Kelly, who ran from the Seventh Ward.[64]

For the coal operators, victories in city elections and injunctions from the courts propped up their interests, but they were disappointed with their representative in Congress. In October 1913, the congressional district had a special election to replace John W. Davis, who resigned to become the U.S. solicitor general. Democrat Matthew M. Neely swept to an easy victory. In Fairmont, only the old union neighborhoods of the South Side refused to give Neely overwhelming support. But Neely proved to be an independent Democrat, attracted to the reform spirit of the liberal wing of the party rather than the segment dominated by the Watson-Fleming interests. Indeed, Neely proved his support for unions in March 1914, when he asked for an investigation of Judge Dayton for his willingness to issue injunctions against organized labor. Throughout the spring of 1914, the antiunion operators suffered additional setbacks. While Neely's investigation of Dayton proceeded in Congress, the U.S.

Court of Appeals overturned Dayton's *Hitchman Coal & Coke* decision. Clearly, sentiment for reform was growing in "that corrupt stronghold of Watson and the scab coal barons."[65]

Although unrest and conflict characterized labor relations in the coal fields surrounding Fairmont, the glass industry offered the city some stability. The Monongah plant "experienced an exceptionally good run" in 1914 and employed nearly 800 workers, more than 200 of whom were members of AFGWU Local 49. The Fairmont Window Glass Company still provided jobs for about 150 (about 50 union members), and the Owens bottle factory earned praise as "the most up-to-date bottle manufacturing plant in the world." About 300 men worked at the Fairmont plant, and Owens opened a second factory in Clarksburg, about fifteen miles to the south.[66] Steady work and wages, as well as the popularity of reformers in both the Democrat and the Republican parties, diminished support for political alternatives. In November 1914, Socialists failed to capture more than 8 percent of the vote in any city district; in most, the party carried less than half that. Neely gained reelection with wide margins in Marion County, especially in the precincts where coal miners made up a majority of the voters and in the east end precincts near the Owens factory. Ironically, he faired less well in the union glassworker neighborhood on the South Side, a testament to the reluctance of glass union members to break with the high-tariff policies of the Republicans.[67]

Open Shop Triumphant

The years of World War I continued the changes overtaking Fairmont. The city grew in size from under 10,000 to 17,851. Three of every four adult citizens were native-born of native parents, about one-sixth of the adults were either immigrants or the children of immigrants, and one out of twenty was African American. Both the black and the immigrant populations increased slightly during the decade, despite a flurry of anti-immigrant sentiments. Fairmont was a city conducive to home ownership; owners or people in the process of owning occupied 4 of every 9 homes in the city. The war years also were a potential boon to manufacturing. Between 1914 and 1919, the value of the city's manufactures nearly doubled, from $4.4 million to $8.3 million. Factories employed nearly 2,000 workers, 56 percent of them in the Monongah and Owens glass plants.[68] Still, Marion County's economy remained dependent on coal. The per capita value added by manufacturing stood at $112, well below the state average, and stood at less than one-fourth of that for the northern panhandle. Moreover, not all shared equally in the growth Fairmont did experience. More than half of the city's manufacturing workers toiled more than forty-eight hours per week for wages that dipped below the state average.[69]

Few industries had done better than glass during the war. In West Virginia, the value of manufactured glass tripled. In pressed and blown glassware, the value of the product doubled; in bottles and building glass (windows and plate), the value grew by nearly three and a half times. The glass industry of Fairmont, however, was less vibrant. On the positive side, the Owens plant in Fairmont expanded production, continuing as an important part of the company that dominated the glass bottle industry. In 1921, the GBBA noted that despite its efforts to accommodate union strategies to mass production, the manufacturers chose a program of "open-shop reactionaryism." Giving back wages and making concessions to productivity made no impact on the directors of the huge Owens Company, which continued to operate nonunion.[70]

At the other end of town, the Fairmont Window Glass Company shut its doors at the end of the war, no longer able to compete with the mass-production giants Pittsburgh Plate Glass and Libbey-Owens-Ford. About 60 union members lost their jobs. In the middle, the Monongah Glass Company continued to negotiate with AFGWU Local 49, but it began to slowly scale back production. The stalwart company of the South Side had employed as many as 800 workers at the start of World War I, but employed only 500 by the end. By the mid-1920s, Monongah had dismantled the tanks in several of its factory buildings and concentrated production on automatic-machine-made tumblers and bottles. Shortly afterward, the owners sold out to the Hocking/Lancaster Glass conglomerate.[71]

The city's political climate had also weathered dramatic changes. In the summer of 1914, the state's Yost Law went into effect, providing enforcement for West Virginia's prohibition of liquor sales. Immigrants, who generally opposed the law, felt the brunt of the police crackdown on drinking. Resentment slowly built to a boiling point. When a group of immigrant miners threw down their tools in a wildcat strike in February 1915, they took out their frustrations on Constable William Riggs and his posse when they attempted to restore order. The immigrants attacked all of the law enforcers but singled out Riggs because of his role in enforcing the Yost Law, and the constable died from his beating.[72] Such incidents sparked a growing hostility toward immigrants, especially Italians, the largest concentration of foreigners in the area. In the minds of many, Italians were associated with a growing "lawless element" in the city. In the years leading up to World War I, the Fairmont newspapers frightened readers with stories about the existence of a "Black Hand" gang, thought to be behind a number of murders and other crimes. A sensational trial in March 1915 convicted five of the leaders of the Black Hand group, which informants accused of engaging in bootlegging, extortion, gambling, and acts of violence.[73]

Coal operators and city authorities successfully meshed anti-immigrant sentiments with antilabor and anti-Socialist fears. The Consolidation Coal Company hired a "secret service" to intimidate UMW organizers, and the Fairmont city council passed a law that banned public addresses without the permission of the mayor or police chief. The involvement of the United States in World War I only intensified this connection. The presence of large numbers of foreigners in Marion County and the importance of coal to the national economy and the war effort made the Fairmont field ripe for U.S. Bureau of Investigation agents who watched the scene closely and fueled suspicion. Then the "high demand for coal, the scarcity of labor, [and] the sympathetic attitude of the Wilson administration toward unions" revitalized the UMW in 1917, according to historian Michael Workman. This combination looked like a recipe for violence.[74]

Fortunately for Fairmont, Clarence Watson had aspirations to return to the U.S. Senate. Since senators now were elected by popular votes rather than by state legislatures, Watson realized he needed to build a popular base, a lesson he had learned too late to try and regain the seat he had previously held in 1916. What better way for a coal operator to win friends than to negotiate with the UMW, since coal miners made up over 75,000 of the state's 175,000 wage earners. By 1918, a large portion of the 17,000 miners in the Fairmont field had become union members, and Watson had the endorsement of West Virginia's UMW leaders. Unfortunately for Watson, after a brief period of Democratic victories between 1910 and 1913, the state was again solidly Republican, and he lost the election by nearly 18,000 votes.[75]

Ironically, the Watson-Fleming interests ceded the open shop in the coal fields just as the unions in the glass industry, which they had feared for two decades, faded in significance. The opportunity to encourage a high-wage, diversified economy had faded as well. By 1930, Marion County had a smaller portion of its labor force in manufacturing than did the state as a whole, and much less than neighboring Harrison County. In addition, Marion County's industrial base lagged well behind, despite the presence of one of the leading glass manufacturing companies in the nation.[76]

Meanwhile, the city government tried to make certain that local control would remain outside the influence of popular politics. In 1919, the city commissioners urged the state legislature to again revise Fairmont's charter, this time increasing the salary of the city commissioners while eliminating the popularly elected city council. Citizens adopted the new charter by a vote of 1,851 to 713.[77] Nevertheless, the strong but conservative labor unions in Fairmont had a considerable presence. Fred Wilson, a member of the Boilermakers Union, served as mayor for twelve years; union carpenter Clyde Morris won election as the director of water and sewers; and former blacksmith L. D. Snider became chief of police.[78] In state and national politics, Fairmont helped steer the path to the Democratic dominance of the state that would begin in the New Deal. In 1922, favorite son Matthew Neely succeeded where Clarence Watson had failed, using UMW support to gain a seat in the U.S. Senate. As West Virginia broke with its three decades of voting Republican, Neely took advantage of the base he had built in Marion County to become the leader of the state Democrats and governor in the 1940s. Starting in the 1920s, Neely defied the coal operators in his party and his county by advocating repeal of the regressive state sales tax and substituting a severance tax on coal, oil, and gas. But he had more success in riding his base to electoral victories than in overcoming the entrenched resistance to reform in the state legislature.[79]

The glass industry had once appeared to be a harbinger of a modern industrial economy of high wages and diversity in Fairmont. But despite its success in attracting firms, the fear of industry's impact on the dominant resource export economy had stifled investment in manufacturing. By the time coal operators accepted unionization, the glass industry no longer offered the potential to create large numbers of high-wage jobs. Although Fairmont played an important role in ushering in West Virginia's New Deal regime, the resurgence of unionized glassworkers would follow, not lead.

7 Into the Depression

In the spring of 1934, glassworker Lilburn Jay was on the verge of fulfilling a dream of bringing collective bargaining to workers at the Pittsburgh Plate Glass plant in Clarksburg. The declining wages and working conditions caused by the Great Depression and the passage of the National Industrial Recovery Act (NIRA) a year earlier had started a flurry of organizing in flat-glass production. Glen McCabe, president of the lone remaining craft organization in the industry, the Window Glass Cutters League of America (WGCLA), saw the opportunity to revive unionism in flat-glass manufacture and spread its benefits to unskilled and semi-skilled workers. When the WGCLA balked at including unskilled workers who might quickly outvote them and take control of the union, McCabe resigned as president and started an industrial union, the Federation of Flat Glass Workers (FFGW). In January 1934, the FFGW brought Rolland Brothers and Adamston Flat Glass to the bargaining table.[1]

But Lilburn Jay had seen earlier dreams collapse. Now over 50, Jay had been working in the flat-glass industry for more than three decades. Born in Indiana in 1882, Jay and his brother Don had witnessed the restructuring of window-glass manufacture. In 1901, Lilburn Jay was involved in the first efforts of the Knights of Labor to organize the semiskilled snappers, men who were increasingly important to the work of blowers and gatherers in the larger factories. Sometime in the years before World War I, Jay and his brother followed the migration of the industry to West Virginia. Again, he played an active role in the unsuccessful movement of snappers to gain acceptance in the NWGW, and he eventually joined the independent union of snappers headquartered in Clarksburg.[2] Unfor-

tunately, the snappers were no more successful at surviving in a restruc-
tured, mass-production industry than were the blowers, gatherers, and
flatteners of the NWGW.

Possibilities emerged anew in the changing social and political climate of the New Deal. Industrial unionism promised less skilled operators like Lilburn Jay the chance to have a say in the terms and conditions
of employment in all branches of the industry. Moreover, the resurgence
of organized labor in glass towns opened up opportunities for working
people to exert a greater influence in the governance of their communities and perhaps in their state. Indeed, in what seemed like a remarkably
short time, glassworkers participated in the emergence of a movement
that threatened to reshape the political economy of West Virginia. Before
the decade was over, the state ranked among the nation's leaders in union
density, and the Democratic Party put a stop to nearly four decades of
virtually uninterrupted Republican control. Men (the industrial union
movement in West Virginia did not allow women anything approaching
an equal voice) like Lilburn Jay, who had been unable to participate fully
in organized labor's program, now elbowed aside those skilled workers
who had struck bargains with Republican politicians and employers who
had tried to buy labor peace with sops to a select craft elite. However,
this process followed different paths with differing results in each branch
of the industry and in each of the glass towns included in this study.

Although glassworkers helped challenge the power relations of labor
and capital in West Virginia, the various branches of the glass industry ultimately had less impact in reshaping the state's economic structure. The
coal industry continued to attract much of the investment capital and to
get favorable treatment in the state's tax policies. As a result, labor force
participation rates remained considerably below the nation's, and both
population growth and manufacturing employment stagnated. Moreover,
those industries that dominated in the state had relatively high propor-
tions of low-skilled and low-wage jobs. Even glass manufacture, once the
domain of a labor aristocracy, now paid wages below the industrial average.[3] Thus, the occupational and industrial structures of West Virginia
left the state poorly equipped for sustained economic development.

In this chapter, then, I will survey the progress of the glass industry
in West Virginia during the 1920s and 1930s. Next, I will explore the developments in Moundsville, Clarksburg, and Fairmont in the depression
decade, paying attention to the ways that past restructurings in each
branch of the industry led to dissimilar reactions to the upheavals of the
1930s. Third, I will examine glass manufacturing within the state's political economy and suggest some of the limitations facing both workers and

communities as they sought to influence the direction of economic and social policies. Finally, I will summarize some of the findings resulting from this study of restructuring and struggles over the political economy of West Virginia from 1890 into the 1930s.

West Virginia Glass in the Interwar Years

Technological changes in production and the collapse of the unions in parts of the industry, combined with the market disruption of World War I, played havoc with American glass manufacturing in the 1920s. The dramatic decline in glass imports and a growing market for American exports during the war years stimulated an overexpansion of capacity. For example, in window glass, imports dropped from more than 1 million square feet in 1911 to less than 100,000 square feet each year between 1917 and 1920. Meanwhile, the dollar value of exports multiplied 10 times between 1914 and 1916, and doubled again by 1919. However, by 1922, imports were greater and exports less than they had been before the war.[4] Other branches experienced less severe fluctuations, but each branch faced significant challenges. In bottle manufacture, for example, Prohibition had hurt demand and had cut into the bar trade, important consumers of glass tumblers. As a result, the number of wage earners in the glass industry, which peaked at 77,520 in 1919, dropped to under 55,000 in 1921, before leveling off at around 67,000 between 1925 and 1929.[5]

West Virginia's share of the glass industry continued to grow during the 1920s. While glass plant employment in 1914 stood at just under 9,000, the number swelled to 13,144 by 1929. At the start of the depression, the state ranked a close second to Pennsylvania in its number of glass factories (59 to 58). But the Mountain State typically attracted the less efficient parts of the industry. Although the state accounted for 22 percent of the plants, West Virginia employed only 15.3 percent of the industry's workers and produced only 13.8 percent of its total value. Each of its glassworkers made only $3,700 worth of ware, compared to the $4,100 produced by the average American glassworker.[6] Interestingly, however, annual earnings of West Virginia glassworkers surpassed the industry's national average, peaking at just under $1,400 in 1929. Labor costs, in fact, had not been the most important factor in plant location; the ratio of wages to the value added by manufacturing in the glass industry had steadily declined from 65 percent in 1910 to just over 40 percent by 1930.[7]

The onset of the depression only added to the dramatic fluctuations in the state's glass industry. By 1932, glass factories in West Virginia employed only 8,759 men and women, and average annual earnings had plummeted by more than one-third in three years. But the long history of regulatory collective bargaining in the industry facilitated the development of codes once the NIRA was passed in 1933. In fact, several of the larger glass companies, including Owens-Illinois and Hazel-Atlas, welcomed the NIRA for the stability it brought to what had become an industry characterized by excess capacity and cutthroat competition in the 1920s. Unions actually helped equalize wages and restrict the entry of new competitors. Labor and management "cooperated closely on legislative matters and spoke with one voice at hearings concerning the tariff or Prohibition repeal," according to historian Colin Gordon.[8]

Glass employment thus rebounded fairly quickly with the coming of the New Deal, returning to predepression employment levels in West Virginia by 1935. Annual earnings recovered more slowly, but by 1937 they approached predepression levels. A survey of the industry in the state in 1938 showed that there were sixty-two plants producing an annual product of nearly $50 million (see map 6). More than 45 percent of the workers produced glass tableware, which totaled just 28 percent of the annual product value. West Virginia had six factories making bottles and glass containers, but they employed 1 out of 4 glassworkers and produced 37 percent of product value. Six flat-glass factories had 2,588 employees (about one-fifth of the state's glassworkers) producing just about the same volume of sales as the much larger number of tableware workers. The remaining twenty-nine glass plants made lamp chimneys, illuminating ware, marbles, mirrors, and a variety of other products. Together they accounted for less than 9 percent of the workers in the industry and only 7 percent of the product value.[9] Thus, the recovery of West Virginia's glass industry during the depression relied on plants at the lower end of the industry, as measured by capital investment, product value, and size of factory.[10]

Although the glass industry maintained its importance in West Virginia's manufacturing employment during the depression, jobs in the industry lost ground in compensation, relative to others. Annual earnings in glass sank below the state average for the first time in 1931 and stayed there. Glass continued to be an important industrial sector, but the signs of future decline were already becoming clear. Capital investment in glass plants in 1935 was only 72 percent of what it had been in 1929 (a $6 million decline), and the value of the product did not surpass predepression levels until the 1940s.[11] In short, the glass industry was beginning yet another phase of restructuring, complicated by the presence of unionism that included unskilled and semiskilled workers. This

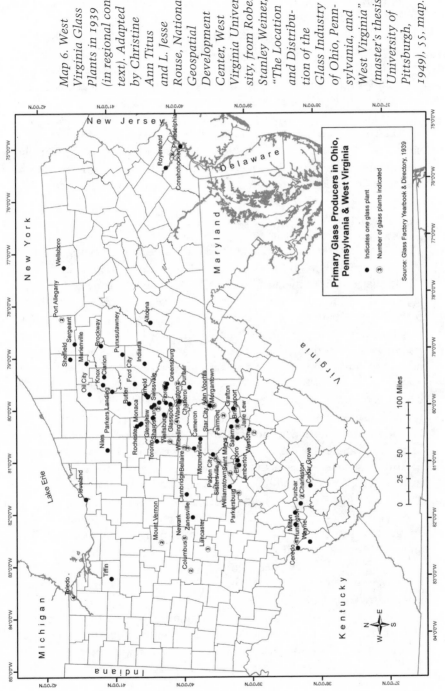

Map 6. West Virginia Glass Plants in 1939 (in regional context). Adapted by Christine Ann Titus and L. Jesse Rouse, National Geospatial Development Center, West Virginia University, from Robert Stanley Weiner, "The Location and Distribution of the Glass Industry of Ohio, Pennsylvania, and West Virginia" (master's thesis, University of Pittsburgh, 1949), 55, map.

Primary Glass Producers in Ohio, Pennsylvania & West Virginia

● Indicates one glass plant

③ Number of glass plants indicated

Source: Glass Factory Yearbook & Directory, 1939

time, work rules and labor costs would be a major factor in the relocation of the industry into new areas.[12]

The fluctuations in the glass industry that characterized the interwar
years rippled through West Virginia's glass towns with decidedly different
frequency and intensity. Each branch of the industry experienced expan-
sions and contractions, and both manufacturers and workers in tableware,
flat-glass, and bottle plants adopted various strategies to deal with the
problems and opportunities presented. In many respects, the different
restructuring processes of the branches in the years from 1890 to 1920
shaped the ways that each branch of the industry would develop during
the ensuing generation. To understand the beginnings of a new wave of
restructuring, it is important to return to West Virginia's glass towns.

Moundsville and Tableware

The glass tableware industry had to adapt to a number of changes in the
interwar years. The revival of international competition at the end of
World War I meant an eightfold increase of imports during the decade.
This came at the same time that the passage of Prohibition limited the
market for the bar trade. Plants making tumblers, goblets, and bar goods
saw their product value stagnate or decline during the 1920s. Happily
for workers in Moundsville, Fostoria Glass Company was at the cutting
edge of the emergence of a new market in fine quality glass dinnerware
for the home. W. A. B. Dalzell, Fostoria's manager, pioneered in adding a
design department, "which promptly broke away from the tired look of
imitation cut glass and introduced a new line of pastel tableware that gave
Fostoria high visibility in the department store business," according to
historian Regina Lee Blaszczyk. The company responded to the expansion
of American consumerism and credit purchasing with increased output,
lower prices, and a revved-up pace of design and innovation.[13]

As a result, Fostoria's labor–management relations settled into a
period of calm, with employment levels remaining steady and wages
ample. This was reinforced by a concerted campaign of Americanization
and repressive state institutions. The passage of a state constabulary law,
the governor's advocacy of committees of public safety to combat labor
militancy, and the use of both state and federal troops against strike actions, from Weirton in the northern panhandle to Matewan at the state's
southern tip, sent a chilling message to union activists. In the 1928 presidential election, Marshall County voters gave the Republicans nearly a
2-to-1 margin, while Socialists polled a mere 39 votes out of over 14,000.
Even Local 10's leadership seemed to fall in line with Fostoria's manage-

ment in supporting the Republicans. Guy Alexander served as a local officer and a Republican town official, and the union worked closely with
management in lobbying for the Tariff Act of 1930.[14]

Fostoria's relatively stable relations with its unionized skilled workers extended even into the early years of the depression. Conditions for
Local 10, however, stood in stark contrast to those for the majority of
the flints. The nation's economic collapse hurt the union; membership
declined from 6,880 in 1929 to 5,636 in 1933. Production of goblets and
tumblers in 1931 slumped to 28 percent of 1925 levels.[15] Fostoria was
also an island of stability in Marshall County's sea of economic decline.
Moundsville lost population during the 1930s, and the county's population was lower in 1950 than it had been in 1930. Local 10 tried to respond
to the economic hardship in the area, but the flints also confronted some
cutbacks by 1931, at which time the local negotiated with management
to distribute work time equally among its members.[16]

Hard times eventually began to disrupt the harmonious Republican
political climate of Moundsville. In 1930, Marshall County sent two
Democrats and only one Republican to the state legislature. The county
also voted overwhelmingly for Democrat Matthew M. Neely for the U.S.
Senate, while sending a Republican to the House of Representatives.
Two years later, Marshall County voters turned in Democratic Party
majorities in every political race, coinciding with the start of thirty-six
years of Democrat dominance in the state.[17] At the national level, West
Virginia joined the emerging Democratic coalition that inaugurated the
New Deal.

Equally important, the depression prompted union organizing drives
among Fostoria's unskilled and semiskilled workers. While Local 10 of
the AFGWU had settled into a mutually accommodating relationship
with the company, seven of every ten workers at Fostoria were not represented. The earlier restructuring of the glass tableware industry had
moved factories to small towns where they did not compete for labor, but
it left skilled workers ("flints") at the head of production teams. Flints,
not machines, set the pace, and they also directed the process and wielded
authority.[18]

The arrival of the New Deal improved the climate for miscellaneous
workers to organize. In fact, the passage of the NIRA and the development of codes to govern wages and working conditions actually encouraged miscellaneous workers to form unions so that they could have a
voice in the shaping of the codes. Throughout the industry, local unions
of miscellaneous workers emerged after 1933; Fostoria's local first appeared in 1935 as Federal Labor Union Number 20129. However, the

Illus. 17. "Birds Eye View of Fostoria Glass Works." By the 1930s, the *Fostoria Glass Company dominated the north end of Moundsville, thriving due to its design department. Postcard, ca. 1930s. From the collections of the Corning Museum of Glass.*

long-established relationship between the flints and the companies actually discouraged the creation of unions independent of the AFGWU. Tableware employers hoped to avoid dealing with more militant industrial unions. In addition, miscellaneous employees generally worked under the supervision of Local 10 members; some were the children and spouses of craftsmen, and others hoped to move into a craft apprenticeship. Consequently, in 1936, the unions of miscellaneous workers chose to affiliate as branches of the AFGWU, despite the fact that the parent union limited the miscellaneous workers (who outnumbered the crafts by more than 2 to 1) to only 16 of 190 delegates at the union convention. This essentially prevented them from assuming union leadership and muted their voice in the collective bargaining process.[19]

Miscellaneous workers at Fostoria became Branch 507 of the AFGWU in September 1936, inheriting some aspects of the business unionism that increasingly characterized the flints. Indeed, Branch 507 leadership was exclusively male in the 1930s and 1940s, although women made up a significant portion of the membership. In fact, the achievement of a collective bargaining agreement coincided with a lowering of the minimum wage rates for women.[20] In other areas, the craftsmen in Local 10 pressured the miscellaneous workers to defer to conservative union practices. Fostoria's management implemented a bonus system in the late 1930s that benefited Local 10 far more than Branch 507. When the miscellaneous workers complained and threatened to take action, Local 10 brought in the national officers to quash unrest. Ultimately, the craftsmen agreed to a seniority plan that allowed members of Branch 507 to be promoted into craft jobs in exchange for their support.[21] Other conflicts between the two locals also jeopardized the flints' control. For example, Branch 507 members at times refused to work with abusive craftsmen who practiced "unfair tactics towards the members of our Union."[22]

Nevertheless, in Moundsville, as in the tableware industry generally, the existing craft union subsumed the organization of unskilled workers and imposed much of the conservative business unionism on the miscellaneous workers. More militant workers eventually moved on, leaving Branch 507 in the hands of more compliant employees. Many of Branch 507's officers had family members in Local 10; others planned on becoming skilled workers and moving into the craft side of production.[23] In the end, the restructuring of the tableware industry between 1900 and the 1920s had left the work process and the craft union pretty much intact. These factors shaped the type of unionism that emerged when new opportunities arose in the 1930s.

Clarksburg Flat Glass

The restructuring of the window-glass industry before World War I had more profound results. Window-glass manufacturing became a capital-intensive, mass-production process. Moreover, the same process also transformed plate glass manufacture, which combined what had once been two separate branches, into a single flat-glass industry. For West Virginia, this meant a drastic reduction in the number of plants operating in the state, from twenty-one in 1910 to six in 1938. But flat-glass manufacturing survived in the state. Industry leaders—the Libbey-Owens-Ford Company and Pittsburgh Plate Glass—built factories in Clarksburg and Charleston, and older companies, like Rolland Brothers and Adamston Flat Glass, modernized their plants and merged to form the Fourco Company. Flat glass, like all industries, suffered with the onset of the depression, but rebounded to produce over $100 million worth of glass in 1937, and employed 2,800 West Virginians by the late 1930s.[24]

After the mid-1920s, the union presence in the industry all but vanished, however. Only the WGCLA, with a total national membership of about 1,000, survived in the new mechanized environment. The absence of unions did not greatly reduce the annual earnings of workers, since they had been making concessions to help the hand plants survive for years, but it left them at the mercy of a faster pace, more intense supervision, deteriorating working conditions, and a more authoritarian style of management in the machine plants.[25] In Clarksburg, flat-glass workers gained employment at one of two Fourco plants or at Pittsburgh Plate Glass. By early 1933, these three factories nearly matched the employment levels of the eight window-glass companies that had operated in the city in 1920. Moreover, these factories hired many former window-glass craftsmen and their sons, since they valued their insights for monitoring conditions at the tank, the drawing chamber, and the annealing lehr.[26]

Because West Virginia had been the last bastion of the NWGW, it was also home to the resurgence of unionism in the industry in 1933. Many former union members worked at one of the city's flat-glass plants in the 1930s. They shared a heritage of labor activism, bolstered by the French, Belgian, and English immigrant communities that had been the backbone of the cooperative factories and the local Socialist politics. Such men never lost their attachment to unionism, even though they had to hide it while working at the Pittsburgh Plate Glass or Fourco plants.[27] Then, window-glass worker Emil "Bud" Walz recalled, "the NRA [National Recovery Administration] came in and we were oh-so-proud. . . . The [government officials] put big posters up with the blue eagle on them, and we were proud of that. It was an opportunity to organize, but it wasn't easy. I gave Glen McCabe and the cutters all the credit in the world, they slipped around and signed cards." Indeed, the WGCLA and its president, Glen McCabe, recognized the desire on the part of flat-glass workers to restore union conditions to the industry.[28]

First, McCabe had to overcome the resistance of the WGCLA. He proposed to take the industrial workers into the WGCLA in much the same way that the flints eventually did. However, the craftsmen in flat glass had a long history of rejecting the recruitment of less skilled workers, and they feared being overwhelmed by thousands of industrial workers, particularly since the WGCLA was so small. When the league rejected McCabe's plan in July 1934, he formed the Federation of Flat Glass Workers and began a monthly journal, the *Flat Glass Worker*, to coordinate the union drive. Once he made the move, McCabe needed to overcome the objections of the companies. Here, his experience with regulatory unionism paid dividends. He promised the Fourco plants in Clarksburg

(Rolland Brothers and Adamston Flat Glass, where the old NWGW had deep roots) that if they recognized the FFGW, he would cooperate with them to strengthen NRA regulation and ensure industry stability. Then he used contracts with Fourco to obtain contracts from Pittsburgh Plate Glass and Libbey-Owens-Ford.[29]

Because of McCabe's influence, the relations between the WGCLA and the FFGW began amicably. However, following his resignation from the WGCLA and forming of the FFGW, tensions emerged. The FFGW went on strike in January 1936 over seniority rights and protection of bargaining unit work, issues the cutters deemed "trivial." Meanwhile, verbal threats from the industrial workers prevented cutters from crossing the picket lines. Harry Nixon, secretary of the WGCLA, wrote: "I don't think our men can work without risking lives."[30] Subsequently, the FFGW annoyed the cutters by siding with the fledgling Committee on Industrial Organization, which would soon become the Congress of Industrial Organizations (CIO). In addition, McCabe's tendency to run the FFGW the same way he had previously run the WGCLA generated internal resistance. A significant portion of the membership did not have connections to the earlier regulatory unionism. Men like Lilburn Jay had been denied the chance to join the NWGW on several occasions. Now that they had gained collective bargaining agreements, they bristled at the peremptory way McCabe operated. For example, he treated the union newspaper as his own private property, and he often settled workplace disputes without input from local or national officers. Most annoying to local leaders like Jay, however, was McCabe's insistence on using the WGCLA's "divide and conquer" bargaining strategy. Officers in the big Pittsburgh Plate Glass and Libbey-Owens-Ford locals sought to establish uniform wages and contract terms in industry-wide pattern bargaining.[31]

In the winter of 1936–37, the conflict between McCabe and the leaders of the big locals came to climax. During negotiations with Pittsburgh Plate Glass, McCabe insisted that the locals hold out for the closed shop, which the company refused to grant. The Pittsburgh Plate Glass local officers, in contrast, wanted uniform pay scales, a grievance procedure, seniority improvements, and some limitations on the authority of the foremen. Frustrated with McCabe, local officers led their members on strike. In December, the Libbey-Owens-Ford contracts also expired, and these locals joined the strike, severely taxing the union's resources. Local leaders blamed McCabe for botching the strike strategy, and eventually forced a settlement that gave the local union leaders most of what they wanted—union recognition, a grievance system with protections against unfair discharge, posted seniority lists for promotions and layoffs, and promises by both Pittsburgh Plate Glass and Libbey-Owens-Ford officials of future pattern bargaining.[32]

The FFGW executive board, dominated by the leaders of the big locals and headed by Lilburn Jay, was not finished with McCabe, however; they brought charges against him for misappropriation of union funds. McCabe challenged the charges at Jay's own Pittsburgh Plate Glass Local 2 in Clarksburg. In February 1937, while Jay presided over an executive board meeting that suspended McCabe, Local 2 recommended disciplinary action against Jay. For the next six months, the FFGW was embroiled in a struggle for control of the union. Ultimately, the CIO decided against McCabe, who eventually returned to the WGCLA and the American Federation of Labor.[33]

For Lilburn Jay and the PPG workers, the conflict demonstrated the lingering impact of the earlier restructuring of the industry. The craft, ethnic, and familial networks that had provided the roots for the earlier growth of cooperatives, labor unions, and socialism in Clarksburg did not adapt easily to the workplace contractualism of the mass-production unions. Many Clarksburg FFGW members had loyalties to the craft outlook of the old NWGW; Local 2 voted to withhold payments to the national union, to oust Jay from office, and to petition Pittsburgh Plate Glass to fire him.[34] Fortunately for Jay and the workers, cooler heads prevailed. The Clarksburg locals accommodated themselves to the new leadership of the FFGW, and Jay kept his job at Pittsburgh Plate Glass, but it would be a decade before he would again serve as a local union officer. The three flat-glass plants in Clarksburg settled into a stable relationship with the FFGW that provided around 1,500 good, union-wage jobs, making the industry the most important local employer. But in the 1950s, the flat-glass industry gradually reduced West Virginia's share of domestic production.[35]

Fairmont Glass Containers

As the glass bottle and container industry entered the post–World War I era, it was dominated by two companies, the Owens West Virginia Bottle Company (which became Owens-Illinois in 1929) and the Hartford-Empire conglomerate. Between the two of them they controlled the domestic market, through machinery license agreements, and consistently exported more than $3 million worth of containers per year. When the two joined together in a crosslicensing agreement in 1924, they accounted for 96 percent of the container production in the United States. Both companies had plants in Fairmont, which employed about one-third of the state's glass container workforce. Overall, West Virginia factories made up between 10 and 12 percent of the glass container industry between the two world wars.[36]

However, because of the Owens Company's antipathy to organized labor, the fate of members of the GBBA was rocky. Local 79 had established a foothold at the Monongah Glass Company, which was part of the Hartford group. But in the immediate post–World War I years, the power of the Owens plants forced the GBBA to make concessions. The union presented itself as a reliable organization of "practical American workmen" that would help employers rid their factories of "Poles, Hungarians, Italians and Slavs" and still make a profit.[37] Even that was not enough for the dominant companies. Early in the 1920s, Local 79 faded from existence, and Fairmont's glass container industry was "open shop" territory. Only a small flame of trade unionism flickered; J. H. Nichols, who worked at Owens, served on the board of directors that established the Fairmont Labor Temple in June 1921.[38]

Ironically, as glass unions disappeared from Fairmont in the 1920s, the local labor movement continued to have a notable presence. The building trades unions and the railroad brotherhoods complemented organizations of the printing trades, machinists, letter carriers, musicians, and the remnants of the UMW locals that had been recognized by Clarence Watson to bolster his political ambitions. When the depression arrived, organized labor had some clout, particularly since one of the local political leaders, Matthew M. Neely, was considered a friend of labor. After the passage of the NIRA, the UMW quickly reversed the declining fortunes of coal miners, and GBBA Local 79 resurfaced at the declining Monongah factory. In addition, a union of aluminum workers and two steel workers' locals appeared by 1936.[39]

At the Owens-Illinois plant, workers failed to join in labor's resurgence. However, the company was certainly aware of a changed labor relations environment; plant managers moved quickly to implement an extensive program of clubs, recreation, health care, insurance, food service, and communications with employees to diminish the perceived need for an independent union. The company fostered a "family feeling" in the plant through bowling teams, weekend trips, holiday festivities, dances, gun clubs, a weekly magazine, and a welfare council. It also gained the loyalties of most employees through a medical program that offered sick benefits, "including hospital, doctor, drugs, etc.," according to one fifty-year veteran. The commanding place of Owens-Illinois meant that the company offered steady employment at decent wages to generations of families.[40] To workers like Helen Frankman, who began at Owens-Illinois as a twenty-year-old facing the worst of the depression, the company "gave new strength and a resurgence of hope to thousands of desperate and hungry people." Another simply recalled: "My life with the Company has been good. If I could go through these years again, I would."[41]

The earlier restructuring of the glass container industry did not leave a vibrant union heritage at the Owens-Illinois plant. When it opened in 1910, it was already a highly mechanized, mass-production facility that did not rely on skilled labor, and consequently it avoided hiring union members. Instead, Owens-Illinois staffed its Fairmont factory with large numbers of unskilled immigrants and young male and female migrants from the local countryside and the deep South.[42] Few had expectations of a voice in the terms and conditions of employment in the factory. Not until 1944 did Owens-Illinois employees choose to bring unionism to the Fairmont plant. By then, the GBBA had organized most of the industry and had established a stable collective bargaining relationship with the most important companies, as well as the government agencies that regulated production and labor during World War II.[43] During the war, employment at Owens-Illinois grew to around 1,400, and Locals 248 and 249 became fixtures in Fairmont's labor movement for the next three decades. But Owens-Illinois was rapidly losing its command of the industry, and the postwar era would bring a new round of restructuring to bottle manufacturing.[44]

The Changing Political Economy of West Virginia

In West Virginia, the depression years marked a dramatic shift in partisan politics. Through the 1920s, the Republicans dominated the state, holding the state senate consistently and losing control of the governor's office and the House of Delegates only once. State political leaders of both parties utilized the hysteria generated by the post–World War I Red Scare to solidify a conservative, probusiness environment. In conjunction with voluntary associations, like the American Constitutional Association and the West Virginia Federation of Women's Clubs, or with business groups, like the Chamber of Commerce and the Manufacturers Association, politicians won support for loyalty oaths, constabulary bills, and educational reforms that promoted individual initiative, the protection of private property, faith in the benefits of free enterprise, and "public consent to elite principles of social organization," according to historian John Hennen.[45] Generally, this political climate favored the Republicans, who represented the politics of big business and a conservative social order. Indeed, the decline in unionization rates in branches of the glass industry paled in comparison to the defeat of organizing drives in the steel industry of the northern panhandle and the destruction of the UMW in the state, especially following the disastrous 1924 strike in the northern West Virginia fields.[46]

The depression thus came early to West Virginia, and the shift from the Republican Party followed apace. Per capita incomes in the state plummeted from 78.9 percent of the national average in 1920 to 65.7 percent by 1929, as coal mining wages declined. As early as 1928, Democrat Matthew M. Neely nearly upset Republican Henry D. Hatfield in the race for the U.S. Senate seat. In Marion and Harrison counties, which were home territory for Neely and where coal miners made up a substantial voting block, Neely carried majorities. By 1930, the tide had turned; Neely won the Senate seat by 133,000 votes, as glass towns voted better than 2 to 1 in his favor. Starting in 1932, the state entered a period of almost complete domination by the Democrats. For the next three decades, the party controlled 74 percent of the seats in the House of Delegates and 71 percent of the state senate seats; only once did the Republicans win the governor's race.[47]

The shift in party allegiance did not pay immediate dividends to Democrats, who hoped for a more liberal political agenda. Before the Democrats took over, the state government passed the Tax Limitation Amendment in 1932, which made it difficult to raise taxes. When the Democrats assumed control of the state in 1933, they faced growing financial burdens for public programs with insufficient funds. Unfortunately, they chose to meet their responsibilities by imposing regressive sales taxes, even on food and medicine. Public services remained "chronically underfinanced," and the state proved unable to assert its control over West Virginia's abundant resources and natural wealth.[48] Even when the Democrats assumed control, the situation did not change greatly. The Democrats were deeply divided between "Southern-style" politicians from the party's longtime Democratic counties below the Kanawha River and the more liberal New Deal Democrats who rallied around Neely. While Neely, as the U.S. senator, had the advantage of doling out federal patronage, the "State House" faction of conservative southern Democrats had control over state patronage, which was growing rapidly in the 1930s. State budget problems also made it difficult for West Virginia to reap the full benefits of federal relief programs.[49]

Unions in the state, however, did grow in political influence. The UMW rapidly organized coal miners, and organized labor resurfaced in the glass, steel, and major manufacturing industries. Their increasing clout was evident in the hotly contested campaign of 1936, when they helped return Neely to the Senate and thwarted the ambitions of the maverick Democrat Rush Dew Holt. The unions' influence reached fruition in 1940 when they played a key role in helping the liberals defeat the State House faction in the Democratic primaries and then in electing Neely as governor of West Virginia. Still, Neely faced conservative legislators in his own party who prevented him from totally reorienting state politics. A bitter conflict between the CIO and the AFL made the situation worse by dividing the labor movement, one key source of Neely's support.[50]

For the UMW, the most powerful union in the state, federal and state legislation improved its members' economic position. Although many historians and economists have judged the New Deal policies a failure in solving the long-term problems of the coal industry, the short-term benefits in West Virginia were substantial. By 1940, coal mining was employing a larger share of the state's workforce than in 1930 (from 19 percent to 20.4 percent), and paying good wages. The same was not true for manufacturing, which declined from 23.4 percent of the state's labor force in 1930 to 17.6 percent a decade later. Investment in the coal industry did not attract, and possibly discouraged, investment in value-added manufacturing. The state continued to suffer from low labor participation rates, a poorly differentiated occupational structure, and underfunded public services and schools that might have provided opportunities for economic development.[51] When the coal industry finally declined in the 1950s, the state was ill prepared to adapt.

The glass industry, which had once seemed so promising as a way to help diversify the state's political economy, was unequal to the task. Employment and investment in glass manufacturing stopped growing in the 1920s. The industry's share of manufacturing capital invested declined from 5.1 percent in 1909 to 2.6 percent by 1948, despite the enormous advances in mechanization. Furthermore, wages in the industry did not keep pace. Finally, even the glass factories that survived were increasingly owned by absentee corporations that had no more interest in the state's political economy than did the more famous coal, oil, and gas companies. The restructuring of the glass industry in the post–World War II era would resemble the "capital moves" so ably described by scholars like Jefferson Cowie, Barry Bluestone, and Bennett Harrison.[52]

Conclusion

Like Lilburn Jay, whose story opened this chapter, West Virginia once dreamed of a different future. The state had abundant natural resources that might have enabled it to join the great manufacturing belt of the North rather than remaining tied to the backward and dependent economic periphery of Appalachia and the South. The state could not compete with the well-established centers of steel production by the 1890s, but a restructuring of glass manufacturing held out promise. The industry needed natural gas, which was available and plentiful in West Virginia; it needed skilled craftsmen, who were concentrated in nearby Pennsylvania; and it needed local boosters, who would welcome factories and high-wage, unionized workers to their communities. In the 1890s, the state had all three. Indeed, some entrepreneurs believed that glass manufacturing might be only the first of many industries that would follow. Factories that added value to the state's resources and diversified its occupational structure would be beneficial to its future economic development.

For a generation, glass manufacturing fulfilled much of its promise. Particularly along the Ohio River and in the upper Monongahela valley regions, glass factories contributed to the reshaping of the cultures and economies of towns like Moundsville, Clarksburg, and Fairmont. Local wealth increased, civil society became more vibrant and diverse, and new opportunities flourished for people in the area. These parts of West Virginia expected a future that resembled the prosperity and growth of the industrial core, not the poverty of the dependent periphery. As economic geographer Doreen Massey suggests, "new sets of relations between activities in different places, new spatial forms of social organization, new dimensions of inequality and new relations of dominance and dependence" came to characterize these towns.[53] Politics also looked different. Old elites and local political leaders, whose power had derived from control of the land and the county courthouse, now had to compete with manufacturers, developers, immigrant craftsmen, and groups of unskilled workers. A new middle class, as well as working people, ran for office, contested elections, and offered different visions of what society should be and what government should do.

But the restructuring of the glass industry was not finished, and the battle for the political economy of West Virginia was not won. By the end of World War I, large corporations controlled bottle and window manufacture. Locally owned and controlled factories went out of business as mechanized, capital-intensive production dominated those branches. Unions, which had given voice to at least a significant portion of the workforce, disappeared, and with them went some of the political muscle they had brought to the debate over the state's economic policies. In the branch of the industry where West Virginia remained strong—glass tableware—wages, product value, productivity, and the union were weak.

The coal operators, both inside and outside the state, increasingly controlled the debate over the political economy of West Virginia. In an intensely competitive industry, they sought any advantage. Freedom from the high wages and work rules of unionized miners and relief from the taxes that might be used to improve the state's public services and infrastructure were critical to their profits. They opted for a low-wage economy and limited government. Leaders of this group fought off efforts at tax reform in the early 1900s, the movement for social democracy during the World War I era, and eventually the liberalism of the New Deal. The promise that the glassworkers had generated of union wages, collectively bargained working conditions, and a political voice did not completely vanish, but their vision of West Virginia's future did not prevail. For most of the twentieth century, the state's coal producers thrived as a result. Much of the rest of the population continues to suffer the consequences.

Today, little glass manufacturing remains in the state. Yet another round of industry restructuring has nearly eliminated the flat-glass and container branches, although several tableware and art-glass factories continue to operate. They are a small part of what once was the state's largest manufacturing industry, although the shells of old buildings and the furnace smokestacks can still be seen—in places where it is difficult to imagine that scores of French, Belgian, German, and English craftsmen once dominated the community and were a critical part of a development faith.

NOTE ON SOURCES

In a sense, this is really two projects; one concerns the restructuring of the glass industry between 1890 and the 1920s, and the other is the story of the possibilities of reshaping the political economy of West Virginia—possibilities that emerged and failed during that period—told through case studies of three towns that had dreams of creating a diversified industrial society. The sources, as well as the projects themselves, inevitably overlapped, since they were so intertwined. Since I have provided complete citations in the notes, this note will only survey the most useful primary sources in the development of my arguments.

For the glass industry restructuring, the two weekly journals provided the most essential material. The *National Glass Budget*, representing the opinions of the manufacturers, and the *Commoner and Glassworker*, which was the voice of the skilled workers in the industry, offered a wealth of insights about the markets, the technologies, the labor situations, the corporate strategies, and the political environments that transformed glass manufacturing during this crucial period. Both weeklies also illuminated the human costs (in addition to the triumphs) of industrial restructuring, the missing pieces in the otherwise excellent studies completed now more than a half-century ago. Finally, both of these weeklies attest to the global context of the labor movement, technology transfer, managerial initiatives, and markets that caused and shaped the restructuring of the industry. Reading either weekly, one can easily see that the fate of a German or Belgian immigrant in a small West Virginia town involved factors in Europe and the Americas, and those immigrants were keenly aware of that fact.

I have to admit to a strange pastime, relishing the published volumes of the U.S. Census Bureau, especially those from 1860 through the 1920s. The volumes covering population, religion, and manufacturing are virtual treasure troves of fascinating information concerning the stuff of labor and social history. For the glass industry, the decennial compilations, starting with Joseph D. Weeks's unparalleled *Report on the Manufacture of Glass*, in United States Census Bureau, *Tenth Census (1880): Report on the Manufactures* (Washington, D.C.: Government Printing Office, 1883) made my job of charting changes in the size of factories, the composition of the workforce, the productivity and earnings of the workers, and the capital investment in the industry much easier than it might have been. Useful insights into the thinking of manufacturers and union leaders can be gleaned from reading testimonies in the nineteen-volume *Report on the Relations and Conditions of Capital and Labor Employed in Manufacturers and General Business,* produced by the U.S. Industrial Commission (Washington, D.C.: Government Printing Office, 1901), especially vol. 7, and by U.S. labor commissioner Carroll D. Wright's special report, *Regulation and Restriction of Output: Eleventh Special Report of the Commissioner of Labor* (Washington, D.C.: Government Printing Office, 1904). My conclusions about the changing ethnic makeup of the glass industry workforce relied heavily on the excellent volumes published by the U.S. Immigration Commission, especially *Reports: Immigrants in Industries,* pt. 12, *Glass Manufacturing* (Washington, D.C.: Government Printing Office, 1911). Work in the Census Bureau's manuscript census schedules for Harrison, Marion, and Marshall counties in West Virginia (1900, 1910, 1920)—held at the West Virginia and Regional History Collection (WVRHC), in the West Virginia University Libraries—confirmed those insights. Two dissertations, Richard John O'Connor, "Cinderheads and Iron Lungs: Window-Glass Craftsmen and the Transformation of Workers' Control, 1880–1905" (University of Pittsburgh, 1991), and Dennis Michael Zembala, "Machines in the Glasshouse: The Transformation of Work in the Glass Industry, 1820–1915" (George Washington University, 1984), greatly facilitated my reconstruction of the restructuring of glass manufacturing.

My work on the political economy of West Virginia involved more manuscript research and reading of newspapers. For my overview, the papers of politicians certainly laid bare many of their assumptions and strategies. Particularly useful were the papers of Stephen B. Elkins, Nathan Goff Jr., John W. Mason, A. Brooks Fleming, and Albert B. White, all in the WVRHC. The WVRHC also has a terrific collection of reports from state agencies, including the West Virginia Bureau of Mines, the West Virginia Department (or Bureau) of Labor (cited throughout as the Department of Labor's *Biennial Reports,* for convenience, and the West Virginia commissioner of banking. Critical to my overview were two dissertations, Richard Mark Simon, "The Development of Underdevelopment: The Coal Industry and Its Effect on the West Virginia Economy, 1880–1930" (University of Pittsburgh, 1978), and Michael E. Workman, "Political Culture and the Coal Economy: 1776–1933" (West Virginia University, 1995).

My case study of Moundsville benefited from the records of Local 10 of the AFGWU (at the WVRHC), which are relatively complete and include rich minutes of meetings beginning in 1891. Also useful were notes on reminiscences of several former workers at the Fostoria Glass Company given to me by Paul Myers, the business agent of the AFGWU and a former Fostoria glassblower himself. To follow political and social developments in the town, I used the *Moundsville Echo,* the *Moundsville Journal,* and the Socialist newspaper the *Wheeling Majority.* The manuscript census schedules of Marshall County for 1900, 1910, and 1920 provided snapshots of Fostoria's workforce.

For Clarksburg, the papers of Nathan Goff Jr., Matthew S. Holt (in the Rush D. Holt collection) and Harvey Harmer (all in WVRHC) illuminated key political developments. The Joseph Slight Papers at the Ohio Historical Society (available on microfilm) are essential to understanding Local Assembly 300 of the Knights of Labor and the National Window Glass Workers. What a terrific source for understanding the craftsman's empire! The *Clarksburg Telegram*, the *Salem Express*, and the *Clarksburg News* were essential for town life and politics, and the *National*, the monthly organ of the National Window Glass Workers, helped clarify the World War I era. The manuscript census schedules for Harrison County (1900–20) first demonstrated to me the size of the Francophone neighborhood in Clarksburg. Finally, the records of the National Window Glass Workers are available in the records of a successor organization, the Window Glass Cutters League of America (WVRHC).

Since Fairmont had a far less significant union presence, there was less to draw on for the union scene. The Hulett Nestor Papers (WVRHC), however, offered some insights into a vibrant labor movement. The papers of A. B. Fleming are very rich on local coal operators' flirtation with a manufacturing base, followed by a rigid emphasis on the imperatives of a low-wage coal export economy. The *Fairmont Free Press* or *Farmer's Free Press*, the *Fairmont Times*, and the *Fairmont Index* illuminate daily life and politics in the town, and manuscript census schedules are especially useful for charting the impact of mass-production technologies on workforce composition. Finally, the scrapbooks of Matthew M. Neely (WVRHC) chronicle the rise of a fascinating state political figure.

Following the glass industry into the depression decade meant returning to U.S. Census Bureau and West Virginia Department of Labor publications. However, the papers of Branch 507 of the AFGWU, the records of Local 2 of the Federation of Flat Glass Workers, and the Hulett Nestor Papers (all in WVRHC) enabled glimpses into the difficult transition from craft to industrial unionism that characterized all three towns.

NOTES

Abbreviations

AFGWU	American Flint Glass Workers Union
FFGW	Federation of Flat Glass Workers
LA 300	Local Assembly 300, Knights of Labor
Mss. Census	U.S. Census Bureau, manuscript census schedules for Harrison, Marion, and Marshall counties, West Virginia (1900, 1910, 1920), WVRHC
NWGW	National Window Glass Workers
Slight Papers	Joseph Slight Papers (microfilm), Ohio Historical Society, Columbus
USCB	U.S. Census Bureau
USCL	U.S. Commissioner of Labor
USIC	U.S. Immigration Commission
WGCLA	Window Glass Cutters League of America
WVDL	West Virginia Department of Labor
WVRHC	West Virginia and Regional History Collection, West Virginia University, Morgantown, West Virginia

Introduction

1. *Commoner and Glassworker,* Oct. 2, 1909, 3.

2. Richard Peet, "The Geography of Class Struggle and the Relocation of United States Manufacturing Industry," in Peet, ed., *International Capitalism and Industrial Restructuring: A Critical Analysis* (Boston: Allen and Unwin, 1987), 47.

3. Richard Franklin Bensel, *The Political Economy of American Industrialization, 1877–1900* (New York: Cambridge University Press, 2000), 27.

4. Doreen Massey, *Spatial Divisions of Labor: Social Structures and the Geography of Production,* 2d ed. (New York: Routledge, 1995), 3.

5. Michael Storper and Richard Walker, *The Capitalist Imperative: Territory, Technology, and Industrial Growth* (New York: Blackwell, 1989), 91; Peet, *International Capitalism,* 47.

6. See the tables in Pearce Davis, *The Development of the American Glass Industry* (Cambridge, Mass.: Harvard University Press, 1949), 280–93; and table 1.2 here.

7. Warren C. Scoville, *Revolution in Glassmaking: Entrepreneurship and Technological Change in the American Industry, 1880–1920* (Cambridge, Mass.: Harvard University Press, 1948).

8. Testimony of Henry Clay Fry, in U.S. Industrial Commission, *Report on the Relations and Conditions of Capital and Labor* (Washington, D.C.: Government Printing Office, 1901), 7:896.

9. Jefferson Cowie, *Capital Moves: RCA's Seventy-Year Quest for Cheap Labor* (Ithaca, N.Y.: Cornell University Press, 1999); John Bradbury, "The Social and Economic Imperatives of Restructuring: A Geographic Perspective," in Audrey Kobayashi and Suzanne Mackenzie, eds., *Remaking Human Geography* (Boston: Unwin Hyman, 1989), 25.

10. Massey, *Spatial Divisions of Labor*, 3.

11. Davis, *Development*, vii; Scoville, *Revolution*, vii–viii.

12. Peet, "Geography of Class Struggle," 43.

13. Cowie, *Capital Moves*, 4–6, has extended the debate on deindustrialization, but I would add that even this argument understates the movements associated with capitalist production. Scholars like Dirk Hoerder note the importance of "labor migrations" long before factories began moving to new locations. See Hoerder, *Cultures in Contact: World Migrations in the Second Millenium* (Durham, N.C.: Duke University Press, 2002).

14. John Alexander Williams, "The New Dominion and the Old: Ante-Bellum and Statehood Politics as the Background of West Virginia's 'Bourbon Democracy,'" *West Virginia History* 33 (July 1972): 329–42; Dwight B. Billings and Kathleen M. Blee, *The Road to Poverty: The Making of Wealth and Hardship in Appalachia* (New York: Cambridge University Press, 2000), 131–33.

15. Paul Salstrom, *Appalachia's Path to Dependency: Rethinking a Region's Economic History, 1730–1940* (Lexington: University Press of Kentucky, 1994), chap. 2.

16. Helen Matthews Lewis, Linda Johnson, and Donald Askins, eds., *Colonialism in Modern America: The Appalachian Case* (Boone, N.C.: Appalachian Consortium Press, 1978); Ronald D. Eller, *Miners, Millhands, and Mountaineers: Industrialization of the Appalachian South, 1880–1930* (Knoxville: University of Tennessee Press, 1982); John Alexander Williams, *West Virginia and the Captains of Industry* (Morgantown: West Virginia University Library, 1976), 1–16.

17. For the earlier intrusion of a market economy into Appalachia, see the essays in Mary Beth Pudup, Dwight B. Billings, and Altina L. Waller, eds., *Appalachia in the Making: The Mountain South in the Nineteenth Century* (Chapel Hill: University of North Carolina Press, 1995). For the ethnic diversity of the region, see Ken Fones-Wolf and Ronald L. Lewis, eds., *Transnational West Virginia: Ethnic Communities and Economic Change, 1840–1940* (Morgantown: West Virginia University Press, 2002).

18. John Alexander Williams, "Appalachia as Colony and as Periphery: A Review Essay," *Appalachian Journal* 6 (winter 1979): 161. An excellent overview and critique of this literature is in Michael E. Workman, "Political Culture and the Coal Economy in the Upper Monongahela Region, 1776–1933" (Ph.D. diss., West Virginia University, 1995), chap. 1.

19. David S. Walls, "Internal Colony or Internal Periphery? A Critique of Current Models and an Alternative Formulation," in Lewis, Johnson, and Askins, *Colonialism in Modern America*, 319–49; Salstrom, *Appalachia's Path*; Richard M. Simon, "The Development of Underdevelopment: The Coal Industry and Its Effect on the West Virginia Economy, 1880–1930" (Ph.D. diss., University of Pittsburgh, 1978); Ronald L. Lewis, *Transforming the Appalachian Countryside:*

Railroads, Deforestation, and Social Change in West Virginia, 1880–1920 (Chapel Hill: University of North Carolina Press, 1998).

20. Storper and Walker, *The Capitalist Imperative,* 123.

21. Bensel, *Political Economy of American Industrialization,* 49–51. Bensel's discussion of the politics of uneven economic development in the United States was critical to my analysis.

22. Williams, *Captains of Industry,* 17–18.

23. Bensel's emphasis on the importance of these differences is exceptional; see his *Political Economy of American Industrialization,* 506–9.

24. Cowie, *Capital Moves,* 6; Massey, *Spatial Divisions of Labor,* 3.

25. The phrase "regulatory unionism" comes from the insightful work of Colin Gordon. See his *New Deals: Business, Labor, and Politics in America, 1920–1935* (New York: Cambridge University Press, 1994), 110–13.

26. Workman, in "Political Culture," makes a strong case for the importance of these indigenous operators in rethinking the political economy of the state.

27. Even the Owens-Illinois factories in Fairmont and Clarksburg considered relocating because of the problems that flooding and strong winds posed for furnaces. Scoville, *Revolution,* 296.

Chapter 1: The Emergence and Crisis of the Dual Monopoly

1. U.S. Industrial Commission, *Report on the Relations and Conditions of Capital and Labor Employed in Manufactures and General Business,* 19 vols. (Washington, D.C.: Government Printing Office, 1901), 7:102. See also "Digest," 7:166–69.

2. U.S. Industrial Commission, *Report,* 7:46 (Campbell), 107–11 (Hays), 832–37 and 900–901 (National Glass Company executives), and 933–34 (Kunzler).

3. The phrase "bilateral monopoly" comes from Pearce Davis, *The Development of the American Glass Industry* (Cambridge, Mass.: Harvard University Press, 1949), 126. For the 1880s, see USCB, *Eleventh Census (1890): Report on Manufacturing Industries,* pt. 3 (Washington, D.C.: Government Printing Office, 1895), 313.

4. USCB, *Manufactures 1905,* pt. 3, *Special Reports on Selected Industries* (Washington, D.C.: Government Printing Office, 1908), 840.

5. Davis, *Development,* 27–35; Dennis Michael Zembala, "Machines in the Glasshouse: The Transformation of Work in the Glass Industry, 1820–1915" (Ph.D. diss., George Washington University, 1984), 33–56.

6. Warren C. Scoville, *Revolution in Glassmaking: Entrepreneurship and Technological Change in the American Industry, 1880–1920* (Cambridge, Mass.: Harvard University Press, 1948), 9–13.

7. Zembala, "Machines," 57.

8. Davis, *Development,* 98–117, 133–39. Discussion of the importance of the tariff in American political debate during industrialization is in Richard Franklin Bensel, *The Political Economy of American Industrialization, 1877–1900* (New York: Cambridge University Press, 2000), 458–68.

9. *American Pottery and Glassware Reporter,* May 15, 1879, as quoted in Zembala, "Machines," 103. See also Davis, *Development,* 116–17; Zembala, "Machines," 85–110.

10. Joseph D. Weeks, *Report on the Manufacture of Glass*, in USCB, *Tenth Census (1880): Report on the Manufactures* (Washington, D.C.: Government Printing Office, 1883), 11; Scoville, *Revolution*, 23–29, 39–43. For a theoretical analysis of how industries produce regions, see Michael Storper and Richard Walker, *The Capitalist Imperative: Territory, Technology and Industrial Growth* (Oxford: Blackwell, 1989), 70–98.

11. U.S. Industrial Commission, *Report*, 7:896; Scoville, *Revolution*, 28–29. For the geography of uneven industrialization in the United States, see Bensel, *Political Economy*, chap. 2.

12. Weeks, *Report*, 8; Zembala, "Machines," 85–110.

13. *Hunt's Merchants Magazine and Commercial Review*, Oct. 1846, 418, quoted in Davis, *Development*, 84.

14. Deming Jarves quoted in Scoville, *Revolution*, 38.

15. Thompson quoted in U.S. Industrial Commission, *Report*, 7:833, *National Glass Budget*, Aug. 10, 1901, 1. For the experiments in the use of lime, see Davis, *Development*, 152–56.

16. Weeks, *Report*, 7.

17. Davis, *Development*, 156–57; Thomas W. Rowe and Harry H. Cook, *History of the American Flint Glass Workers' Union of North America, 1878–1957* (Toledo: AFGWU, [1957]), 5–9.

18. Rowe and Cook, *History*, 10–12.

19. Carroll D. Wright, *Regulation and Restriction of Output: Eleventh Special Report of the Commissioner of Labor* (Washington, D.C.: Government Printing Office, 1904), 624–27.

20. Ken Fones-Wolf, "Work, Culture and Politics in Industrializing West Virginia: The Glassworkers of Clarksburg and Moundsville, 1891–1919," *West Virginia History* 58 (1999–2000): 2–4.

21. Rowe and Cook, *History*, 13–19.

22. Davis, *Development*, 159–64.

23. Drawn from Weeks, *Report*, 14; USCB, *Eleventh Census (1890): Manufacturing*, pt. 3, 332–33; USCB, *Manufactures 1905*, pt. 3, 848–49.

24. USCB, *Eleventh Census (1890): Manufacturing*, pt. 3, 314, 332–33.

25. USCB, *Manufactures 1905*, pt. 3, 848–49; testimony of Henry Clay Fry, in U.S. Industrial Commission, *Report*, 7:896; Davis, *Development*, 293.

26. Testimony of John Kunzler, AFGWU president, in U.S. Industrial Commission, *Report*, 7:933–34; Rowe and Cook, *History*, 30–38.

27. Rowe and Cook, *History*, 38; *National Glass Budget*, June 17, 1899, 1; Davis, *Development*, 229–39. An excellent description of restructuring that helps provide a framework for this analysis is in John Bradbury, "The Social and Economic Imperatives of Restructuring: A Geographic Perspective," in Audrey Kobayaski and Suzanne Mackenzie, eds., *Remaking Human Geography* (Boston: Unwin Hyman, 1989), 21–39.

28. USCB, *Manufactures 1905*, pt. 3, 848.

29. See debates, *Commoner and Glassworker*, Oct. 28, 1899, 1, and the rejoinder, Nov. 4, 1899, 12.

30. USCB, *Manufactures 1905*, pt. 3, 848.

31. Hugh D. Hindman, *Child Labor: An American History* (London: Sharpe, 2002), chap. 5. For the geography of protective legislation, see Elizabeth S. Cle-

mens, *The People's Lobby: Organizational Innovation and the Rise of Interest Group Politics in the United States, 1890–1925* (Chicago: University of Chicago Press, 1997), 76.

32. *National Glass Budget,* Jan. 3, 1903, 6. Also see *Commoner and Glass-worker,* Oct. 9, 1897, 16; and testimony of John Kunzler, U.S. Industrial Commission, *Report,* 7:937.

33. USIC, *Reports: Immigrants in Industries* (Washington, D.C.: Government Printing Office, 1911), pt. 12, *Glass Manufacturing,* 51.

34. Testimony of Kunzler, Fry, and Addison Thompson (secretary, National Glass Company), all in U.S. Industrial Commission, *Report,* 7:829–35, 895–903, and 931–38; USCB, *Manufactures 1905,* pt. 3, 848–49.

35. See, especially, David Montgomery, *The Fall of the House of Labor: The Workplace, the State, and American Labor Activism, 1865–1925* (New York: Cambridge University Press, 1987), 261–65.

36. Fry testimony in U.S. Industrial Commission, *Report,* 7:898–99.

37. This struggle had much to do with the development in the 1830s of clear flint bottles, which began to substitute for the common "green" or amber metal used for bottles.

38. Zembala, "Machines," 90. Davis, *Development,* 141–42, sees the process differently, arguing that they maintained their skill.

39. Davis, *Development,* 142–43; Wright, *Regulation of Output,* 632.

40. Lee W. Minton, *Flame and Heart: A History of the Glass Bottle Blowers Association of the United States and Canada* (n.p.: Glass Bottle Blowers Association, 1961), 6–18; Scoville, *Revolution,* 200–201.

41. Weeks, *Report,* 14; Scoville, *Revolution,* 12, 201.

42. Davis, *Development,* 145–46; Minton, *Flame and Heart,* 13–18.

43. Wright, *Regulation of Output,* 633–34.

44. USCB, *Eleventh Census (1890): Manufacturing,* pt. 3, 314, 336–37.

45. Hays testimony in U.S. Industrial Commission, *Report,* 7:107.

46. Wright, *Regulation of Output,*635.

47. Minton, *Flame and Heart,* 19–31; Scoville, *Revolution,* 151–54.

48. *National Glass Budget,* June 25, 1898, 1; Scoville, *Revolution,* 178–79.

49. *National Glass Budget,* May 20, 1899, 1.

50. Minton, *Flame and Heart,* 27–31; USCB, *Manufactures 1905,* pt. 3, 848–49.

51. Hays testimony in U.S. Industrial Commission, *Report,* 7:102–12; USCB, *Manufactures 1905,* pt. 3, 848.

52. Statement of Belle Vernon manufacturer Robert Schmertz, quoted in Richard John O'Connor, "Cinderheads and Iron Lungs: Window-Glass Craftsmen and the Transformation of Workers' Control, 1880–1905" (Ph.D. diss., University of Pittsburgh, 1991), 31–32.

53. This description relies heavily on Zembala, "Machines," 40–41; and O'Connor, "Cinderheads," 15–16.

54. Davis, *Development,* 118–39; O'Connor, "Cinderheads," 29–31; Weeks, *Report,* 14.

55. LA 300, Minutes, Aug. 17, 1879, Dec. 30, 1881, in Slight Papers, reel 1; Norman J. Ware, *The Labor Movement in the United States 1860–1895: A Study in Democracy* (New York: Vintage Books, 1964), 160.

56. O'Connor, "Cinderheads," chap. 2; David Montgomery, *Workers' Control in America: Studies in the History of Work, Technology and Labor Struggles* (New York: Cambridge University Press, 1979), pp. 15–16; Wright, *Regulation of Output,* 600–624.

57. Testimony of James Campbell (former president of LA 300), in U.S. Industrial Commission, *Report,* 7:44; Ken Fones-Wolf, "Immigrants, Labor and Capital in a Transnational Context: Belgian Glass Workers in America, 1880–1925," *Journal of American Ethnic History* 21 (winter 2002): 63.

58. Wright, *Regulation of Output,* 600–601; Davis, *Development,* 126–32; O'Connor, "Cinderheads," chap. 2; Scoville, *Revolution,* 12.

59. The four crafts were not evenly distributed. Gatherers and blowers made up about 75 percent of the members; flatteners generally numbered about 1 for every 4 blowers, and cutters 1 for every 3 blowers. Wright, *Regulation of Output,* 607.

60. Richard O'Connor, "Technology and Union Fragmentation in American Window Glass, 1880–1920" (unpublished paper, in my possession, 1991), 4–5.

61. R. A. Parkin, *The Window Glass Makers of St. Helens* (Sheffield, England: Society of Glass Technology, 2000), 40–48.

62. LA 300, Minutes, Apr. 19, 1889, Slight Papers, reel 7; O'Connor, "Cinderheads," 175.

63. O'Connor, "Cinderheads," chaps. 3–4; testimony of James Campbell and A. M. Hammett (WGCLA), U.S. Industrial Commission, *Report,* 7:46, 922–25.

64. O'Connor, "Cinderheads," 223; O'Connor, "Technology and Union Fragmentation"; E. H. Gillot, *A History of Trade Unions in the Window Glass Industry* (Columbus, Ohio, 1943); Scoville, *Revolution,* 315.

65. *National Glass Budget,* Nov. 11, 1899, 1; May 26, 1900, 15; June 16, 1900, 1.

66. USCB, *Manufactures 1905,* pt. 3, pp. 844–45. Unfortunately, the census tables figure wages on the average number of workers employed during the year, which seriously understates the total number of workers in the industry when plants are not operating for six months. Although the number of firms in building glass (window and plate firms) grew by 24 percent during the 1890s, the "average" number of workers reported in the census declined from 11,982 to 11,902. My estimate, based on LA 300 membership, suggests that there would have been about 11,800 workers in window glass alone, and perhaps another 4,500 in plate glass. If this is correct, average wages in building glass in 1900 would not be $759 but $590.

67. Zembala, "Machines," 67–72.

68. On Pittsburgh, see O'Connor, "Cinderheads," chaps. 2–3.

69. *National Glass Budget,* Apr. 6, 1901, 5, Feb. 27, 1904, 1; *Commoner and Glassworker,* Dec. 23, 1899, 3; Oct. 13, 1900, 6; O'Connor, "Cinderheads," 161–62.

70. Scoville, *Revolution,* chap. 4. Owens remained sympathetic to unions in principle, but not in practice, throughout his career, see 215–16.

71. The elaboration of these changes is presented in detail in Zembala, "Machines," chap. 3.

72. Testimony of Thompson and Fry, in U.S. Industrial Commission, *Report,*

7:838, 895; *Commoner and Glassworker*, Dec. 25, 1897, 16; *National Glass Budget*, Nov. 10, 1906, 1.

73. Fry testimony, in U.S. Industrial Commission, *Report*, 7:899.

74. In 1898, the industry journal claimed that trusts were "a necessity" for the survival of the industry, but just a year later it denounced the window-glass union as a devious "trust." See *National Glass Budget*, Dec. 10, 1898, 1, Sept. 30, 1899, 4.

75. Scoville, *Revolution*, vii; Zembala, "Machines," 23–27.

Chapter 2: Workers and the Revolution in Glassmaking

1. The portrait of Jeannette comes from USIC, *Reports: Immigrants in Industries*, pt. 12, *Glass Manufacturing* (Washington, D.C.: Government Printing Office, 1911), 33–34 (hereafter cited as USIC, *Glass Manufacturing*). See also Richard O'Connor, "Technology and Union Fragmentation in American Window Glass, 1880–1900" (unpublished paper in my possession, 1991).

2. There has been a flood of important new work analyzing the transnational spaces forged by workers in the great labor migrations of the nineteenth and twentieth centuries. The most important is Dirk Hoerder's magisterial *Cultures in Contact: World Migrations in the Second Millennium* (Durham, N.C.: Duke University Press, 2002). While much of this work explores the contemporary scene, an excellent overview of the historical roots is provided in Ewa Morawska, "Immigrants, Transnationalism, and Ethnicization: A Comparison of This Great Wave and the Last," in Gary Gerstle and John Mollenkopf, eds., *E Pluribus Unum? Contemporary and Historical Perspectives on Immigrant Political Incorporation* (New York: Russell Sage Foundation, 2001).

3. Pearce Davis, *The Development of the American Glass Industry* (Cambridge, Mass.: Harvard University Press, 1949), chaps. 8–10; Warren Scoville, *Revolution in Glassmaking: Entrepreneurship and Technological Change in the American Industry, 1880–1920* (Cambridge, Mass.: Harvard University Press, 1948), chaps. 6–8.

4. USCB, *Manufactures 1905*, pt. 3, *Special Reports on Selected Industries* (Washington, D.C.: Government Printing Office, 1908), 837. For opposition to women in the industry, see the debates in the *Commoner and Glassworker*, Oct. 28, 1899, 1, and Nov. 4, 1899, 12.

5. USIC, *Glass Manufacturing*, 16–25, 65–69. For a brilliant overview of the transatlantic labor migrations, see Dirk Hoerder, "An Introduction to Labor Migration in the Atlantic Economies, 1815–1914," in Hoerder, ed., *Labor Migration in the Atlantic Economies: The European and North American Working Classes During the Period of Industrialization* (Westport, Conn.: Greenwood Press, 1985), 3–31.

6. For example, the plant superintendent of the newly mechanized factory at New Eagle, Pennsylvania, told investigators from the U.S. Immigration Commission that he "was opposed to using the class of immigrant labor represented by the Slovaks, Poles, and Italians." USIC, *Glass Manufacturing*, 34.

7. USIC, *Glass Manufacturing*, 18, table 10; Ken Fones-Wolf, "Work, Culture and Politics in Industrializing West Virginia: The Glassworkers of Clarksburg and

Moundsville, 1891–1919," *West Virginia History* 58 (1999–2000): 4. On the ethnic characterization of the AFGWU, see *National Glass Budget*, Aug. 31, 1904, 1.

    8. USIC, *Glass Manufacturing*, 17, table 9, 36; Davis, *Development*, 205–25.

    9. R. A. Parkin, *The Window Glass Makers of St. Helens* (Sheffield, England: Society of Glass Technology, 2000), 92–93.

    10. USIC, *Glass Manufacturing*, 16, table 8. See also the descriptions of the Jeannette pattern replicated in Arnold, Kane, New Eagle, and Charleroi, Pennsylvania, 29–36. For the best overview of the window-glass industry and its impact on the workforce, see Richard John O'Connor, "Cinderheads and Iron Lungs: Window-Glass Craftsmen and the Transformation of Workers' Control, 1880–1905" (Ph.D. diss., University of Pittsburgh, 1991).

    11. USCB, *Manufactures 1905*, pt. 3, table 2, 840–41; USIC, *Glass Manufacturing*, 23–56.

    12. USIC, *Glass Manufacturing*, 29–32.

    13. For the tramping tradition of craftsmen in both Europe and the U.S., see Jules Tygiel, "Tramping Artisans: The Case of the Carpenters in Industrial America," *Labor History* 22 (1981): 348–76; William S. Pretzer, "Tramp Printers: Craft Culture, Trade Unions and Technology," *Printing History* 12 (1984): 3–6; and E. J. Hobsbawm, *Labouring Men: Studies in the History of Labour* (London: Wiedenfield and Nicholson, 1964), 41–74. A cursory read of 1890s issues of the *National Glass Budget* and *Commoner and Glassworker*, the former a weekly journal for glass manufacturers and the latter a weekly for glassworkers, shows how attuned people in the industry were to developments all over the world.

    14. Scoville, *Revolution*, 315.

    15. USCL, *Regulation and Restriction of Output: Eleventh Special Report* (Washington, D.C.: Government Printing Office, 1904), 599–662 (hereafter USCL, *Regulation of Output*).

    16. USCL, *Regulation of Output*, 43, 61–62.

    17. USCL, *Regulation of Output*, 66–69, 73.

    18. USCL, *Regulation of Output*, 113. For a classic description of unskilled immigrant labor, see Michael J. Piore, *Birds of Passage: Migrant Labor and Industrial Societies* (New York: Cambridge University Press, 1979).

    19. According to USIC, *Glass Manufacturing*, 75, table 49, the average annual income for Italian households was $549, for Slovaks $648, and for Poles $752. Information on persons per room is available in table 67, p. 93.

    20. USIC, *Glass Manufacture*, 149, 183–87. Although the community is not named in the study, it appears to be Charleroi, Pennsylvania (40 miles south of Pittsburgh on the Monongahela River).

    21. For the strategies of unskilled workers in other industries in southwestern Pennsylvania, see John Bodnar, *Workers' World: Kinship, Community, and Protest in an Industrial Society, 1900–1940* (Baltimore: Johns Hopkins University Press, 1982); Mildred Allen Beik, *The Miners of Windber: The Struggles of New Immigrants for Unionization, 1890s–1930s* (University Park: Pennsylvania State University Press, 1996); John Bodnar, *Steelton: Immigration and Industrialization, 1870–1940* (Pittsburgh: University of Pittsburgh Press, 1977).

    22. USIC, *Glass Manufacturing*, 29–30.

    23. USIC, *Glass Manufacturing*, 66–68.

    24. Davis, *Development*, 218; USIC, *Glass Manufacturing*, 73.

25. USIC, *Glass Manufacturing*, 75, 81, 83, 85.

26. Much of this discussion of snappers relies on the excellent work of O'Connor, "Cinderheads," 172–83.

27. *Commoner and Glassworker*, June 9, 1900, as quoted in O'Connor, "Cinderheads," 177.

28. *National Glass Budget*, June 16, 1900; *Commoner and Glassworker*, Oct. 14, 1905, both quoted in O'Connor, "Cinderheads," 177–78.

29. The later efforts to gain admittance to the National Window Glass Workers is discussed in Ken Fones-Wolf, "From Craft to Industrial Unionism in the Window-Glass Industry: Clarksburg, West Virginia, 1900–1937," *Labor History* 37 (winter 1995–96): 35.

30. Robert S. Lynd and Helen Merrell Lynd, *Middletown: A Study in Modern American Culture* (New York: Harcourt, Brace and World, 1956), 51–52.

31. A sampling of these pictures is in *Lewis W. Hine: Children at Work*, edited by Vicki Goldberg (New York: Prestel, 1999), 78–85.

32. U.S. Industrial Commission, *Report on the Relations and Conditions of Capital and Labor Employed in Manufactures and General Business* (Washington, D.C.: Government Printing Office, 1901), 7:110, 835.

33. Walter I. Trattner, *Crusade for the Children: A History of the National Child Labor Committee and Child Labor Reform in America* (Chicago: Quadrangle Books, 1970), 77. See also Hugh D. Hindman, *Child Labor: An American History* (London: Sharpe, 2002), 121–51.

34. *National Glass Budget*, Jan. 21, 1905, 1.

35. Fones-Wolf, "Work, Culture and Politics," 11; *National Glass Budget*, Mar. 18, 1899, 1, Apr. 8, 1899, 1.

36. USIC, *Glass Manufacturing*, 275–77; Trattner, *Crusade for the Children*, 78; *National Glass Budget*, Feb. 8, 1911, 6.

37. Quoted in Trattner, *Crusade for the Children*, 78.

38. *National Glass Budget*, Jan. 21, 1905, 1; Scoville, *Revolution*, 321; USIC, *Glass Manufacturing*, 329.

39. Charles Forman, *Industrial Town: Self Portrait of St. Helens in the 1920s* (London: Cameron and Taylor, 1978), 15; Patricia Penn Hilden, *Women, Work, and Politics: Belgium, 1830–1914* (London: Oxford University Press, 1993), 186, 254–60.

40. *Commoner and Glassworker*, Oct. 28, 1899, 1; Nov. 4, 1899, 12.

41. USCB, *Manufactures 1905*, pt. 3, 840, 844, 848; USIC, *Glass Manufacturing*, 69, 76, 123.

42. For the sinking of *La Bourgogne* and the harrowing story of the lone glassworker survivor, Ernest Delmotte, see *National Glass Budget*, July 16, 1898, 2; Oct. 1, 1898, 1; *Commoner and Glassworker*, July 9, 1898, 1, and Aug. 20, 1898, 2.

43. *National Glass Budget*, Nov. 12, 1898, 1; Jan. 19, 1901, 1–2.

44. *Commoner and Glassworker*, Dec. 25, 1897, 16; Dec. 23, 1899, 3; Aug. 31, 1901, 1.

45. *Commoner and Glassworker*, Jan. 4, 1908, 2. For Owens's attitudes toward unions and the relationship with Rowe, see Scoville, *Revolution*, 215–16, 275–76.

46. USIC, *Glass Manufacturing*, 66–68, tables 38–40.

47. USCL, *Regulation of Output*, 634–35.

48. USIC, *Glass Manufacturing*, 75, 81, 85, 89–90, 113.

49. USIC, *Glass Manufacturing*, 130–31, 139–40.

50. For Pittsburgh, see Francis G. Couvares, *The Remaking of Pittsburgh: Class and Culture in an Industrializing City, 1877–1919* (Albany: State University of New York Press, 1984), chap. 2; and O'Connor, "Cinderheads," 57–58. For newer glass towns, see the descriptions of "representative localities" in USIC, *Glass Manufacturing*, 27–41.

51. An excellent description of this process is in Peggy Levitt, *The Transnational Villagers* (Berkeley: University of California Press, 2001), 7–9.

52. David Montgomery, *Workers' Control in America: Studies in the History of Work, Technology, and Labor Struggles* (New York: Cambridge University Press, 1979), 15–16; Fones-Wolf, "Work, Culture and Politics," 2–5; USCL, *Regulation of Output*, 637–40.

53. Fones-Wolf, "Work, Culture and Politics," 4–5; O'Connor, "Cinderheads," chap. 2.

54. O'Connor, "Cinderheads," 110–17.

55. *National Glass Budget*, June 2, 1900. For other descriptions of carnivals and festivals, see *Commoner and Glassworker*, June 2, 1900, and Sept. 7, 1901 (Matthews, Ind.); Aug. 20, 1898 (Wheeling, W.V.); June 13, 1908 (Pt. Marion, Pa.).

56. Ken Fones-Wolf, "Immigrants, Labor and Capital in a Transnational Context: Belgian Glass Workers in America, 1880–1925," *Journal of American Ethnic History* 21 (winter 2002): 71; *Commoner and Glassworker*, Nov. 25, 1899, 7.

57. *Commoner and Glassworker*, July 28, 1900, 13; Oct. 13, 1900, 15; May 21, 1910, 13–14; July 16, 1910, 13.

58. USIC, *Glass Manufacturing*, 184; *Commoner and Glassworker*, Sept. 7, 1901, 15.

59. Fones-Wolf, "Work, Culture and Politics," 8–13; Fones-Wolf, "Immigrants, Labor and Capital," 73; USIC, *Glass Manufacturing*, 183–84.

60. *National Glass Budget*, Feb. 4, 1899, 3. For the depth of this identity, see O'Connor, "Cinderheads," 110–37.

61. Lee W. Minton, *Flame and Heart: A History of the Glass Bottle Blowers Association of the United States and Canada* (n.p.: GBBA, 1961), 23–43.

62. Thomas W. Rowe and Harry H. Cook, *History of the American Flint Glass Workers' Union of North America, 1878–1957* (Toledo: AFGWU, [1957]), 31.

63. O'Connor, "Cinderheads," chap. 4.

64. *National Glass Budget*, Mar. 4, 1899, 4; June 20, 1903, 3.

65. USCL, *Regulation of Output*, 636, 648; *Commoner and Glassworker*, Jan. 1, 1898, 12.

66. *Commoner and Glassworker*, Mar. 17, 1900, 2; Mar. 16, 1901, 10.

67. Rowe and Cook, *History*, 32–33.

68. *National Glass Budget*, Jan. 4, 1902, 6.

69. *National Glass Budget*, May 16, 1903, 6. For reasons for the appeal of the protective tariff to industrial workers, see Richard Franklin Bensel, *The Political Economy of American Industrialization, 1877–1900* (New York: Cambridge University Press, 2000), 148.

70. *Commoner and Glassworker*, Oct. 13, 1900, 6 (Wellsburg); May 5, 1899, 12, and Dec. 27, 1902, 1 (Matthews, Ind.); Sept. 12, 1903, 8 (Hayes).

71. Rowe and Cook, *History*, 39, 42; *National Glass Budget*, Aug. 27, 1898, 6.

72. *Commoner and Glassworker*, Mar. 30, 1900, 14, Dec. 1, 1900, 14, July 21, 1900, 15. See also Daisy E. DeVreese, "Belgium," in *The Formation of Labour Movements, 1870–1914: An International Perspective* (Leiden: Brill, 1990), 25–55.

73. *Commoner and Glassworker*, Aug. 31, 1901, 3; Oct. 27, 1900, 1.

74. *National Glass Budget*, Nov. 11, 1898, 6; Feb. 4, 1899, 3; Jan. 26, 1901, 2; July 27, 1901, 1.

75. *National Glass Budget*, July 27, 1901, 1; June 29, 1901, 6; Sept. 28, 1901, 6; Oct. 19, 1901, 8.

76. *National Glass Budget*, Aug. 6, 1898, 1; Aug. 20, 1898, 4; Jan. 7, 1899, 4; Oct. 20, 1900, 6; Dec. 29, 1900, 6.

77. LA 300, Minutes, Mar. 11, 1899, May 5, 1899, Sept. 1, 1900, all in Slight Papers, reel 7; *National Glass Budget*, Mar. 9, 1901, 1; Sept. 28, 1901, 6; Fones-Wolf, "Immigrants, Labor and Capital," 68–69.

78. Rowe and Cook, *History*, 35, 39; *National Glass Budget*, July 25, 1903, 4; Dec. 12, 1903, 6.

79. *National Glass Budget*, Jan. 7, 1905, 1.

Chapter 3: The Development Faith and the Glass Industry

1. See, among others, David Alan Corbin, *Life, Work, and Rebellion in the Coal Fields: The Southern West Virginia Miners, 1880–1920* (Urbana: University of Illinois Press, 1981), chap. 1; Ronald L. Lewis, *Transforming the Appalachian Countryside: Railroads, Deforestation, and Social Change in West Virginia, 1880–1920* (Chapel Hill: University of North Carolina Press, 1998), chap. 2; Ronald D. Eller, *Miners, Millhands, and Mountaineers: Industrialization of the Appalachian South, 1880–1930* (Knoxville: University of Tennessee Press, 1982), chap. 2.

2. Michael E. Workman, in his thoughtful dissertation, distinguishes the north-central coal fields from the more heavily studied southern West Virginia fields, especially in regard to both local investment and a more diversified economy. See his "Political Culture and the Coal Economy in the Upper Monongahela Region, 1776–1933" (Ph.D. diss., West Virginia University, 1995), chap. 4.

3. *West Virginia State Gazetteer and Business Directory 1891–92* (Detroit: R. L. Polk, 1891), 29, included in Ronald L. Lewis and John C. Hennen Jr., *West Virginia: Documents in the History of a Rural-Industrial State* (Dubuque, Iowa: Kendall/Hunt, 1991), 156–57.

4. John Alexander Williams, "The New Dominion and the Old: Ante-bellum and Statehood Politics as the Background of West Virginia's 'Bourbon Democracy,'" *West Virginia History* 33 (July 1972): 342.

5. Ken Fones-Wolf, "Caught between Revolutions: Wheeling Germans in the Civil War Era," in Ken Fones-Wolf and Ronald L. Lewis, eds., *Transnational West Virginia: Ethnic Communities and Economic Change, 1840–1940* (Morgantown: West Virginia University Press, 2002), 20–23.

6. Gordon B. McKinney, *Southern Mountain Republicans, 1865–1900: Politics and the Appalachian Community* (Chapel Hill: University of North Carolina Press, 1978), 41–44.

7. Lewis, *Transforming the Appalachian Countryside*, especially chap. 8; Williams, "New Dominion," 352; Patrick A. Carone, "The Governor as a Legislator in West Virginia" (Ph.D. diss., Duke University, 1969), 110.

8. John Alexander Williams, *West Virginia and the Captains of Industry* (Morgantown: West Virginia University Library, 1976), 7–10.

9. Richard Franklin Bensel, *The Political Economy of American Industrialization, 1877–1900* (New York: Cambridge University Press, 2000), chap. 3.

10. Richard Mark Simon, "The Development of Underdevelopment: The Coal Industry and Its Effect on the West Virginia Economy, 1880–1930" (Ph.D. diss., University of Pittsburgh, 1978), 289.

11. Festus Summers, *Johnson Newlon Camden: A Study in Individualism* (New York: Putnam, 1937), 164, 248–49; Williams, *Captains of Industry*, 7–16.

12. Summers, *Camden*, chap. 7 (quotation, 194); Charles M. Pepper, *The Life and Times of Henry Gassaway Davis, 1823–1916* (New York: Century, 1920), 27–29, 96–103.

13. Corbin, *Life, Work, and Rebellion*, 2–4.

14. West Virginia Tax Commission, *Second Report: State Development* (Wheeling, 1884), 1–3, included in Lewis and Hennen, *West Virginia*, 158–60.

15. See, for examples, Williams, *Captains of Industry*; Eller, *Miners, Millhands, and Mountaineers*; and Helen M. Lewis and Edward E. Knipe, "The Colonialism Model: The Appalachian Case," in Helen Matthews Lewis, Linda Johnson, and Donald Askins, *Colonialism in Modern America: The Appalachian Case* (Boone, N.C.: Appalachian Consortium Press, 1978), 9–31.

16. Simon, "Development of Underdevelopment," 307–14; Workman, "Political Culture," chap. 4.

17. In addition to the sources in note 16, see the rejoinder by David Walls, "Internal Colony or Internal Periphery? A Critique of Current Models and an Alternative Formulation," in Lewis, Johnson, and Askins, *Colonialism*, 319–50.

18. Simon, "Development of Underdevelopment," 288–91.

19. Paul Salstrom, *Appalachia's Path to Dependency: Rethinking a Region's Economic History, 1730–1940* (Lexington: University Press of Kentucky, 1994), 28–33; *Appletons' Annual Cyclopaedia and Register of Important Events of the Year 1892* (New York: Appleton, 1893), 794–95; Commissioner of Banking of the State of West Virginia, *Tenth Annual Report, 1910* (Charleston, W.V.: Tribune, 1911), 6; Bensel, *Political Economy*, 62.

20. Salstrom, *Appalachia's Path to Dependency*, 29.

21. Bensel, *Political Economy*, 47–54; *Official Directory, West Virginia Democratic State Committee, with the Vote of the State* (Charleston, W.V.: M. W. Donnally, 1894), 6–22.

22. Williams, *Captains of Industry*, 7–16.

23. William A. MacCorkle, "Address to the Columbian Exposition," in *Public Papers of Governor Wm. A. MacCorkle, of West Virginia* (Charlestown, W.V.: Moses W. Donnelly, 1897), 21–34.

24. Williams, *Captains of Industry*, 17–21, 172–73. See also Jeffery B. Cook, "The Ambassador of Development: Aretas Brooks Fleming, West Virginia's Political Entrepreneur, 1839–1923" (Ph.D. diss., West Virginia University, 1998), 161–84.

25. Stanley B. Parsons, Michael J. Dubin, and Karen Toombs Parsons, *United*

States Congressional Districts, 1883–1913 (New York: Greenwood Press, 1990), 159.

26. Nathan Goff Jr. to *Toledo Blade,* Nov. 24, 1887; W. J. W. Cowden to Goff, Sept. 12, 1888, Nathan Goff Jr. Papers (hereafter Goff Papers), WVRHC, box 9.

27. There are reports of mass meetings of miners and mine laborers from Coal Valley (Feb. 6, 1888), Fayette County (Jan. 30, 1888), the Caperton mines (Jan. 23, 1888), and Stone Cliff (Jan. 25, 1888), among others, in Goff Papers, box 9. See also Wheeling Potters Protective Tariff Club to Goff, Mar. 6, 1888; and Nail City Lodge # 3, AAISW (Amalgamated Association of Iron and Steel Workers) to Goff, Mar. 13, 1888, Goff Papers, box 9. The confluence of party constituencies and party economic programs is discussed in Jeffrey A. Jenkins, Eric Schickler, and Jamie L. Carson, "Constituency Cleavages and Congressional Parties: Measuring Homogeneity and Polarization, 1857–1913," *Social Science History* 28 (winter 2004): 537–73.

28. Quotation from H. R. Riddle to William H. H. Flick, Aug. 16, 1888, cited in McKinney, *Southern Mountain Republicans,* 152. There is much information on the contest between Goff and Elkins for control of the Republican party and its patronage in 1888 in the John W. Mason Papers, WVRHC, box 2. For information on Elkins, see Williams, *Captains of Industry,* 3–7; and McKinney, *Southern Mountain Republicans,* 150–60.

29. Williams, *Captains of Industry,* 57–64.

30. S. C. Neale to Elkins, July 17, 1894, Stephen B. Elkins Papers, WVRHC, box 4. See also Elkins to H. G. Davis, Dec. 14, Dec. 19, 1893, Feb. 10, Feb. 21, 1894, Elkins Papers, box 4.

31. Henry G. Davis to H. G. Buxton, Nov. 10, 1894, cited in Williams, *Captains of Industry,* 66.

32. Nominating address of Alex R. Campbell to House of Delegates, Jan. 22, 1895, Elkins Papers, box 4.

33. Nathan B. Scott to John W. Mason, Jan. 25, 1897, A. B. White to Mason, Feb. 25, 1897, Elkins to Mason, Mar. 11, Apr. 14, 1897, all in Mason Papers, box 3; Robert E. Murphy, *Progressive West Virginians: Some of the Men Who Have Built Up and Developed the State of West Virginia* (Wheeling: Wheeling News, 1905), 1, 43.

34. Elkins to Mason, Apr. 10, Apr. 25, 1896, Mason Papers, box 3. Scott feared that McKinley's eventual election would hurt Elkins and his wing of the party. See Scott to Elkins, Dec. 5, 1896, Elkins Papers, box 4.

35. Bensel, *Political Economy,* 276–77; Carone, "Governor as Legislator," 110.

36. Simon, "Development of Underdevelopment," 287, 294; Williams, *Captains of Industry,* 59.

37. Simon, "Development of Underdevelopment," 302–6; Corbin, *Life, Work, and Rebellion,* 4–9; Joe William Trotter, *Coal, Class, and Color: Blacks in Southern West Virginia, 1915–32* (Urbana: University of Illinois Press, 1990), 16–23.

38. Workman, "Political Culture," 149–53.

39. Gibson Lamb Cranmer, *History of Wheeling City and Ohio County, West Virginia and Representative Citizens* (Chicago: Biographical, 1902), 317–23.

40. Workman, "Political Culture," chap. 4; Charles Henry Ambler, *West Virginia: The Mountain State* (New York: Prentice-Hall, 1940), 621.

41. *Commoner and Glassworker,* Dec. 25, 1897, 16, Dec. 23, 1899, 3; Williams, *Captains of Industry,* 3; Murphy, *Progressive West Virginians,* 4; Cranmer, *History of Wheeling,* 327–28.

42. See, for example, N. B. Scott to A. B. White, Nov. 7, 1902; and S. B. Elkins to White, Feb. 9, Feb. 19, 1903, all in White Papers, WVRHC, box 33, and W. J. Showalter to Elkins, Oct. 16, 1906, Elkins Papers, box 8.

43. Williams, *Captains of Industry,* 203–6, brilliantly explains the operation of the archaic tax system inherited from "colonial Virginia."

44. Nicholas Clare Burckel, "Progressive Governors in the Border States: Reform Governors of Missouri, Kentucky, West Virginia and Maryland, 1900–1918" (Ph.D. diss., University of Wisconsin, 1971), 292–97; David T. Javersak, "The Ohio Valley Trades and Labor Assembly: The Formative Years, 1882–1915" (Ph.D. diss., West Virginia University, 1977), 105–10; Williams, *Captains of Industry,* 203–4.

45. Williams, *Captains of Industry,* 220–21; Elmer Guy Hendershot, "Tax Reforms in West Virginia during the Administration of Governor Albert Blakeslee White" (master's thesis, West Virginia University, 1949), 29–40.

46. Elkins to White, Oct. 30, 1903, White Papers, box 35. See also William N. Miller to White, Oct. 9, 1903, Elkins to White, Jan. 19, 1904, and Scott to White, Jan. 22, Jan. 27, Feb. 29, 1904; all in White Papers, box 35.

47. Burckel, "Progressive Governors," 302; Williams, *Captains of Industry,* 232.

48. A. B. White, "First Biennial Message to the Legislature," in *Public Addresses of Albert Blakeslee White, A.M., Governor of West Virginia, during His Term of Office* (Charleston, W.V., 1905), 117.

49. George W. Atkinson, "The New Old Dominion," in *Public Addresses, Etc. of Geo. W. Atkinson, LL.D., D.C.L., Governor of West Virginia during His Term of Office* (Charleston, W.V., 1901), 25. Simon, "Development of Underdevelopment," chap. 11, goes into great detail on the problems that overinvestment in coal created for the development of the state's economy.

50. This description of restructuring draws on the analysis of Anne E. Mosher, *Capital's Utopia: Vandergrift, Pennsylvania, 1855–1916* (Baltimore: Johns Hopkins University Press, 2004), 4–8. For the glass industry, the relevant works are: Warren C. Scoville, *Revolution in Glassmaking: Entrepreneurship and Technological Change in the American Industry, 1880–1920* (Cambridge: Harvard University Press, 1948); and Pearce Davis, *The Development of the American Glass Industry* (Cambridge: Harvard University Press, 1949). Although neither refers to restructuring, the process they describe fits with Mosher's analysis.

51. Robert Stanley Weiner, "The Location and Distribution of the Glass Industry of Ohio, Pennsylvania and West Virginia" (master's thesis, University of Pittsburgh, 1949), 21–22, 29–35; Richard John O'Connor, "Cinderheads and Iron Lungs: Window-Glass Craftsmen and the Transformation of Workers' Control, 1880–1905" (Ph.D. diss., University of Pittsburgh, 1991), 155–67.

52. *West Virginia Geological Survey,* vol. 1, *A: Petroleum and Natural Gas Precise Levels* (Morgantown: New Dominion, 1904), 29–30.

53. Dennis Zembala, "Machines in the Glasshouse: The Transformation of Work in the Glass Industry, 1820–1915" (Ph.D. diss., George Washington University, 1984), 170–76; Gary Everett Baker, "The Flint Glass Industry in Wheeling, West Virginia: 1829–1865" (master's thesis, University of Delaware, 1986), 124.

54. *National Glass Budget,* Aug. 4, 1900, 6.

55. *Commoner and Glassworker,* July 14, 1900, 16, Dec. 23, 1899, 8.

56. USCB, *Manufactures 1905,* pt. 3, *Special Reports on Selected Industries* (Washington, D.C.: Government Printing Office, 1908), 840–41, 866–69.

57. USCB, *Manufactures 1905,* pt. 3, 840, 866.

58. Scott to White, Nov. 7, 1902, Jan. 27, 1904. For the glass industry's pride in Scott, see *Commoner and Glassworker,* May 5, 1900, 3.

59. *Commoner and Glassworker,* Feb. 10, 1900, 13; *National Glass Budget,* Dec. 10, 1910, 6; Frederick A. Barkey, *Cinderheads in the Hills: The Belgian Window Glass Workers of West Virginia* (Charleston: West Virginia Humanities Council, 1988).

60. USCB, *Fourteenth Census (1910),* vol. 4, *Population* (Washington, D.C.: Government Printing Office, 1923), 1039–42; vol. 10, *Manufactures, 1919,* 831–32.

61. Scoville, *Revolution,* 211–12, 296; *National Glass Budget,* Nov. 21, 1914, 2; Mar. 11, 1916, 14.

62. *National Glass Budget,* June 19, 1909, 8, Dec. 5, 1914, 1, Apr. 3, 1915, 1; W. J. Showalter to Elkins, Oct. 16, 1906, Elkins Papers, box 8.

63. Bensel, *Political Economy,* chap. 4; Gerald W. Johnson, "West Virginia Politics: A Socio-Cultural Analysis of Political Participation" (Ph.D. diss., University of Tennessee, 1970), 45; Evelyn L. K. Harris and Frank J. Krebs, *From Humble Beginnings: West Virginia State Federation of Labor, 1903–1957* (Charleston: West Virginia Labor History Publishing Fund, 1960), 1–6.

64. Harris and Krebs, *Humble Beginnings,* 519; Bensel, *Political Economy,* 211.

65. *West Virginia Legislative Hand Book and Manual and Official Register, 1916* (Charleston, W.V., 1916), 701–8; Johnson, "West Virginia Politics," 45.

66. Simon, "Development of Underdevelopment," 283.

Chapter 4: Moundsville

1. *Commoner and Glassworker,* Oct. 18, 1902, 10. The incorporation agreement is included in *Acts of the Legislature of West Virginia, 1889* (Charleston, W.V.: Moses W. Donnelly, 1889), 278–79.

2. On the earlier development, see Gary Everett Baker, "The Flint Glass Industry in Wheeling, West Virginia: 1829–1865" (master's thesis, University of Delaware, 1986); and Dennis Michael Zembala, "Machines in the Glasshouse: The Transformation of Work in the Glass Industry, 1820–1915" (Ph.D. diss., George Washington University, 1984), chap. 3.

3. J. H. Brantner, *Historical Collections of Moundsville, West Virginia* (Moundsville: Marshall County Historical Society, 1947), 65, 108–9, 126, 138–45; J. H. Newton, G. G. Nichols, and A. G. Sprankle, *History of the Pan-Handle; Being Historical Collections of the Counties of Ohio, Brooke, Marshall and Hancock, West Virginia* (Wheeling: J. A. Caldwell, 1879), 384–93.

4. USCB, *Tenth Census (1880): Report on the Productions of Agriculture* (Washington, D.C.: Government Printing Office, 1883), 139, 175; USCB, *Tenth Census (1880): Report on Manufactures* (Washington, D.C.: Government Printing Office, 1883), 370; *History of the Pan-Handle,* 391–92.

5. USCB, *Tenth Census (1880): Population* (Washington, D.C.: Government Printing Office, 1883), 84, 364, 445; USCB, *Tenth Census: Manufactures*, 370; Anne Kelly Knowles, "Wheeling and the Welsh: A Geographical Reading of *Life in the Iron Mills*," in Ken Fones-Wolf and Ronald L. Lewis, eds., *Transnational West Virginia: Ethnic Communities and Economic Change, 1840–1940* (Morgantown: West Virginia University Press, 2002), 218–22.

6. John Alexander Williams, *West Virginia and the Captains of Industry* (Morgantown: West Virginia University Library, 1976), 113.

7. USCB, *Eleventh Census (1890): Population* (Washington, D.C.: Government Printing Office, 1895), 355, 435, 557; USCB, *Eleventh Census (1890): Manufacturing* (Washington, D.C.: Government Printing Office, 1895), 626–27.

8. Brantner, *Historical Collections*, 73; Robert E. Murphy, *Progressive West Virginians: Some of the Men Who Have Built Up and Developed the State of West Virginia* (Wheeling: Wheeling News, 1905), 117.

9. Murphy, *Progressive West Virginians*, 21, 43, 107, 115. For Mason's importance in the state in the 1880s and early 1890s, see his correspondence, especially Stephen B. Elkins to Mason, Apr. 6, 1888, Jan. 3, 1889, Feb. 2, 1889, John W. Mason Papers, WVRHC, box 2. Unfortunately, Mason's papers do not detail his involvement with the company.

10. Zembala, "Machines in the Glasshouse," 174–76; Joseph D. Weeks, *Report on the Manufacture of Glass* (Washington, D.C.: Government Printing Office, 1883), 78–79.

11. *Commoner and Glassworker*, June 2, 1900, 12; AFGWU, Local 10, Minutes, Jan. 23, 1892, in American Flint Glass Workers Union Records, WVRHC (hereafter AFGWU Local 10 Minutes).

12. *Commoner and Glassworker*, Oct. 18, 1902, 10; Don Moore and Hazel Weatherman, *Fostoria: Its First Fifty Years* (Springfield, Mo.: Weathermans, 1972), ix–x; *Moundsville Echo*, Nov. 13, 1891, Jan. 29, 1892.

13. This information comes from the Sanborn Insurance Atlases for Moundsville, 1893 and 1898. Quotation from *Commoner and Glassworker*, Oct. 18, 1902, 10.

14. Joe Flaherty to Harry Cook, June 9, 1937, Laurell to Cook, June 10, 1937, Crow to Cook, June 6, 1937, copies in my possession, supplied by Paul Myers, former business agent of Local 10.

15. *Moundsville Echo*, Nov. 27, 1891, Jan. 22, Mar. 4, Apr. 1, 1892.

16. Mss. Census, 1900, Marshall County; interview by Paul Myers of Guy Alexander and Robert Knoll [ca. 1979], transcript in my possession, 3; *Moundsville Echo*, Feb. 26, 1892. The census manuscripts for 1900 reveal that only 9 of 97 craftsmen were homeowners. They also reveal that about 40 percent of them were born in West Virginia, most likely all of them in the northern panhandle, the only area in the state where they could have apprenticed for the trades.

17. *Moundsville Echo*, Mar. 4, Apr. 22, 1892, Apr. 28, May 5, 1893.

18. *Moundsville Echo*, Jan. 29, Sept. 16, Nov. 18, 1892, Oct. 5, 1893, Jan. 4, 1895.

19. *Moundsville Echo*, Sept. 2, 1892, Feb. 17, Sept. 15, 1893, Oct. 5, 1894.

20. AFGWU Local 10 Minutes, Jan. 7, Mar. 4, 1893, Mar. 4, 1895, Jan. 18, 1896. For the Catholic preference for the Democrats, see Richard Jensen, *The Winning of the Midwest: Social and Political Conflict, 1888–1896* (Chicago: University of

Chicago Press, 1971), and Paul Kleppner, *The Cross of Culture: A Social Analysis of Midwestern Politics* (New York: Free Press, 1970). For an analysis of the complicating factors to a strict ethnocultural politics introduced by union membership, see Julie Greene, *Pure and Simple Politics: The American Federation of Labor and Political Activism, 1881–1917* (New York: Cambridge University Press, 1998).

21. *Moundsville Echo*, Nov. 20, 1896, Jan. 4, 1895, May 13, 1904, Mar. 30, 1906; Ken Fones-Wolf, "Work, Culture and Politics in Industrializing West Virginia: The Glassworkers of Clarksburg and Moundsville, 1891–1919," *West Virginia History* 58 (1999–2000): 1–23.

22. USCB, *Eleventh Census (1890): Manufactures*, pt. 3, 314, 332–33.

23. This is covered in the testimony of AFGWU president John Kunzler, in U.S. Industrial Commission, *Report on the Conditions of Capital and Labor Employed in Manufactures and General Business*, 19 vols. (Washington, D.C.: Government Printing Office, 1901), 7:933–34; and in Thomas W. Rowe and Harry H. Cook, *History of the American Flint Glass Workers' Union of North America, 1878–1957* (Toledo: AFGWU, [1957]), 30–38.

24. AFGWU Local 10 Minutes, Sept. 30, Oct. 21, 1893, Feb. 17, Apr. 21, May 19, Sept. 1, 1894, Apr. 18, June 19, 1896.

25. AFGWU Local 10 Minutes, Apr. 15, Nov. 4, Nov. 18, 1893. The arduous process of setting the pot is described in the *National Glass Budget*, June 6, 1903, 1.

26. AFGWU Local 10 Minutes, Oct. 19, 1895, Apr. 18, May 12, June 19, July 21, 1896.

27. AFGWU Local 10 Minutes, May 22, 1897, Jan. 15, May 7, June 18, Aug. 6, Nov. 15, 1898, Feb. 4, Apr. 10, 1899.

28. U.S. Industrial Commission, *Report*, 7:933–94; *Commoner and Glassworker*, Jan. 15, 1898, 16, Oct. 13, 1900, 6; AFGWU Local 10 Minutes, Aug. 5, 1899.

29. U.S. Industrial Commission, *Report*, 7:933–94; *Commoner and Glassworker*, Oct. 27, 1900, 1.

30. Testimony of Addison Thompson and Henry Clay Fry, in U.S. Industrial Commission, *Report*, 7:828–41, 895–906.

31. *Commoner and Glassworker*, Mar. 23, 1901, 3, Apr. 6, 1901, 8; Moore and Weatherman, *Fostoria*, xiii.

32. *West Virginia State Gazetteer and Business Directory, 1900–1901* (Detroit: R. L. Polk, 1900), 342–47; *Moundsville . . . The Coming Industrial City of West Virginia* (Moundsville: Moundsville Development Co., [1904]), 6–9.

33. WVDL, *Fifth Biennial Report, 1901–2* (Charleston, W.V., 1902), 70–74; Mss. Census, 1910, Marshall County; *Moundsville Echo*, Feb. 12, 1897, Feb. 9, 1900.

34. Moore and Weatherman, *Fostoria*, xiv; John W. Kirk, *Progressive West Virginians* (Wheeling: Wheeling Intelligencer, 1923), 449. On the importance of the Pittsburgh High School's commercial program, especially for allowing young men and women to cross class barriers, see Ileen A. DeVault, *Sons and Daughters of Labor: Class and Clerical Work in Turn-of-the-Century Pittsburgh* (Ithaca, N.Y.: Cornell University Press, 1990).

35. *Moundsville Echo*, June 29, 1896; *Commoner and Glassworker*, Oct. 18, 1902, 10, Nov. 8, 1902, 3, Jan. 3, 1903, 4; *National Glass Budget*, Apr. 19, 1902, 8.

36. Moore and Weatherman, *Fostoria*, xiv; interview by Paul Myers of Howard Denoon, [ca. 1977], transcript in my possession, 15.

37. Mss. Census, 1900, 1910, 1920, Marshall County. Samples were based on 144 workers in 1900, 456 in 1910, and 234 in 1920. See also Fones-Wolf, "Work, Culture and Politics," 2–4.

38. This comes from the 456 workers included in the Mss. Census, 1910, Marshall County.

39. *Moundsville Echo*, Jan. 26, 1900, Mar. 15, 1901, June 19, 1908; *Commoner and Glassworker*, June 27, 1903, 7.

40. *Moundsville Echo*, July 3, 1896, Jan. 3, 1902, Dec. 2, 1904, Apr. 19, 1907; *Commoner and Glassworker*, Oct. 19, 1907, 12, May 30, 1908, 9, Mar. 27, 1909, 7.

41. *Commoner and Glassworker*, Dec. 5, 1908, 8; *Moundsville Echo*, Jan. 3, Jan. 17, Apr. 11, June 27, 1902, Jan. 1, 1904, Jan. 5, 1906. For religious figures, see USCB, *Religious Bodies: 1906* (Washington, D.C.: Government Printing Office, 1910), 1:369–70, and USCB, *Religious Bodies: 1916* (Washington, D.C.: Government Printing Office, 1920), 1: 325–26. The rate of growth for Marshall County was 22.5 percent; the rate of increase for members of religious bodies was 46.3 percent.

42. Jake Crimmel to Harry Cook, June 5, 1937, copy in my possession; AFGWU Local 10 Minutes, Feb. 17, 1894, June 19, 1896, Aug. 6, 1898, Feb. 14, 1902. For the importance of rituals to the Knights of Labor, see Robert Weir, *Beyond Labor's Veil: The Culture of the Knights of Labor* (University Park: Pennsylvania State University Press, 1996).

43. *National Glass Budget*, Aug. 13, 1904, 1; *Commoner and Glassworker*, July 17, 1909, 6, July 16, 1910, 6, Dec. 24, 1910, 14.

44. AFGWU Local 10 Minutes, Aug. 27, 1903, Nov. 21, 1908, Jan. 16, 1909, Jan. 22, Apr. 2, 1910; Owen Lovejoy, "Child Labor in the Glass Industry," *Annals of the American Academy of Political and Social Science* (March 1906): 35–41; Hugh Hindman, *Child Labor: An American History* (London: Sharpe, 2002), 121–51.

45. *National Glass Budget*, Jan. 3, 1903, 6; *Moundsville Echo*, Oct. 21, Dec. 2, 1904.

46. *Moundsville Echo*, Feb. 16, 1900, Dec. 23, 1904, Aug. 9, 1907.

47. *Moundsville Echo*, Apr. 1, Apr. 8, Apr. 15, 1904; *Commoner and Glassworker*, June 6, 1903, 4. The boys' strike was not even mentioned in the AFGWU Local 10 Minutes.

48. *Moundsville Echo*, Mar. 11, 1904, Nov. 8, 1907; AFGWU Local 10 Minutes, Sept. 16, 1899, Jan. 16, 1904; interview by Paul Myers of Guy Alexander and Robert Knoll, [ca. 1977], transcript in my possession. See also John William Larner Jr., "The Glass House Boys: Child Labor Conditions in Pittsburgh's Glass Factories, 1890–1917," *Western Pennsylvania Historical Magazine* 48 (Oct. 1965): 355–64.

49. AFGWU Local 10 Minutes, Sept. 16, 1899.

50. Mss. Census, 1910, Marshall County.

51. *National Glass Budget*, Aug. 13, 1904, 1, Mar. 9, 1907, 6.

52. Rowe and Cook, *History*, 41–45; *National Glass Budget*, Jan. 24, 1903, 6, July 25, 1903, 4.

53. *Commoner and Glassworker*, May 16, 1908, 12, Sept. 4, 1909, 7; *National Glass Budget*, July 29, 1905, 6, May 1, 1909, 1, Mar. 26, 1910, 1.

54. Moore and Weatherman, *Fostoria*, xv; AFGWU Local 10 Minutes, Dec. 6, 1902, Jan. 2, Dec. 10, 1904, Oct. 7, 1905; *Moundsville Echo*, Jan. 3, 1902, Feb. 20, 1903, Apr. 1, Apr. 8, 1904. See also Fones-Wolf, "Work, Culture and Politics," 11.

55. Interview by Paul Myers of Guy Alexander and Robert Knoll, 10, 14–17; *Moundsville Echo*, May 27, 1904, Feb. 10, 1905, Feb. 21, 1907. For Local 10 leaders, see AFGWU Local 10 Minutes.

56. *Moundsville Echo*, May 13, 1904, Mar. 30, Apr. 6, 1906, Jan. 4, Mar. 22, May 3, 1907.

57. *Wheeling Majority*, May 12, 1910; *Moundsville Echo*, May 8, 1908; *Commoner and Glassworker*, Nov. 14, 1908, 6.

58. The Democratic platform is in *Moundsville Echo*, Oct. 25, 1912.

59. *Wheeling Majority*, July 13, 1911; *Moundsville Echo*, Feb. 12, 1912.

60. AFGWU Local 10 Minutes, Apr. 2, 1910, Jan. 13, June 1, Sept. 7, 1912; *National Glass Budget*, June 15, 1912, 1, July 6, 1912, 5, Aug. 2, 1913, 8; *Wheeling Majority*, Apr. 21, 1910, June 27, 1912.

61. *Moundsville Journal*, Nov. 10, 1910, Jan. 19, 1911; *Wheeling Majority*, Jan. 26, 1911.

62. The platform was carried in its entirety in the *Wheeling Majority*, Feb. 23, 1911.

63. *Moundsville Journal*, Mar. 16, 1911; *Moundsville Echo*, Mar. 17, 1911.

64. *Moundsville Echo*, Nov. 8, 1912, Mar. 21, 1913; *Moundsville Journal*, Oct. 18, 1912, Nov. 7, 1912.

65. See the steady coverage in the *Wheeling Majority* in the fall of 1911.

66. *Moundsville Echo*, Dec. 8, 1911, Mar. 19, 1915. The state Democratic platforms are in *West Virginia Legislative Hand Book and Manual and Official Register, 1916* (Charleston, W.V.: Tribune, 1916), 701–8, 738–42.

67. Williams, *Captains of Industry*, 242–46.

68. *Moundsville Echo*, Mar. 19, 1915, Nov. 10, 1916; *Moundsville Journal*, Mar. 18, 1915. The Republican newspaper began publishing in 1910.

69. *National Glass Budget*, Sept. 28, 1912, 1, Aug. 2, 1913, 1; interview by Paul Myers of Howard Denoon, 1, 5, 10.

70. *National Glass Budget*, May 16, 1914, 4; *Moundsville Echo*, July 31, 1914.

71. Pearce Davis, *The Development of the American Glass Industry* (Cambridge, Mass.: Harvard University Press, 1949), 239–41; Colin Gordon, *New Deals: Business, Labor, and Politics in America, 1920–1935* (New York: Cambridge University Press, 1994), 110–13.

72. Louis C. Martin, "Causes and Consequences of the 1909–1910 Steel Strike in the Wheeling District" (master's thesis, West Virginia University, 1999); David T. Javersak, "The Ohio Valley Trades and Labor Assembly: The Formative Years, 1882–1915" (Ph.D. diss., West Virginia University, 1977).

73. Interview by Paul Myers of Howard Denoon, 6–10; interview by Paul Myers of Guy Alexander and Robert Knoll, 1–4; AFGWU Local 10 Minutes, Mar. 7, Sept. 5, 1914, Aug. 5, 1915, June 2, Dec. 1, 1917; Moore and Weatherman, *Fostoria*, 73–74.

74. USCB, *Manufactures 1919* (Washington, D.C.: Government Printing Office, 1923), 1598; *National Glass Budget*, Feb. 5, 1916, 3, Apr. 22, 1917, 7, Sept. 2, 1917, 1.

75. Interview by Paul Myers of Howard Denoon, 11–13.

76. *Moundsville Echo,* Apr. 6, Apr. 20, 1917, Mar. 22, Apr. 12, Apr. 19, Sept. 20, 1918.

77. See for example, John Hennen, *The Americanization of West Virginia: Creating a Modern Industrial State, 1916–1925* (Lexington: University Press of Kentucky, 1996); Charles H. McCormick, *Seeing Reds: Federal Surveillance in the Pittsburgh Mill District, 1917–1921* (Pittsburgh: University of Pittsburgh Press, 1997); and David A. Corbin, *Life, Work, and Rebellion in the Coal Fields: The Southern West Virginia Miners, 1880–1922* (Urbana: University of Illinois Press, 1981).

78. AFGWU Local 10 Minutes, Apr. 6, May 4, June 1, June 29, 1918, Feb. 1, Nov. 1, Dec. 7, 1919.

79. *Moundsville Echo,* Mar. 16, 1917, Nov. 8, 1918, Mar. 21, 1919.

80. USCB, *Biennial Census of Manufactures, 1921* (Washington, D.C.: Government Printing Office, 1924), 929–33; AFGWU Local 10 Minutes, Sept. 4, 1920, Apr. 2, 1921, Feb. 4, 1922.

81. *National Glass Budget,* Sept. 13, 1920, 12; Rowe and Cook, *History,* 62–65.

82. *Speeches and Addresses of William Clarke, President of the American Flint Glass Workers' Union of North America,* ed. Kathryn L. Meagher and Edward J. Howard (Toledo: AFGWU, n.d.), 117, 125–35; Rowe and Cook, *History,* 70.

83. Moore and Weatherman, *Fostoria,* xvi; W. F. Dalzell to J. W. Martin, secretary, Local Union Number 10, Mar. 31, 1928, AFGWU Local 10 Records.

84. WVDL, *Eighteenth Biennial Report, 1925–26* (Charleston, W.V.: Jarrett, 1928), 83; *Nineteenth Biennial Report, 1927–28* (Charleston, W.V.: Tribune Co., 1926), 80–82; Warren C. Scoville, *Revolution in Glassmaking: Entrepreneurship and Technological Change in the American Industry, 1880–1920* (Cambridge, Mass.: Harvard University Press, 1948), 317.

85. Mss. Census, 1920, Marshall County; *Polk's Moundsville Directory, 1924–25* (Pittsburgh: R. L. Polk, 1924); *Polk's Moundsville Directory, 1929–30* (Pittsburgh: R. L. Polk, 1929); *Service Recognition Dinner for Employees, Fostoria Glass Company* (Moundsville, 1949).

86. Mss. Census, 1920, Marshall County. Based on 425 Moundsville glassworkers.

87. WVDL, *Nineteenth Biennial Report, 1927–28,* 80–82; *West Virginia Legislative Hand Book and Manual and Official Register* (Charleston, W.V., 1933), 423, 711.

88. USCB, *Fourteenth Census (1920): State Compendium, West Virginia* (Washington, D.C.: Government Printing Office, 1925), 9, 11, 83. For the importance of the concentration of manufacturing areas, see Richard N. Simon, "The Development of Underdevelopment: The Coal Industry and Its Effect on the West Virginia Economy, 1880–1930" (Ph.D. diss., University of Pittsburgh, 1978), 287–93.

89. *Moundsville Echo,* Mar. 21, 1919, Mar. 16, 1923; AFGWU Local 10 Minutes, Dec. 5, 1927, Jan. 9, Feb. 7, 1928.

Chapter 5: Clarksburg

1. *National Glass Budget*, Sept. 28, 1901, 6.
2. *Clarksburg Telegram*, Jan. 6, 1905; Dorothy Davis, *History of Harrison County, West Virginia* (Clarksburg: American Association of University Women, 1970), 759–62.
3. William H. Harbaugh, *Lawyer's Lawyer: The Life of John W. Davis* (New York: Oxford University Press, 1973), 8–10.
4. John Alexander Williams, *West Virginia and the Captains of Industry* (Morgantown: West Virginia University Library, 1976), 113.
5. Williams, *Captains of Industry*, 46–51; Gordon B. McKinney, *Southern Mountain Republicans 1865–1900: Politics and the Appalachian Community* (Chapel Hill: University of North Carolina Press, 1978), 150–58.
6. Nathan Goff Jr. to *Toledo Blade*, Nov. 24, 1887, in Nathan Goff Jr. Papers, WVRHC, box 9.
7. "Public Meeting of miners and mine laborers of Coal Valley, West Virginia," Feb. 6, 1888; Wheeling Potters Protective Tariff Club to Goff, Mar. 6, 1888; and Nail City Lodge Number 3, AAISW to Goff, Mar. 13, 1888; W. J. W. Cowden to Goff, Sept. 12, 1888, all in Goff Papers, box 9.
8. G. Wayne Smith, *Nathan Goff, Jr.: A Biography* (Charleston: West Virginia Education Foundation, 1959), chap. 8. For the machinations behind the scenes in West Virginia, consult Williams, *Captains of Industry*, 46–51; and McKinney, *Southern Mountain Republicans*, 150–58.
9. *Clarksburg News*, Apr. 23, 1897, Mar. 18, 1898; Smith, *Nathan Goff, Jr.*, 209–12.
10. Davis, *Harrison County*, 674, 696, 732–39; Smith, *Nathan Goff, Jr.*, 210–17. For the characterization of the *Telegram*, see the *Clarksburg News*, June 17, 1897, which claimed that the paper was for those who choose corporations over people.
11. Davis, *Harrison County*, 728; Smith, *Nathan Goff, Jr.*, 216–17.
12. Davis quoted in Harbaugh, *Lawyer's Lawyer*, 39.
13. *Clarksburg News*, Aug. 20, Aug. 27, 1897; Harbaugh, *Lawyer's Lawyer*, 38–41.
14. Harbaugh, *Lawyer's Lawyer*. Davis, despite some Progressive credentials, also never completely lost his father's affinity for the small-government, agrarian wing of the Democratic Party. Davis eventually served as the chief legal counsel for the defense in the famous *Brown v. Board of Education* case in the 1950s.
15. *Clarksburg News*, Oct. 7, Oct. 14, Nov. 11, 1898; *Clarksburg Telegram*, Oct. 21, 1898; Harbaugh, *Lawyer's Lawyer*, 51–53.
16. Festus Summers, *Johnson Newlon Camden: A Study in Individualism* (New York: Putnam, 1937), 541–45; Williams, *Captains of Industry*, 138–39, 200–201; Harbaugh, *Lawyer's Lawyer*, 46–50; Jeffery B. Cook, "The Ambassador of Development: Aretas Brooks Fleming, West Virginia's Political Entrepreneur, 1839–1923" (Ph.D. diss., West Virginia University, 1998), chap. 5.
17. Contrast the content of the *Clarksburg Telegram* (Republican) with the *Clarksburg News* (Democrat) during the local and state elections of 1898 and 1899. For a brilliant analysis of how the two mainstream parties conducted a politics of "class warfare," at least on the surface, see Mark Wahlgren Summers,

Party Games: Getting, Keeping, and Using Power in Gilded Age Politics (Chapel Hill: University of North Carolina Press, 2004), chap. 11.

18. Davis, *Harrison County*, 81; USCB, *Twelfth Census (1900): Population*, pt. 1 (Washington, D.C.: Government Printing Office, 1901), 409.

19. LA 300, Minutes, Apr. 19, 1889, Slight Papers, reel 7 (hereafter LA 300 Minutes).

20. Pearce Davis, *The Development of the American Glass Industry* (Cambridge, Mass.: Harvard University Press, 1949), 138–39; Ken Fones-Wolf, "Immigrants, Labor and Capital in a Transnational Context: Belgian Glass Workers in America, 1880–1925," *Journal of American Ethnic History* 21 (winter 2002): 66–67.

21. Richard John O'Connor, "Cinderheads and Iron Lungs: Window-Glass Craftsmen and the Transformation of Workers' Control, 1880–1905" (Ph.D. diss., University of Pittsburgh, 1991), 155–56, 175.

22. I have written on this in several other places. See "Immigrants, Labor and Capital," 63–66; and Ken Fones-Wolf, "Transatlantic Craft Migrations and Transnational Spaces: Belgian Window Glass Workers in America, 1880–1920," *Labor History* 45 (Aug. 2004): 299–321.

23. *National Glass Budget*, Oct. 19, 1901, 8.

24. LA 300 Minutes, Mar. 24, May 19, 1888, Apr. 19, May 17, Aug. 16, Oct. 4, 1889; Leon Watillon, *The Knights of Labor in Belgium* (Los Angeles: Institute of Labor Relations, 1959). Colin Gordon characterizes the labor relations system of the window-glass industry as "regulatory unionism," implying that both employers and workers gained from a system that regulated entrance to key production jobs as well as output, thereby eliminating competition and maintaining high wages and prices. See *New Deals: Business, Labor, and Politics in America, 1920–1935* (New York: Cambridge University Press, 1994), 110–13.

25. This is discussed fully in O'Connor, "Cinderheads," 142–55.

26. Details are in O'Connor, "Cinderheads," chap. 4. Ethnic aspects are covered in the *National Glass Budget*, Dec. 3, 1898, 1, June 16, 1900, 1, Sept. 28, 1901, 6.

27. *National Glass Budget*, Dec. 3, 1898, 1, Nov. 22, 1902, 1; LA 300 Minutes, Sept. 1, 1900. For an excellent overview of the Belgian labor movement and its ideology, see Daisy E. DeVreese, "Belgium," in Marcel Van der Linden and Jurgen Rojahn, eds., *The Formation of Labour Movements, 1870–1914: An International Perspective* (Leiden: Brill, 1990), 25–55.

28. *Commoner and Glassworker*, Dec. 23, 1899, 8; *Clarksburg News*, Sept. 1, 1899; Dorothy Davis, *Harrison County*, 759.

29. *National Glass Budget*, Sept. 16, 1899, 2. On North View, see *Clarksburg News*, Mar. 18, 1898, June 2, 1899.

30. *Clarksburg Telegram*, Jan. 18, 1901; *Commoner and Glassworker*, Jan. 19, 1901, 1; Davis, *Harrison County*, 771.

31. Davis, *Harrison County*, 767; WVDL, *Tenth Biennial Report, 1909–10* (Charleston, W.V.: News Mail, 1910), 33, 38.

32. Davis, *Harrison County*, 277; *Harrison County Heritage* (Clarksburg: Harrison County Genealogical Society, 1995), 191.

33. *Clarksburg Telegram*, Oct. 18, 1901; *Clarksburg News*, Aug. 29, 1905, Apr. 9, 1906; *Polk's Clarksburg City Directory, 1909–10* (Pittsburgh: R. L. Polk, 1909).

34. Based on a sample of 244 workers in the window-glass industry taken from Mss. Census, 1910, Harrison County. Rates for glass craftsmen were 13.6 percent

of household heads; for semiskilled workers 47.1 percent; and for unskilled workers 30.8 percent.

35. *Clarksburg News,* Mar. 14, 1904, June 13, 1906, Sept. 14, 1906, Mar. 20, 1909; *Clarksburg Telegram,* Sept. 9, 1904, Aug. 25, 1905.

36. *Clarksburg News,* Apr. 9, 1906, Nov. 22, 1906; *Clarksburg Telegram,* Jan. 18, 1901, Feb. 3, 1905.

37. See note 34.

38. *Clarksburg News,* Apr. 5, 1905, Jan. 6, 1906, Feb. 27, 1907; Harbaugh, *Lawyer's Lawyer,* 37.

39. "Autobiography," box 1, and scrapbooks, box 4, Harvey W. Harmer Papers, WVRHC; *Clarksburg Telegram,* Apr. 6, 1906.

40. *Clarksburg News,* Jan. 4, 1909; *Commoner and Glassworker,* Sept. 12, 1908, 11, Nov. 28, 1908, 12.

41. Interview with George DelForge, in Frederick A. Barkey, *Cinderheads in the Hills: The Belgian Window Glass Workers of West Virginia* (Charleston: West Virginia Humanities Council, 1988), 29.

42. *Commoner and Glassworker,* Sept. 7, 1901, June 13, 1908; *Harrison County Heritage,* 66; Fones-Wolf, "Immigrants, Labor and Capital," 71–72; Barkey, *Cinderheads in the Hills,* 23–35.

43. *Clarksburg News,* Sept. 1, 1905; *Clarksburg Telegram,* Oct. 4, 1901. A similar view of the insularity of a Belgian glassworker community in Russia is contained in Vladimir Ronin, "Les Ouvrier Wallons dans la Region de Petersbourg en 1900," *Revue Belge d'Histoire Contemporaine* 25 (1994–95): 79–97.

44. *Clarksburg News,* Feb. 19, 1906, Aug. 21, 1908, Aug. 27, 1908.

45. *Clarksburg News,* Oct. 22, 1906, July 17, 1908; Adrian DeMeester interview in Barkey, *Cinderheads in the Hills,* 26.

46. Glassworker participation in parades and rallies for Debs is described in *Clarksburg Telegram,* Oct. 18, 1901. Also see M. S. Holt to *Appeal to Reason,* Nov. 2, 1911, in Rush Dew Holt Papers, WVRHC, box 183.

47. *Clarksburg Telegram,* Dec. 27, 1907; *Clarksburg News,* Aug. 21, Aug. 27, 1908.

48. *Clarksburg Telegram,* Oct. 28, Oct. 30, Nov. 3, 1908.

49. *National Glass Budget,* Dec. 3, 1898, 1, June 29, 1901, 6, July 27, 1901, 1, Sept. 7, 1901, 6.

50. *National Glass Budget,* Nov. 15, 1902, 6; Apr. 18, 1903, 1, June 3, 1904, 4.

51. *National Glass Budget,* May 16, 1903, 6. See also O'Connor, "Cinderheads," chap. 5, for a thorough elaboration of the breakdown of LA 300.

52. *Commoner and Glassworker,* Apr. 27, 1907, 12.

53. *Clarksburg News,* Dec. 14, 16, 17, 27, 1907, Jan. 9, 1908; *Commoner and Glassworker,* Dec. 21, 1907, 1; Jan. 4, 1908, 5, Jan. 25, 1908, 1.

54. *Commoner and Glassworker,* June 26, 1909, 10, July 3, 1909, 10, July 17, 1909, 14, Sept. 3, 1910, 12.

55. *National Glass Budget,* Aug. 10, 1907, 6; Apr. 18, 1908, 1; *Commoner and Glassworker,* Feb. 22, 1908, 4, May 8, 1909, 1, 4.

56. *Commoner and Glassworker,* June 13, 1908, 11, Nov. 14, 1908, 10, Dec. 5, 1908, 13; *Wheeling Majority,* June 27, 1912. See also Mss. Census, 1910, Harrison County. For a more extensive look at the Belgian influence, see Fones-Wolf, "Transatlantic Craft Migrations."

57. See, among other works, Joan Scott, *The Glassworkers of Carmaux: French Craftsmen and Political Action in a Nineteenth-Century City* (Cambridge, Mass.: Harvard University Press, 1974); Bernard H. Moss, *The Origins of the French Labor Movement, 1830–1914: The Socialism of Skilled Workers* (Berkeley: University of California Press, 1976); Carl Strikwerda, *A House Divided: Catholics, Socialists, and Flemish Nationalists in Nineteenth-Century Belgium* (New York: Rowman and Littlefield, 1997).

58. *Commoner and Glassworker,* June 6, 1908, 12, Oct. 31, 1908, 16.

59. *Clarksburg News,* Jan. 16, Feb. 5, Feb. 13, 1909; *Commoner and Glassworker,* Jan. 9, 1909, 13, Feb. 27, 1909, 1, 11.

60. *Clarksburg News,* Jan. 7, Feb. 10, 1909; *Clarksburg Telegram,* Apr. 6, 1910.

61. *Clarksburg Telegram,* Nov. 3, Nov. 9, 1910; Harbaugh, *Lawyer's Lawyer,* 64–65.

62. *Commoner and Glassworker,* Feb. 25, 1911, 12.

63. Harbaugh, *Lawyer's Lawyer,* 76–78; NWGW, Minutes, Oct. 24, 1913, Slight Papers, reel 8.

64. *Clarksburg Telegram,* Jan. 5, 1912; *Clarksburg Exponent,* Jan. 3, 1913.

65. Demographic information is based on a sample of 400 glassworkers from the Mss. Census schedules, 1920, Harrison County; and the membership ledgers of the NWGW, 1921, WGCLA Records, WVRHC. The Socialist and cooperative backgrounds of the Belgians are discussed in DeVreese, "Belgium," 45–49; and Fones-Wolf, "Craft, Ethnicity, and Identity: Belgian Glassworkers in West Virginia, 1898–1940," in Ken Fones-Wolf and Ronald L. Lewis, *Transnational West Virginia: Ethnic Communities and Economic Change, 1840–1940* (Morgantown: West Virginia University Press, 2002), 113–34.

66. *Clarksburg Telegram,* Nov. 7, 1912, Jan. 3, 1913, Jan. 2, 1914, Nov. 7, 1914, Jan. 8, 1915; *Salem Express,* Oct. 17, 1913. For an overview of the Socialist movement in Adamston, see *Socialists in a Small Town: The Socialist Victory in Adamston, West Virginia* (Buckhannon, W.V.: n.p., 1992).

67. NWGW Minutes, Aug. 27, 1911, Slight Papers, reel 8; *Commoner and Glassworker,* Jan. 28, 1911.

68. *Wheeling Majority,* July 13, 1911, Aug. 14, 1913. See also Lynn Vacca, "Weir, Ernest Tener," in *American National Biography* (New York: Oxford University Press, 1999), 22:903–4.

69. *Wheeling Majority,* June 12, Aug. 14, Sept. 4, 1913; NWGW Minutes, Feb. 1, 1913, Slight Papers, reel 8; *Salem Express,* May 23, 1913, Jan. 16, May 1, 1914.

70. *The National* (organ of the NWGW), Oct. 1915, 7–13, 19–21; *Salem Express,* Feb. 13, Mar. 20, 1913.

71. *Commoner and Glassworker,* Sept. 17, 1910, 13, Jan. 14, 1911, 5; *Salem Express,* July 4, 1913, May 1, 1914; *Socialists in a Small Town,* 5; *Wheeling Majority,* Nov. 20, 1913. For a more general discussion of the Socialist appeal in West Virginia, see Frederick Allan Barkey, "The Socialist Party in West Virginia from 1898 to 1920: A Study in Working Class Radicalism" (Ph.D. diss., University of Pittsburgh, 1971), chap. 2.

72. In fact, when the semiskilled snappers went on strike in Harrison County in March 1916, the blowers and gatherers performed their tasks until the strike was defeated by the manufacturers. See *Salem Express,* Mar. 24, 1916.

73. This is discussed in Ken Fones-Wolf, "A Craftsman's Paradise in Appalachia: Glassworkers and the Transformation of Clarksburg, 1900–1933," *Journal of Appalachian Studies* 1 (fall 1995): 73–75. For an example of craft socialism in another context, see Moss, *Origins of the French Labor Movement.*

74. *Salem Express*, June 5, 1914; Davis, *Harrison County*, 767; *National Glass Budget*, Nov. 21, 1914, 2.

75. *National Glass Budget*, July 4, 1914, 5.

76. *Salem Express*, Aug. 14, Aug. 21, Aug. 28, 1914; *National Glass Budget*, Sept. 12, 1914, 12.

77. *Salem Express*, Aug. 1914–July 1917, provides the best coverage of these activities. See also *National*, Nov. 1916, 11, June 1917, "honor roll" insert.

78. *Clarksburg Telegram*, Jan. 7, 9, Nov. 9, 1916; *Salem Express*, July 2, July 9, Oct. 22, 1915, Sept. 7, 1916, Mar. 29, May 31, 1917.

79. *Clarksburg Telegram*, Jan. 5, 1917; *Five Years of the Council-Manager Government in Clarksburg, West Virginia* (Clarksburg: City of Clarksburg, 1926) 1, 5, 11; *Police Journal*, special issue devoted to Clarksburg, September 1923; Agent 35 to C. E. Smith, Oct. 18, 1919, and Agent 37 to Smith, Oct. 25, 1919, in C. E. Smith Papers, WVRHC. For the climate of superpatriotic oppression in the state generally, see John C. Hennen, "The Americanization of West Virginia: Creating a Modern Industrial State, 1916–1925" (Ph.D. diss., West Virginia University, 1993), 178–214.

80. *National Glass Budget*, June 26, 1915, 5, July 17, 1915, 1; *National*, July 1916, 18–21, Nov. 1917, 18–20; USCB, *Manufactures 1919* (Washington, D.C.: Government Printing Office, 1923), 1598; Robert Lookabill, "The Hand Window Glass Worker in West Virginia: A Study of His Skill, Union Organization and Life Style" (master's thesis, Marshall University, 1971), 61–64.

81. E. H. Gillot, *A History of Trade Unions in the Window Glass Industry* (Columbus, Ohio: WGCLA, 1943), 11; Lookabill, "Hand Window Glass Worker," 65–67; *National Glass Budget*, Mar. 11, 1916, 3.

82. *National*, Dec. 1922, 20; Feb. 1923, 3–11.

83. NWGW, Executive Board Minutes, Dec. 20, 1920, WGCLA Records, WVRHC, ser. 7, box 9; *National*, Sept. 1922, 23–27, Apr. 1923, 24–25.

84. USCB, *Biennial Census of Manufactures 1927* (Washington, D.C.: Government Printing Office, 1930), 864; Davis, *Harrison County*, 278, 767–68.

85. USCB, *Manufactures 1919*, 1596. Of course, window-glass plants in Clarksburg accounted for the majority of workers employed in factories owned by individuals, partnerships, and cooperatives in 1914.

86. "The Passing of the National Window Glass Workers," *Monthly Labor Review* 29 (Oct. 1929): 11–15; Barkey, *Cinderheads in the Hills*, 14–15, 23, 35; Mss. Census, 1920, Harrison County; *Polk's Clarksburg Directory, 1925* (Pittsburgh: R. L. Polk, 1925), and *Polk's Clarksburg Directory, 1935* (Pittsburgh: R. L. Polk, 1935). I checked 211 skilled glassworkers from the 1920 census against both the 1925 and the 1935 city directories—75 percent of the homeowners were present in 1925, and 68 percent were present in 1935. In addition, of the 110 glass craftsmen who remained in the city, 66 were still in glass plants in 1935.

87. *National*, Oct. 1922, 28; WVDL, *Twentieth Biennial Report, 1929–30* (Charleston, W.V.: Jarrett, 1930), 19.

88. Barkey, *Cinderheads in the Hills*, 15–18; Trevor Bain, "The Impact of Tech-

nological Change on the Flat Glass Industry and the Unions' Reactions to Change: Colonial Period to the Present" (Ph.D. diss., University of California, Berkeley, 1964), chap. 3.

89. Davis, *Harrison County,* 271, 278; USCB, *Fifteenth Census (1930),* vol. 4, *Occupations* (Washington, D.C.: Government Printing Office, 1934); USCB, *County Data Book* (Washington, D.C.: Government Printing Office, 1947).

90. USCB, *Census of Religious Bodies: 1926* (Washington, D.C.: Government Printing Office, 1930).

91. Clarksburg had home ownership rates of 42 percent, illiteracy rates of under 3 percent, and average earnings more than $200 above the state average. USCB, *Fourteenth Census (1920): State Compendium: West Virginia* (Washington, D.C.: Government Printing Office, 1925), 11, 30, 41, 83.

92. Davis, *Harrison County,* 719–91; *Five Years of the Council-Manager Government in Clarksburg* (Clarksburg, W.V., 1926), pamphlet, in WVRHC; *Clarksburg Exponent,* May 4, 1927; *West Virginia Legislative Hand Book and Manual and Official Register, 1927* (Charleston, W.V., 1927), 79–86.

93. USCB, *1920 State Compendium,* 89–92.

94. Oscar Chapman, "Report of the Committee on the Upper Monongahela Valley, West Virginia," 1934, mimeograph, WVRHC, 45–46.

95. *West Virginia Legislative Hand Book 1927,* 82–83.

96. Barkey, *Cinderheads in the Hills,* 32, 36.

Chapter 6: Fairmont

1. *Commoner and Glassworker,* May 7, 1910, 16; *National Glass Budget,* Dec. 10, 1910, 6.

2. *National Glass Budget,* Dec. 18, 1909, 6; Dean Six, *West Virginia Glass between the World Wars* (Altgen, Pa.: Schiffer, 2002), 79.

3. *A History of Marion County, West Virginia* (Fairmont: Marion County Historical Society, 1985), 44.

4. Michael E. Workman, "Political Culture and the Coal Economy in the Upper Monongahela Region: 1776–1933" (Ph.D. diss., West Virginia University, 1995), 132–35; Jeffery B. Cook, "The Ambassador of Development: Aretas Brooks Fleming, West Virginia's Political Entrepreneur, 1839–1923" (Ph.D. diss., West Virginia University, 1998), 54–68.

5. A. B. Fleming, "A History of the Fairmont Coal Region," in West Virginia Mining Institute, *Proceedings* (1911), 251–52, as quoted in Workman, "Political Culture," 134.

6. Workman, "Political Culture," 146–47.

7. George A. Dunnington, *History and Progress of the County of Marion, West Virginia* (Fairmont: George A. Dunnington, 1880), 119–21; *Second Annual Report of the Commissioner of Banking, State of West Virginia, 1902* (Charleston, W.V.: Tribune, 1902), 4.

8. USCB, *Thirteenth Census (1910): Statistical Abstract with Supplement for West Virginia* (Washington, D.C.: Government Printing Office, 1913), 576, 592.

9. Festus Summers, *Johnson Newlon Camden: A Study in Individualism* (New York: Putnam, 1937), 277–93; Workman, "Political Culture," 161–66.

10. John Alexander Williams, *West Virginia and the Captains of Industry* (Mor-

gantown: West Virginia University Library, 1976), 44, 55–56; Cook, "Ambassador of Development," 110–13.

11. Cook, "Ambassador of Development," 116–17; Williams, *Captains of Industry,* 57–62.

12. Cook, "Ambassador of Development," 161–84; Paul Gaston, *The New South Creed: A Study in Southern Mythmaking* (Baton Rouge: Louisiana State University Press, 1970).

13. Cook, "Ambassador of Development," 185–86.

14. J. E. Watson to A. B. Fleming, Aug. 18, 1892, in A. B. Fleming Papers, WVRHC; Workman, "Political Culture," 215–17.

15. *Acts of the Legislature of West Virginia, 1893* (Charleston, W.V.: Moses W. Donnally, 1893), 81; Cook, "Ambassador of Development," 187–88.

16. *Acts of the Legislature, 1893,* 174, 185; *West Virginia Gazetteer and Business Directory, 1891–1892* (Detroit: R. L. Polk, 1891), 162; *Fairmont Index,* special ed., Apr. 15, 1892, also quoted in Workman, "Political Culture," 167–69.

17. Williams, *Captains of Industry,* 120. Note, in particular, the small support that the Populist party received in West Virginia in 1892.

18. Gerald W. Johnson, "West Virginia Politics: A Socio-Cultural Analysis of Political Participation" (Ph.D. diss., University of Tennessee, 1970), 50, 68; Williams, *Captains of Industry,* 110–24. For an analysis of the key issues involved in the shift to the Republican Party in the 1890s, see Richard Franklin Bensel, *The Political Economy of American Industrialization, 1877–1900* (New York: Cambridge University Press, 2000).

19. *Fairmont Free Press,* Oct. 21, 1892; *Acts of the Legislature, 1893,* 174, 185.

20. *Fairmont Free Press,* Oct. 7, Oct. 21, 1892, June 2, 1893; *West Virginia Gazetteer, 1891–92,* 162, 164; *Fairmont Index,* Apr. 15, 1892; Workman, "Political Culture," 167–69.

21. *Fairmont Free Press,* Nov. 18, Dec. 2, 1892, Jan. 6, Jan. 20, Feb. 24, 1893.

22. *Fairmont Free Press,* Sept. 23, Oct. 21, Dec. 2, 1892, Jan. 13, Mar. 24, 1893.

23. *West Virginian* (Fairmont), Sept. 21, 1894, Mar. 8, 1895; *Fairmont Free Press,* Feb. 1, Apr. 5, May 24, June 7, Aug. 16, 1895.

24. *Fairmont Free Press,* July 26, 1895; *Commoner and Glassworker,* Dec. 4, 1897, 7.

25. W. A. Ohley to A. B. Fleming, July 29, 1897, Fleming Papers. For a full discussion, see Workman, "Political Culture," 218–20.

26. *West Virginian* (Fairmont), July 30, Aug. 6, Sept. 24, 1897; *Fairmont Free Press,* Nov. 17, 1898.

27. *Fairmont Free Press,* Sept. 6, 27, 1895; *Acts of the Legislature of West Virginia, 1899* (Charleston, W.V.: Press Butter Printing Co., 1899), 71; *Commoner and Glassworker,* June 25, 1898, 3.

28. Owen S. McKinney to Fleming, Jan. 23, 1902, Fleming Papers.

29. Mss. Census, 1900, Marion County (microfilm); WVDL, *Seventh Biennial Report, 1901–1902* (Charleston, W.V.: Tribune, 1902), 70; *Commoner and Glassworker,* Dec. 18, 1897, 6, Dec. 25, 1897, 15, June 25, 1898, 3.

30. *Commoner and Glassworker,* Jan. 26, 1901, 4, Feb. 23, 1901, 12, July 20, 1901, 12; WVDL, *Seventh Biennial Report,* 70.

31. *Fairmont Times,* Oct. 28, Nov. 5, *Fairmont Free Press,* Nov. 27, 1902; Workman, "Political Culture," 220–23.

32. *Fairmont Free Press,* Jan. 23, Mar. 20, 1903.

33. Workman, "Political Culture," 223–28.

34. In 1914, Fairmont had 1,837 wage earners, according to the Census of Manufactures. That year, the state labor bureau reported 890 members of unions in the city. USCB, *Fourteenth Census (1920),* vol. 9, *Manufactures, 1919* (Washington, D.C.: Government Printing Office, 1923), 1589; WVDL, *Twelfth Biennial Report, 1913–14* (Charleston, W.V., 1914), 71–84.

35. USCB, *Thirteenth Census (1910) Abstract,* 576; *Fairmont Free Press,* Jan. 22, 1903; *Industrial Fairmont in 1908: The Coal City of West Virginia and the Ideal Manufacturing Center* (Fairmont: Fairmont Board of Trade, 1908).

36. *National Glass Budget,* May 18, 1907, 8.

37. *National Glass Budget,* Jan. 16, 1904, 2, Dec. 15, 1906, 5.

38. *National Glass Budget,* July 23, 1910, 1; *Industrial Fairmont in 1908,* 82–83.

39. *National Glass Budget,* July 14, 1906, 4, Mar. 2, 1907, 2; *Industrial Fairmont in 1908,* 82–83.

40. *National Glass Budget,* Jan. 7, 1905, 1, Apr. 14, 1906, 1; *Commoner and Glassworker,* Apr. 18, 1908, 8–9; *Fairmont Free Press,* Mar. 19, 1903.

41. Mss. Census, 1910, Marion County. My sample of the unskilled included 148 workers who were identified as working in glass factories.

42. *Commoner and Glassworker,* Aug. 25, 1900, 14, May 18, 1901, 12, May 25, 1901, 12, Oct. 5, 1907, 11, Mar. 26, 1910, 5. The fight between the GBBA and the AFGWU is covered in Thomas W. Rowe and Harry H. Cook, *History of the American Flint Glass Workers' Union of North America, 1878–1957* (Toledo: AFGWU, [1957]), 40–47.

43. Mss. Census, 1910, Marion County. Of 120 skilled glassworkers who were household heads, only 6 were homeowners; 50 more were boarders, and 38 lived with their parents.

44. *Fairmont Free Press,* Jan. 28, 1904, Oct. 5 1905, Apr. 26, 1906; *Fairmont Times,* Jan. 8, Mar. 1, 1909; Workman, "Political Culture," 200–201.

45. *National Glass Budget,* July 25, 1908, 1.

46. Matthew M. Neely, scrapbooks, Matthew M. Neely Papers, WVRHC; *Fairmont Free Press,* Feb. 27, Mar. 5, Mar. 24, 1908; *Commoner and Glassworker,* Oct. 23, 1909, 13.

47. *Fairmont Free Press,* Nov. 4, 1908; *Fairmont Times,* Feb. 6, Feb. 22, Mar. 22, 1909.

48. *Fairmont Times,* Nov. 8, Nov. 9, 1910; *Wheeling Majority,* Jan. 12, 1911; *Fairmont Free Press,* Feb. 2, 1911.

49. *Commoner and Glassworker,* July 2, 1910, 12, Oct. 22, 1910, 5.

50. Warren C. Scoville, *Revolution in Glassmaking: Entrepreneurship and Technological Change in the American Industry, 1880–1920* (Cambridge, Mass.: Harvard University Press, 1948), 183–84; Six, *West Virginia Glass,* 79.

51. Scoville, *Revolution,* 275–77.

52. Scoville, *Revolution,* 92–110, describes this process in considerable detail.

53. *National Glass Budget,* Aug. 24, 1912, 1; Scoville, *Revolution,* 212, 298–99.

54. Scoville, *Revolution,* 296; *Fairmont Times,* Feb. 14, 1911.

55. *National Glass Budget,* Dec. 15, 1906, 2, July 6, 1912, 8, Aug. 3, 1912, 9; Scoville, *Revolution,* 115, 188.

56. Mss. Census, 1920, Marion County; Kenneth R. Bailey, "A Judicious Mixture: Negroes and Immigrants in the West Virginia Mines, 1880–1917," *West Virginia History* 34 (1973): 141–61.

57. Mss. Census, 1920, Marion County.

58. *Fairmont Times,* Mar. 17, 1912; *Wheeling Majority,* Apr. 18, 1912. For the interweaving of class and ethnic conflict in Fairmont and Marion County, see Charles H. McCormick, "The Death of Constable Riggs: Ethnic Conflict in Marion County in the World War I Era," *West Virginia History* 52 (1993): 33–58.

59. *Fairmont Times,* Nov. 2, 1912; *Wheeling Majority,* Sept. 12, 1912; Workman, "Political Culture," 201; McCormick, "Death of Constable Riggs," 36.

60. *Wheeling Majority,* July 18, 1912; *Fairmont Times,* Nov. 6, 1912.

61. George Gilchrist to A. B. Fleming, Feb. 19, 1913, Fleming Papers; *Wheeling Majority,* Aug. 7, Aug. 14, Sept. 18, 1913. For the importance of the *Hitchman* decision, see William E. Forbath, *Law and the Shaping of the American Labor Movement* (Cambridge, Mass.: Harvard University Press, 1991), 115–17.

62. *Fairmont Times,* Feb. 10, Feb. 19, 1913. On the nondemocratic aspects of the city commission form of government, see James Weinstein, *The Corporate Ideal in the Liberal State: 1900–1918* (Boston: Beacon Press, 1968), chap. 4.

63. *Fairmont Times,* Dec. 10, 1913.

64. *Fairmont Free Press,* Mar. 20, 1903; *Fairmont Times,* Dec. 8, 1913; *Commoner and Glassworker,* Oct. 31, 1908, 13.

65. *Fairmont Times,* Feb. 19, 1914; *Wheeling Majority,* Mar. 5, Mar. 26, Apr. 16, May 14, May 28, 1914. The quotation is from *Wheeling Majority,* Oct. 24, 1912.

66. *National Glass Budget,* Mar. 14, 1914, 13, May 16, 1914, 4, Dec. 4, 1915, 6; WVDL, *Thirteenth Biennial Report, 1915–16* (Charleston, W.V.: Tribune, 1916), 15–16, 30–31.

67. *Fairmont Times,* Nov. 4, Nov. 6, 1914.

68. USCB, *Fourteenth Census (1920): State Compendium: West Virginia* (Washington, D.C.: Government Printing Office, 1925), 30, 41, 85.

69. USCB, *1920 State Compendium,* 83, 88.

70. *National Glass Budget,* Mar. 18, 1916, 1, May 6, 1916, 1; *Bottle Maker* (organ of the GBBA), July 1921, 4, Aug. 1921, 15–21.

71. WVDL, *Fifteenth Biennial Report, 1919–1920* (Charleston, W.V., 1920), 20–23; Six, *West Virginia Glass,* 79–80.

72. McCormick, "Death of Constable Riggs," 38, 40–48.

73. Workman, "Political Culture," 243–51.

74. Charles H. McCormick, *Seeing Reds: Federal Surveillance of Radicals in the Pittsburgh Mill District, 1917–1921* (Pittsburgh: University of Pittsburgh Press, 1997); Workman, "Political Culture," 253–54.

75. Workman, "Political Culture," 256–62.

76. Oscar Chapman, "Report of the Committee on the Upper Monongahela Valley, West Virginia," 1934, mimeograph, WVRHC, 24–25.

77. *Report of the Several Departments under Commission Form of Government, Fairmont, West Virginia, from January 1st, 1914 to July 1st, 1919* (Fairmont: Board of Affairs, 1919), 12.

78. See the historical papers of the Labor Temple and the Monongahela Valley Trades and Labor Assembly, Hulett Nestor Papers, WVRHC; and *R. L. Polk and Co.'s Fairmont City Directory, 1925–1926* (Pittsburgh: R. L. Polk, 1925), 17, 27.

79. John Alexander Williams, *West Virginia: A History* (New York: Norton, 1976), 146, 165–70, 182. See also the clippings relating to Neely's 1922 Senate race and the opposition that ex-governor John Cornwell and Clarence Watson mounted to Neely's severance tax proposals, Neely, scrapbooks.

Chapter 7: Into the Depression

1. The founding of the FFGW is covered in Lowell E. Gallaway, "The Origin and Early Years of the Federation of Flat Glass Workers of America," *Labor History* 3 (1962): 92–102; and Ken Fones-Wolf, "From Craft to Industrial Unionism in the Window-Glass Industry: Clarksburg, West Virginia, 1900–1937," *Labor History* 37 (winter 1995–96): 28–49.

2. *National*, Sept. 1922, 23–27, Apr. 1923, 24–25. Background on Lilburn and Donald Jay from the USCB, Mss. Census, 1920, Harrison County, and the sketch of Lilburn Jay in *The UGCWNA in Pictures* (Columbus, Ohio: United Glass and Ceramic Workers of North America, 1956).

3. Richard Mark Simon, "The Development of Underdevelopment: The Coal Industry and Its Effect on the West Virginia Economy, 1880–1930" (Ph.D. diss., University of Pittsburgh, 1978), 380–85.

4. Pearce Davis, *The Development of the American Glass Industry* (Cambridge, Mass.: Harvard University Press, 1949), 283–84.

5. Stephen Jeckovich, "An Economic Study of the United States Glass Industry, 1899–1947" (Ph.D. diss., University of Pittsburgh, 1961), 57.

6. West Virginia Bureau of Industrial Hygiene, *A Report on the Glass Industry in West Virginia* (n.p.: West Virginia State Health Department, [1938]), 4.

7. WVDL, *Twentieth Biennial Report, 1929–30* (Charleston, W.V.: Jarrett, 1930), 21–22; Jeckovich, "Economic Study," 222.

8. WVDL, *Twenty-Second Biennial Report, 1933–34* (Charleston, W.V.: Jarrett, 1934), 70; Colin Gordon, *New Deals: Business, Labor, and Politics in America, 1920–1935* (New York: Cambridge University Press, 1994), 110–11.

9. Bureau of Industrial Hygiene, *Report on the Glass Industry*, 2.

10. Richard H. Slavin, "The Pressed and Blown Glassware Industry," *West Virginia University Business and Economic Studies* 8 (May 1963): 11.

11. WVDL, *Twentieth Biennial Report*, 21–22, WVDL, *Twenty-Second Biennial Report*, 70, WVDL, *Twenty-Third Biennial Report* (Charleston, W.V.: Jarrett, 1934), 68–71; USCB, *Characteristics of the Population: West Virginia* (Washington, D.C.: Government Printing Office, 1941), 95–96; Bureau of Industrial Hygiene, *Report on the Glass Industry*, 2.

12. See, especially, Trevor Bain, "Industry Relocation and Restrictive Work Practices: The Flat Glass Industry," *Land Economics* 43 (Feb. 1967): 96–100.

13. Regina Lee Blaszczyk, *Imagining Consumers: Design and Innovation from Wedgwood to Corning* (Baltimore: Johns Hopkins University Press, 2000), 129–30.

14. See, especially, John Hennen, *The Americanization of West Virginia: Creating a Modern Industrial State, 1916–1925* (Lexington: Kentucky University Press,

1994); *West Virginia Legislative Hand Book and Manual and Official Register 1930* (Charleston, W.V., 1930), 550–51; interview by Paul Myers of Guy Alexander and Robert Knoll, [ca. 1977], transcript in my possession, 13–14.

15. Thomas W. Rowe and Harry H. Cook, *History of the American Flint Glass Workers of North America, 1878–1957* (Toledo: AFGWU, [1957]), 67, 71; Jeckovich, "Economic Study," 111.

16. Jack Wilbert Gregory, "Economic Survey of the Northern Panhandle of West Virginia" (master's thesis, West Virginia University, 1953), 35–36; AFGWU, Local 10, Minutes, Dec. 1, 1930, Feb. 2, 1931, Oct. 5, 1931, American Flint Glass Workers Union Records, WVRHC.

17. *West Virginia Legislative Hand Book 1933* (Charleston, W.V., 1933), 640–44, 649, 651–54.

18. Slavin, "Pressed and Blown Glassware," 3–7.

19. Gordon, *New Deals*, 111–13; Slavin, "Pressed and Blown Glassware," 23–24.

20. AFGWU Local 507, Minutes of Meetings, Mar. 25, 1939, Mar. 21, 1946, box 1; Minutes, Mar. 21, 1936, box 2, AFGWU Local 507 Records, WVRHC; Slavin, "Pressed and Blown Glassware," 24.

21. AFGWU Local 507, Minutes, Jan. 16, Mar. 21, June 12, 1946, box 1.

22. AFGWU Local 507, Minutes, Apr. 8, 1942, box 1, Dec. 15, 1936, box 2; Harry Cook to J. A. Bamberger, Dec. 5, 1936, AFGWU Local 10 Records, WVRHC, box 6.

23. See, for example, interview by Paul Myers of Guy Alexander and Robert Knoll. See also AFGWU Local 507, Minutes, Apr. 2, 1945, box 1.

24. Frederick A. Barkey, *Cinderheads in the Hills: The Belgian Window Glass Workers of West Virginia* (Charleston: West Virginia Humanities Council, 1988), 15–18; USCB, *Sixteenth Census of the United States (1940): Manufactures* (Washington, D.C.: Government Printing Office, 1942), vol. 2, 73.

25. Barkey, *Cinderheads in the Hills*, 13–19, "The Passing of the National Window Glass Workers," *Monthly Labor Review* (Oct. 1929): 13–16.

26. This is covered in Fones-Wolf, "From Craft to Industrial Unionism." I also thank Rich O'Connor for his insights here.

27. This list was compiled from FFGW Local 2, Minutes, United Glass, Ceramic, and Silica Sand Workers, Local 2, Records, WVRHC, box 1. See also Ken Fones-Wolf, "Transatlantic Craft Migrations and Transnational Spaces: Belgian Window Glass Workers in America, 1880–1920," *Labor History* 45 (Aug. 2004): 314.

28. Barkey, *Cinderheads in the Hills*, 16.

29. Minutes of the wage conference with the Fourco manufacturers, Jan. 24, 1934, WGCLA Records, WVRHC, ser. 4, box 5. This is covered in more detail in Fones-Wolf, "From Craft to Industrial Unionism," 39–40.

30. *Flat Glass Worker*, Jan. 1936, 10; Nixon to Joe Mayeur, Jan. 21, 1936, WGCLA Records, ser. 3, box 5.

31. Trevor Bain, "Internal Union Conflict: The Flat Glass Workers, 1936–1937," *Labor History* 9 (1968): 106–7.

32. This is covered in more detail in Bain, "Internal Union Conflict," 106–7; and Fones-Wolf, "From Craft to Industrial Unionism," 44–46.

33. Much of this is revealed in FFGW Local 2, Minutes, Feb. 14, Feb. 16, Feb. 23, 1937, ser. 1, box 1; James Morris, *Conflict within the AFL* (Ithaca, N.Y.: Cornell University Press, 1958), 267–68.

34. FFGW Local 2, Minutes, Mar. 29, 1937, and Norval Campbell to Howard Halbach, personnel director, Pittsburgh Plate Glass, Mar. 29, 1937, WGCLA Records, ser. 1, box 4. For a description of the "workplace contractualism" of the mass production unions, see David Brody, *In Labor's Cause: Main Themes on the History of the American Worker* (New York: Oxford University Press, 1993), chap. 6.

35. Fones-Wolf, "From Craft to Industrial Unionism," 47–48; Bain, "Industry Location," 97; USCB, *Characteristics of the Population* (1940), 95.

36. Warren C. Scoville, *Revolution in Glassmaking: Entrepreneurship and Technological Change in the American Industry, 1880–1920* (Cambridge, Mass.: Harvard University Press, 1948), 183–85, 247; Slavin, "Pressed and Blown Glassware," 3; USCB, *Sixteenth Census of the United States (1940): Manufactures*, 75–76.

37. *Bottle Maker* (organ of the GBBA), Aug. 1921, 18.

38. See the papers of the Labor Temple Association, Hulett Nestor Papers, WVRHC.

39. List of Fairmont labor organizations, Nestor Papers; Michael E. Workman, "Political Culture and the Coal Economy in the Upper Monongahela Region: 1776–1933" (Ph.D. diss., West Virginia University, 1995), 256–58.

40. For examples of the strong family feelings of many longtime Owens-Illinois employees in Fairmont, see Frank Spevock, *"Plant Three": Keepsake Edition* (Kingwood, W.V.: Shaffer's, 1983), 43.

41. Spevock, *Plant Three*, 38, 43.

42. Mss. Census, 1920, Marion County.

43. Lee Minton, *Flame and Heart: A History of the Glass Bottle Blowers Association of the United States and Canada* (n.p.: Glass Bottle Blowers Association, 1961), 108–10.

44. Minton, *Flame and Heart*, 116–19.

45. Hennen, *Americanization of West Virginia*, chaps. 7–8; quotation, 151.

46. Keith Dix, *What's a Coal Miner to Do? The Mechanization of Coal Mining* (Pittsburgh: University of Pittsburgh Press, 1988), 169–70.

47. Simon, "Development of Underdevelopment," 319–21; Gerald W. Johnson, "West Virginia Politics: A Socio-Cultural Analysis of Political Participation" (Ph.D. diss., University of Tennessee, 1970), 45, 50.

48. John Alexander Williams, *West Virginia: A History* (New York: Norton, 1976), 155.

49. Jerry Bruce Thomas, *An Appalachian New Deal: West Virginia in the Great Depression* (Lexington: University Press of Kentucky, 1998), 211–16; Williams, *West Virginia*, 164–67.

50. Thomas, *Appalachian New Deal*, 223–33.

51. USCB, *Sixteenth Census of the United States (1940): Population*, 3:942–43; Simon, "Development of Underdevelopment," 287.

52. Jefferson Cowie, *Capital Moves: RCA's Seventy-Year Quest for Cheap Labor* (Ithaca, N.Y.: Cornell University Press, 1999); Barry Bluestone and Bennett Harrison, *The Deindustrialization of America: Plant Closings, Community Abandonment, and the Dismantling of Basic Industry* (New York: Basic Books, 1982).

53. Doreen Massey, *Spatial Divisions of Labor: Social Structures and the Geography of Production*, 2d ed. (New York: Routledge, 1995), 3.

INDEX

Adamston Flat Glass Company, 141, 144, 175, 183, 185
African Americans, 12, 61, 99, 115, 148, 167–68, 171
Alexander, Guy, 100, 102, 108, 111
American-born glassworkers, 29, 31–32, 37–40, 111–12, 126, 167–68
American Federation of Labor, 18, 137, 186
American Flint Glass Workers Union, xxvi, 3–4, 8–13, 15, 18, 32, 42, 46, 48, 50–54, 90–91, 93, 95–96, 100–104, 109–10, 157, 164, 182; Branch 507, 182–83; Local 10, 90–93, 96, 98–104, 106–8, 111–12, 180–83; Local 49, 159–60, 171–72
American Window Glass Company, 24, 27, 31, 33, 54, 122, 124, 130–33, 135, 140
anti-Catholicism, 101–3
antiunionism, 27–28, 50–52, 102–4, 108–11, 148, 152, 155–56, 168–71, 187–88
Appalachian economic development, xxii–xxiv, 63–65, 79–80, 190–92
apprentices, 15, 21, 42, 48, 95–96
Atkinson, George, 74, 155–56
Azelvander, "Big Joe", 44–46

Ball Brothers Company, 18, 50
Baltimore & Ohio Railroad, 63, 117, 119, 123, 148–50, 152, 154
banks, banking, xxiii, 64–65, 67, 117–18, 150, 152, 157
Beechnut Packing Company, 148, 163
Belgians, xxvi, 21, 23, 29, 37–38,

47–50, 53–54, 113, 121–22, 124–25, 127–30, 132–35, 137–39, 143, 148, 154, 160, 167, 184, 192
Belgium, 21, 23, 29, 43, 45, 47, 50, 121, 125, 138–39, 168
Belt Line Railway, 153–54, 158
benefit societies, 36–37, 49–50
Bensel, Richard Franklin, xviii, xxv, 66, 69
Benwood, W.V., 84–85
bilateral monopoly. See dual monopoly
birds of passage, 31, 36–37
Blaine, James G., 116
boosters, 61–63, 66–67, 75–77, 85–89, 94, 107, 117–20, 125–26, 138, 144, 152–54, 191
Boreman, Arthur I., 61
bottle industry, xix, xxvii, 14–18, 32–33, 38, 50, 153–57, 160, 163–68, 172, 186–88
Brady, William S., 86, 89, 93–94
Bryan, William Jennings, 69, 119, 133
Burns, Simon, 23, 122
Butler, Benjamin F., 21

Callahan, Frank, 90, 103
Camden, Johnson Newlon, 62–63, 66, 149–51
Cameron, W.V., 87
Campbell, James, 4, 26
Carney, John, 100
Catholics, 37, 90, 98, 100, 102, 143, 161
Central Glass Works (Wheeling), 77, 93, 104

236   *Index*

The University of Illinois Press
is a founding member of the
Association of American University Presses.

———————————————

Composed in 9.5/12.5 Trump Mediaeval
by Jim Proefrock
at the University of Illinois Press
Manufactured by Thomson-Shore, Inc.

University of Illinois Press
1325 South Oak Street
Champaign, IL 61820-6903
www.press.uillinois.edu